Travel Notes
and
·Way Stations

*

a rational ethic

(1997)

Volume Two

*

essay

*

Traumear

The world as an eternal way or as a timely wonder is an imagined world or an image of the world and we have to ask ourselves now how it helps us to see the world after this fashion. We have after all the various beings that make up the world to contend with. Are they too being created or created beings, and if so, will the imaginary beings we create from them likewise be eternal ways or timely wonders?

One notices the difficulty. Always and again the critical spirit enters and before one has overcome it, it has sown the seeds of discord and discontent. Then these too must be overcome.

Our creative imagination of the world and other created beings is therefore wise to take into account this critical spirit and its questionable, doubtful fruits. It comes into the world so that we should gain from it – by quietly overcoming it. In the present case it shows how no sooner have we overcome the pictured world and created a true image of it, right way a tendency announces itself to picture that image. This is indeed one function of the critical spirit, to come up with pictures where only images will do. It comes up with pictures and would have us fall back into them as soon as we have overcome them. So we need to simplify.

Creativity begets criticism. It begets it. We can pretend that creativity and creative imagination should be ideal but then we are confronted by disappointment, so that the worst we can do then is out of idealism deny all connection between our view of creativity and the disappointment. It is the recipe for decay.

Equally we can admit the connection and then dig our heels in somehow in the misguided attempt to prevent such criticism. We set ourselves in all seriousness the task of disallowing that spirit access to our human being and doing. This is the recipe for a morbid dishonesty that always flourishes in the wake of idealism.

1

The third possibility is to espouse criticism and become a critic. Now the bothersome tension between imagination and criticism is gone and we can bask in our superiority. We can enjoy the acquiescence of the like-minded, of those who have connected their identity with the same prejudice – and perish. It may take a long time before we find out, but that is the idea, because by then we are well on our way to having perished.

These three conscious misconceptions of animal being (taking the long view now) that strive for recognition here, are the optimist, the pessimist and the critic. The critic lures the beast so that he may run away from it. The pessimist indulges forever in a struggle with the beast. The optimist says there is no beast and is swallowed by it. The beast is nothing more than the face of rejected (misconceived) animal being. None of the three have what it takes to face the consequences of creative imagination and to overcome them, in the interest of eventual reality.

We can always be sure that the critical spirit is at work in us when 'things' begin to interest us. We may be in a hurry or we may be bored. We may have our best interests at heart but suddenly we take pleasure in being led astray. Certainly this spirit finds its opening during a crisis, and creative imagination moves from crisis to crisis, even as we imagine the world or other created beings either as an eternal way or as a timely wonder. (Let us accept these two for the moment at face value.) The change from one to the other and back again is crucial. The change-over is critical. At that moment the critical spirit may or may not move in. Since we are dealing with spirit we cannot predict its occurrence or movement. All we can do is watch out for it and then persevere with creative imagination. This perseverance is of the essence for our imaginative work because it supplies the ethical backbone. Why should we persevere? Simply for that reason of an ethical content. We will come back to that.

First of all we need to be quite sure of our ability to identify the imaginative impulse which we supply. We must be able to say to ourselves with certitude: "Now I creatively imagine," and our certitude must be based on nothing other than that, imagining, we do. In other words we are not allowed to depend on evidence external to what we do, such as for example a result or a product. Remember that what finally motivates what we do is our human natural affection, and it alone, or all modes of it (creative imagination being one of these), enjoy the testimony of our soul and of the merciful spirit that informs it. The critical spirit, on the other hand, testifies to itself and is pleased with the testimony of products and results. It has its reward. Our peace of mind which it takes from us is one of its many rewards and always therefore our loss.

I know that I imagine a created being not by the effect I have on it or by the success of the image but solely by the way or the wonder of what I do. In addition to that, which we call the inherent identification, we must also then be able to identify the critical spirit by its results – in other words by its works, which are phenomenal. The ethical impulse in our own work is always and again renewed by us as we leave the phenomenal thing to one side and re-commit ourselves imaginatively to the being in hand.

So we must become adept at both inherent and extraneous identification. While we still cling to our own identity we are able to do neither.

*

Returning for a moment to the notion of 'human identity' or 'personal identity' – or rather to what we called identity above and explained as inborn instinct for self-preservation as rejection of soul-appeal : we are bound to admit that human being or personality in the absence of one's soul is a non-starter. It is however not the instinct for preservation which is at fault but rather that it is an attempt to preserve the self rather than one's soul. The connection between soul and human being we can take as read, equally the direct progress from individuality to personality. But a self or an identity allows for nothing more than popularity, where a variety of beings is forfeited on account of an identity of things, and where individualism is bought at the expense of personhood.

However we know now that the ethical issue is not how to prevent identity, i.e. how to prevent reflex reaction against soul-appeal, since an automatic rejection cannot as such be prevented, especially since it commences at birth. Indeed nothing less than merciful intelligence is required if we want to be able to face the facts and make progress in the direction of more life.

In other words, the preservative instinct itself is to be praised and its initial and automatic self-preservative identity is not to be blamed.

Then this self-preservative identity from birth must be clearly understood, for what it amounts to, namely a barrier to soul. If this is not understood, conscious and intentional identity is serviced and defended, and it is this then which incurs guilt and blame. Unconscious self-preservation becomes voluntary and an instinct accidentally <u>compromised</u> at birth is, in addition to this now, <u>sacrificed</u>.

This, incidentally, makes possible a reflection on the difference between ancient and modern morality. Ancient morality endorsed the sacrifice of the self-preservative instinct (of a lame animal) while at the same time upholding the preservative instinct (the pure animal), altogether an impossible situation since the preservative instinct as such only existed as a future hope while the sacrifice of the self-preservative instinct could never be rigorously implemented because this, as was clearly sensed, involved pouring out the baby with the bathwater. A study of ancient cultures in this light shows how much painful effort was involved during a multitude of different attempts to escape from this impossible situation. Modern morality senses that a solution to the problem is near at hand but insists on sacrifice all the same, merely 'correcting' the ancient sacrifice by limiting it as an idea within the boundaries of the spiritual plane. What happens now is that either the will or the intellect is sacrificed, that is to say: either the self-preservative will or the self-preservative intellect, and whichever one is sacrificed, the other one grows rampant. (repent vs rampant).

The contemporary ethical motivation must therefore be to accept the identity of the individual at whatever stage of consciousness and then to appeal to the preservative instinct as such by way of imagination, imaginary being and images. The intention here is that the individual human being will be weaned away from identity, as the preservative instinct is enabled to switch from self to soul. This sounds impossibly complicated and in fact it must truly appear to be impossible if viewed as a once and for all time remedy of an impossible situation; I mean the impossible situation of total self-sacrifice versus self-preservation. What we need to take on board however is that any remedy that is to succeed has to be contemplated as the next single personal act within some unpredictable context. We cannot abide by some recipe, externally imposed, that will allow us to act by ethical rote.

Continuing for the time being with this paradigm of identity and the preservation instinct in the face of soul-appeal, we can see how any act of creative imagination operates as soul-appeal in the guise of merciful spirit. You who <u>imagine</u> creatively are inwardly open to the merciful spirit, to the soul-appeal, against which I in my ignorance have pitted my identity, but you approach me ethically as a human being who has <u>united</u> in himself, just at the moment and for the purpose of a single ethical act, his <u>instinct for preservation</u> *and* <u>his soul</u>, in the absence or

5

to the exclusion of any self-preservative identity. I cannot tell how you have managed this union but it operates in my favour by exerting a powerful attraction. My identity is not challenged, as it would be if self-preservative instinct were active in you, so I can forget about self-defence. But most important for me of course is that powerful sense of soul preservation; it is as yet quite unfamiliar to me and I wonder at it. An experience of wonder has been created in me. The attraction is powerful because my identical self-preservative instinct (that lame animal) senses an opportunity for being healed and even more to the point, because my instinct of preservation as such suddenly suspects that a venue exists for its much greater usefulness. It is as if the born servant, the one whose delight in life is being able to serve, and the one who until now has only been able to serve himself, suddenly saw the opportunity for serving a master. It is the servant-master relation which you make available to me as a going concern in yourself that so astounds me. I sense that you have something much greater than I do but rather than boasting of it to humiliate me and to impress upon me my comparative inferiority or disadvantage you place it at my disposal. It's a bit frightening, to be sure, but only in the sense of awe. What is so intriguing to me is that you seem to be able to serve without demeaning yourself. Quite on the contrary, it makes you admirable in my eyes. How is that done, I would very much like to know, because I want to be able to do it.

Technically what is coming alive in me is the organ of soul preservation.

When I compare the pleasure this organic activity holds out to me to the pleasure I customarily get from successful self-preservation and assertive identity, then this compares indeed as great to little. How petty it seems to me now that I should have wished to survive my fellow man and triumph in the eyes of people! My fear of losing my identity seems so misplaced now. What exactly was it that I was apprehensive of losing?

6

And yet if someone threatened it, I knew only the one response which was defence. It strikes me now as a kind of foolishness. Still, how could I possibly have found out better unless you or someone with your strength had approached me? Was it any surprise that once my identity was unavoidably in place, even at birth, I should seek, in the absence of anything better, to protect it and to establish it on unshakable foundations? Much of my upbringing, most of my education and all of my society was based on survival, survival of the fittest, and fitness was measured in terms of acquired dominance of identity. If by way of my self-preservative identity I could sufficiently domineer, then I could have my way – which in the end only seemed worthwhile, to be sure, if it led to a greater dominance over my fellow man and my environment, indeed over the world. I knew no different until now that you showed me better by doing me good. The good you did me was to implant in me an <u>organ of soul preservation</u>. What begins for me now is the work of doing and undoing. I intend to get strong in terms of soul preservation and soul, and it seems to me even now that I will be able to do this most effectively especially at times when the old habit of self-preservation rears its head or when that tiresome concern over my identity arises. Whatever I do at such times to exercise my organ of soul preservation, under the attractive duress of identity preservation, will do me the most good as foundation, not for my self now, but for myself.

*

It appears that what began in you as a union of preservation instinct and soul was then able to take root in me as an organ of soul preservation. Are we in agreement that I am now better off than you? How is an organ an advance on a union? And does it worry you that suddenly I am better off than you? If it does, then let's face it, yours is the golden opportunity for rendering that union organic in yourself now. Here we have progress indeed! Your initial work in unifying preservation instinct and soul for my sake was of crucial importance because while you were able to overrule your need for phenomenal identity, I was not. I had to be attracted to the power you placed at my service. For me it was not then necessary to work such a union. You had done that for me. I could begin my soul preservational activity organically. When you noticed that, some time later no doubt, you were attacked by jealousy. You had worked diligently for what came to me as a gift. Perhaps I was not even grateful to you right away for what I could not have managed on my own. I have my own temptations now, such as vanity, to test my mettle and temper my organic strength. But the jealousy in your case, if you overcome it, will have pointed the way for you, albeit counterproductively, to your own organic gift.

What is this organic gift of ready soul preservation? How does it compare in effect and function to the union of preservation instinct and soul to which you had originally succeeded? Indeed it seems to me that yours was the labour of prayer and love where mine was the work of grateful-acceptance. What you did when you placed your true soul greatness at the service of someone who was identically great but in truth only little seems to me so much more difficult than my act of acceptance. But now neither one of us wants to waste any time with such artificial comparisons. A third person can learn from all this that in the absence of personal communication and communion the one single advance of ethical importance would not have been achieved: there would have been no organic soul preservation.

Actually we are bound to admit that what I blithely call your achievement of union of soul and preservation-instinct depended itself on your doing it for me, or at least for someone else, other than yourself. Mindful of that, would we not do well to call it <u>communion</u>? The moral, individual activity anticipates the fully ethical, personal activity. The communion makes sense and is powerful in terms of <u>communication</u>. That takes us to the point where I was able to accept what was being

8

offered. It might even be more accurate if instead of acceptance we described it as participation. I joined you, I followed your lead. Well, however we describe it, communication ensued and I became capable of organic soul preservation. Vanity beset me, pretentiousness and presumptuousness. You in turn were attacked by jealousy.

What followed was fully active ethics in that both of us managed to withstand the test and to pass it, which we were able to do equally for ourselves as for one another, or rather for one another in the knowledge that we would both gain equally, and this is <u>community</u>.

*

An organ of soul-preservation? – Organic soul-preservation? – What has happened? What has come about here? Is it not right that we should try to understand?

Whatever is organic, functions spontaneously. Just as we speak of our <u>inner eye</u> as the organ of sight and light, so we have come around now to our <u>brain</u> as the true organ of soul-preservation and world-observation. Just as our eye sheds light on our soul and absorbs light from the world, so does our brain preserve our soul and observe the world. Outwardly our two eyes compare to the two hemispheres of our brain. We say that we use our eyes and that we use our brains (left and right) but we have to be careful here not to be misled by figures of speech. First we have to ask, as usual, is it really ours or are we only pretending that it is. Our eye the organ of sight and light and our brain the organ of soul preservation and world observation are definitely ours, and that means precisely that we no longer have to use them, only to maintain them. In retrospect, once they are ours, we find it difficult in any case to say exactly what we did when we 'used' them. From the 'rational being' point of view, it appears to have been the usual case of wilful or intellectual forcefulness which far from leading to

9

ownership rather wore these organs out. Once we catch ourselves on, we can 'wear them in' again, organically. Part of the maintenance of the organs we own is the repair of the organs we abused. Indeed while we supposed we were using our organs we really abused the organs that were not ours at all. We dimly felt at the time that these organs and others like them should be spontaneously ours but we sensed, we suspected they were not, and so, instead of repairing to the merciful spirit as represented by our soul and establishing the roots of ethical behaviour and action, we aligned ourselves with the modern spirit of ambiguity and presumptuousness and abused or neglected those organs. Different cultures encourage either abuse or neglect. A culture that is world-affirmative in the absence of soul is usually guilty of organ abuse while a world-negating culture would have to answer for their neglect. Finally it makes little difference whether these organs are worn out or incapacitated, for in neither case do we come into their possession, by way of the possession of our soul as the true representation of merciful spirit.

*

Organ maintenance: and ethical contribution to the welfare of the community. "Il faut cultiver notre jardin." Evidently we can do something that assures our ownership and therefore the good functioning of our organs so that there will be neither neglect nor abuse.

Once our soul is our own and we have begun to approach the world with creative imagination, our organs soon follow suit.

Even here, when we say that they "soon" follow suit, we acknowledge the time they take. What we mean is that in the case of our brain for example, during the course of soul preservation and world observation, possession and ownership are effective activities which return this organ to its original mode of being and allow it to function in freedom. <u>Possession</u> and <u>ownership</u>

describe the <u>maintenance</u> we mean here, and the free functioning is then guaranteed in good time. It is guaranteed eternally.

Now if by possession and ownership we mean a doing rather than merely a state, we will have to explain this because commonly to possess or to own something has no effect on it, especially if we own or possess a thing. Perhaps we should emphasize that by organs we do not mean our brains and our eyes, etc. but our brain and our eye. Customarily we refer to our inner eye, to distinguish this from our eyes, but we cannot so readily speak of our inner brain. If our eyes are physical organs, at once mental and bodily, then our eye could by comparison be called a real organ, presumably because we see reality. For the moment let us not worry about what we mean by reality. We have arrived, in our pursuit of the ethical processes, motivations and intentions, at the point where we imagine beings and observe them, (created beings, such as the world). However we know and do well to keep in mind that nothing we can do to created beings in reality can separate or distance us from that uncreated being, which is our soul and from the merciful spirit that informs it.

So we do after all have a serviceable concept of reality here, interestingly enough in terms of animal being. (Remember we are still learning from our response to animal-being affection. We can define reality as world and other created beings in some order of soul. We know that whatever our soul embraces is right away orderly. It is an appreciation of reality after all that allows us initially to perceive that all beings influence us affectionately. Now we know that this occurs in an orderly fashion. Reality embraces the merciful spirit, our soul, and all created beings including the world and ourselves of course.

Returning now to what we called the <u>maintenance</u> and therefore freeing-for-action of our organs, specifically of our brain, we can describe this as a <u>pressing of ourselves into reality</u>.

11

Which cannot make sense while we have no conception of reality such as here set forth. It makes at least superficial sense however that since our organs function freely in reality, we ourselves, if we are not quite real, inhibit to that extent our organs even to the point where we might as well not even have them. On the other hand we can have much more than just a concept of reality. If we are to be in reality we must press into it while we can.

But how does our brain function, spontaneously, now that we know it as the <u>organ of service</u>, i.e. of soul preservation and world observation? To <u>serve</u> means to keep, to hold and to protect. At one and the same time our brain functions to keep our soul, to protect beings and to hold the two together. Once we know this, we are bound to become suspicious of brain power allegedly as a tool for supremacy, so that he with the biggest brain can lord it over the rest.

By the protection of created beings and world in general, by their observation, we mean for example an ongoing and repeated willingness to know them as beings and not as things, which is no small task because every being appears to us first of all as a thing, until our imagination rises to the ethical obligation of perseverance and thoroughness. Also by observation we mean the keeping in mind of ourselves as created beings, albeit with an uncreated soul that longs for us. For if we forget this, and consider ourselves as fundamentally of a different order, we become scourges of our environment. Our brain therefore is to protect the world of beings against our unregenerate selves. This sounds peculiar, because it seems to assume that we might at one and the same time be in the possession of our organic brain and sufficiently removed from reality to abuse the beings of our environment. But of course once we are actually able to observe the world, we are communal beings and responsible for our fellow human beings, as they are for us, so that misconduct in one of us is sooner or later, perhaps even right away, ameliorated by another.

*

The one crucial ethical move on which all our success in the face of world being and beings depends is this pressing of ourselves into reality. If instead we force our selves into the world, we are bound to fail since we forfeit our soul, becoming extinct. The distinction between world and reality has to be kept in mind. <u>Reality</u> embraces merciful spirit, soul, ourselves and world. It is one thing to sustain ourselves in the world at all costs, learning as many survival tactics as possible, and then when the time comes for experience of events that would specifically require our reliance on our soul, which is bound to come to all sooner or later, we break down. Pressing into reality and sustaining ourselves here however is no such thing. Certainly energy and force play a role but we do not identify with these.

The <u>doctrine</u> of <u>energy</u> and <u>force</u> should be tackled simultaneously with the <u>doctrine</u> of <u>organic</u> <u>being</u>.

Energy is unlimited. There is unlimited supply of energy. We have to look into this now in order to be able to make a bit more sense of this pressing-into-reality move. It is precisely because energy is unlimited that it becomes our task then to supply such limits. Modern man rushes into energetic relationships and misconceives his task. A faithful appreciation of energy is required, of energy as elemental and therefore in need of being not rejected or resisted but approached affectionately, with human-natural affection, on ethical grounds. Soon we will discover how this relates to organic being. We still have in mind, I hope, how due to our mortality, to this liability to death of all created beings, we cannot but first resist the approach to us of naturally affectionate beings, and so here too, in the case of this elemental being called energy, we have resisted and –

13

have known force. This turn of phrase: to 'have known' force, is characteristic of a dogmatic tradition but we can resurrect it for our purpose. So much is unavoidable then, that energy affects us and that we forcibly resist it, thereby becoming acquainted with force and also of course with the possibility of pressing it into our service. This temptation is of course totally unethical, all the more so if we attempt some ambivalent modern contractual relation between force and morals. Such a rapprochement is a typically modern attempt at ethics in the absence of soul and merciful spirit. One might call it a modern tragedy. But that by the by. The soundly ethical move looks quite different: we recognize our acquaintance with force, we repent of it even though no court of law could hold us responsible, and we approach this unlimited supply of energy with human-natural affection.

Suddenly we understand how this element energy, as soon as we have enabled it to come into its own, really wants to behave. To put it musically: the horse of our ethical understanding takes energetic wing as Pegasus. Is that too complicated? I hope not.

*

The doctrine of energy brings it to our ken as related to this motion of pressing into reality. This pressing into reality cannot be organic in the sense that we can develop an organ for exerting this motive pressure. It is I myself, not some member of me, that presses into reality. While I do that and once I have done it sufficiently for a time, I begin to understand the true nature of energy which is to <u>empower</u> myself and my organs.

Energy is an element and a being, not a thing. As soon as we imagine energy we come up with a stream of potential strength, with capacity for work, with capability that can be used 'for good or ill'. But this is the picture of it, the phenomenon, not the image. The image of it gives us its true nature and therefore it cannot be for ill. Electricity is not energy but a force. Forces are due to rejected energy, to a resistance of this element being, and therefore unethical. To exert a force means to behave unethically and therefore such behaviour cannot do us good.

When we unavoidably resist energy and know force, we must therefore return to energy as the elemental being that it is and with human-natural affection bring it into its own natural relationship with reality which can be described as fundamental. Energy is truly fundamental to reality.

When we press into reality, we do not do so with force but we do it energetically. At one and the same time, and with the same act, we bring this being into its true relationship to reality and we participate in its fundamental effectiveness.

Our understanding of energy has advanced from when we last thought about it. We have direct and immediate access to it now as a being we do not first have to resist. If we all the same find ourselves involved in the resistant forcefulness we could not avoid, then we all the same apply to the energy that affects us but we respond with human-natural affection and then that being is realized – and we along with it.

We would not get the notion of pressing into reality from out of our self, since our self only resists change – or rather it is a resistance to change. Rather that notion comes to us from the affection of that elemental being energy. Our own human natural affection in turn is necessary if this being it to be realized as fundamentally real. Our own fundamental realization corresponds as we press into reality.

And on that basis our organs are freed.

On that basis then we have, for example, our eye as our organ of sight and our brain as our organ of service.

*

15

It is quite correct that the notion that we might do well to 'press into reality' does not come to us by way of our ego or self, because when we are egoistical we move the side issues of survival into the forefront and judge everything from there, so that we see energy merely as fuel. This is short-sighted and therefore insufficient and misleading. We end up worrying about energy scarcity, an absurd notion, and we run the risk of overweening activity, which is a pity.

Even though a time can come for us when we can press into reality as we wish, we can be sure there was a time when we resisted this fundamental element being called energy, and what did we suppose we were up against then?

We called it <u>panic</u>. While we inadvertently resisted energy we panicked. Everything threatened us. Not that we experienced panic, we just simply did it, and now, in retrospect, we can understand what went on. Perhaps we had several 'panic attacks'? It certainly made us sit up and take notice. To the extent that we did not take notice we went into shock. It can happen so fast, as during a car accident, when for a split second only, perhaps, we panic and then, even if there is no carnal injury, the subsequent shock, or state of shock, can be appreciable. "Phew, that was a close call." The sweat stands out on our forehead.

What we can take for granted here is that reality 'came to us' because we were not ready for it. If we picture the process we feel obliged to say that it came to us and we were not ready for it, but thorough imagination correctly relates the 'coming to us' of reality with our not being ready.

All the same, reality must 'come' to all of us, and everything depends on how soon we sit up and take notice.

So energy, from the rational point of view of being, turns out to be the process of real foundation. If we view reality perhaps a bit more metaphorically as the commonwealth of all beings created or uncreated, then energy is an ambassador from that commonwealth to me, and if I recognize and honour him he will show me how to become a member of that commonwealth. What we called 'pressing into reality' amounts in fact to such an honourable recognition accompanied by the process of membership.

We must keep in mind that as we 'press into reality' something of really fundamental value goes on for which we ourselves are not the first cause. It is more a case of our participation. But we cannot participate unless we have some insight into what is available to us.

On the other hand, unless we get this concept of rational-ethical energy straight in our minds, we will continue to panic and to be shocked. Also we will continue to be swept off our feet by events, because we will again and again build on the bad foundation of energy as fuel for survival, thus misconstruing reality and therefore betraying our own human nature, which longs to be real.

Energy as fuel for survival is either scarce or wasted, so that we have starvation on one side of the globe and butter mountains on the other. There is no measure to it, because of its being a misconception. It lacks both the rational proportion and the ethical dimension. On whatever plane of being it finds currency, we can be sure that peace will be ephemeral and harmony will be destroyed. But proportion and dimension, like peace and harmony, are values in themselves, so that we have them or not, and never in halfway measures.

*

More needs to be said about how we come by this notion to press into reality, so that we may more readily identify it when it occurs to us rather than mistaking it for something else.

17

Initially we panic, we cannot have any doubt about that. Panic is such an all-encompassing fear that we might describe it as a danger to our soul. Now our soul as such cannot of course be in danger, but we might be in danger of losing our soul, and this is indeed where the panic comes in, that energy approaches us and we just might misconceive it as fuel for survival, which misconception would in fact place us in a false position vis-à-vis our soul because we would no longer seek to cooperate with it but instead would try to operate with mechanical force. Those who are not in the possession of their soul, cannot panic and cannot yet learn to press into reality, that goes without saying.

What we automatically do as soon as we panic and as soon as this panic comes over us, is steel ourselves against an imaginary danger. We do this in quite a unique way. It is not the inadvertent resistance of energy we mean here, which results in panic, but the automatic reaction against panic as soon as it sets in. Panic, in that it draws on our entire being, is unusual in this, in that we react to it. And we can observe this reaction. It is as if our hand went up to avert a danger and we observe that our hand goes up – and we discover that we have a hand. That is where the analogy limps of course, since presumably we have known for some time of our hand. Though who knows, perhaps an infant discovers its hands in just that way, after a panic attack. Observe sometime the difference between the baby as its arms flail about and the infant who begins to use his arms, to reach for something.

In any case, what we observe in ourselves as a reaction to panic, is what we use then to press into reality. The proper name for it is <u>strength</u>. Unawares we react to panic, and such a reaction is strong. It is not an energetic, or a forceful, but a strong reaction, and so we become familiar with the strength we can make our own.

This strength we have discovered is in addition to what we need to press into the commonwealth of reality. It is however of the same order as the energy we initially resisted. And, most important, another organ is freed for us, namely our <u>organ of strength, our genitals.</u>

*

We understand now that energy is not fuel for survival but the foundation of reality and that we ourselves have to gain that foundation for ourselves, which we can do by energetically pressing into reality, thereby allowing that being, namely energy, to come into its own on our behalf and participating in its real being as foundation.

In addition to this we understand that in the absence of our soul we cannot help but resist energy, so that we come up with a force, or with forces, which we then mistake for energetic devices as we build ourselves a fool's paradise with a survival kit that really amounts to a rejection of a proper and sound foundation. All the various forces we come up with also have their counterparts of course, namely self-indulgences that are to reward us for the hard, forceful work we do.

So in the absence of our soul, the closest we come to energy is that we mistake it for forces which we try to get under our control and then every once in a while we wonder about the expense. Nevertheless when we compare this expense to the abject horror we associate with the 'thing' that threatens our soulless state with total annihilation, which presumed 'thing' we can still manage to force into the background, then we usually storm ahead – or sink back into debauchery – rather than taking some minor pains to acquire our soul and learn that this horrible 'thing' is what we have made of the energy-being that is willing affectively to supply us with a real foundation for our life.

19

While we are even to some extent in the possession of our soul, however, we can observe a reaction in ourselves to a panic that sets in periodically, and we know now that this panic is to alert us to the danger of compromising our soul due to a misconception of energy as a force. This panic is counterproductive, because by reacting to it we find out about real strength. We still need to make the ethical move of acknowledging this counterproductivity of course. We must use at least some of this strength, to press into reality, otherwise we become prone to panic attacks and to so-called soul-destroying applications of force or indulgences in sensuality. It is while we are to some extent in the possession of our soul, at least aiming and striving for ownership, that true energy makes a stronger appeal, in the name or cause of reality, and our strong panic reactions testify to this. Such reactions are therefore good news and we do well to hear it.

Once again we see how our ethicality is initially in essence an informed response to an appeal from beings to which we are prone to react ignorantly. Part of the task of a work on ethics such as this book is therefore to supply the required and necessary information in one form or another. This however would not be enough, because with all the information in the world we still stand back indifferent and impartial until we are _infected_, as it were, by a personal example or two of how such a proneness, an almost congenital proneness nowadays, to ignorant resistance and blind reaction can be overcome by an eager and knowledgeable response. There are as many ways of setting such personal examples as there are ethically mature human beings; this book is only one of them. It shares with other such examples the necessary characteristic of challenging us to rise to the occasion of it. It is not enough that it should be read and studied. It must also be done.

*

The doctrine of energy and force, we said, must be worked out alongside the doctrine of organic being. So far we have mentioned created being, pertaining to world, and uncreated being, namely merciful spirit and soul. Organic being is not a third category. Being does not break down into categories. On the contrary, organic being is founded in reality and established as organs. Organs are organic beings.

Initially our organs result from ethical behaviour. They are themselves then effective during ethical action. We have mentioned that our pressing into reality frees our organs for action. We know that in the absence of our soul we are not in any real order, so that 'we have eyes but cannot see and ears but cannot hear'. To this we might add that we can force things but have no strength and that we are slaves but cannot serve. In a soul-less state we may loosely talk about our organ of sight but all we really have is external receptors for visual data which are, in their duplicity, causes for confusion. The duplicity stems from the twoness of all such external non-reception. It is, after all, non-reception. We cannot, in the absence of our soul and while we insist on an identity, assimilate or even bear the affection, the affective influence, of created beings around us. It must, and does, occur to us as an attack on our integrity. A contemporary poet might sensibly express his compassion for created beings because they cannot come into their own while human beings do not return their affection. Instead, people play them false. They are bound to appear as things, and thus in duality. By this we do not mean that a thing can be fully appreciated either one way or another, such as when we say that world is an eternal way or a timely wonder. That applies to being and beings. No, in the case of things, they are not equally one or the other but they are neither one nor the other. In fact the only way we can in any sensible way talk about them is in sympathy with those who insist on their identity with them. It is a talking 'as if'. We speak of things 'as if' they existed so that we can all the better appeal to the human nature of those who assume or even insist that they in fact do.

It is not difficult to explain the inherent duplicity of things. We can understand this readily as long as we do not make the attempt through an analysis of things, which must lead to the most complex of confusions, but through insight into beings. Since we are ourselves, and since we are beings, we should not be surprised at the need for perspective when it comes to our knowledge of other beings. Perhaps we have nothing to fear from other beings, so our reasoning goes at the outset, but let us preserve a healthy respect all the same for what can happen, and frequently does, when our knowledge is not based on sound principles and when we betray our humanity through ignorance of ethical expedients and constraints. The process of 'getting to know', we say, shall therefore be respectful, circumspect and introspective. We do well to keep in mind that knowledge, the decision to know, is not out of the blue but is itself a response to the appeal, to us, by beings in our vicinity. This is always so at the start. It is not until we have established organs that we can actually approach other beings in the knowledge of their being.

So this advisedly respectful approach to a relatively new being, this courteous introduction of ourselves, allows us to take into account – and encourages us not to forget to take into account – the uniqueness and individuality of every being; in the present case, of the being we have to do with and of ourselves. If I were to meet you for the first time, to make your acquaintance, this would be managed most sensibly if both of us kept in mind all the time that each one of us, as a human being, has something to offer that cannot be offered by any other being. This should not be confused with the traditional parameter of objectivity versus subjectivity. Either one of us can, after all, be objective or subjective as we wish. What matters during the course of what we should emphatically call ethical knowledge is that the <u>singularity</u> of the being we wish to know and of the being with which or whom we wish to communicate, is understood. All knowledge 'has a hand' in such understanding, which embraces a multitude of cares and anxieties and ambitions, such as that this singularity should be discovered, preserved, respected, upheld and so on.

Our reason for knowledge and the purpose of it finally is a community of beings, and such a community of beings is then how we live in reality. Our singularity, our individuality and uniqueness, must be carried through from birth to a personal maturity. When we meet, you and I, during the process of getting to know each other, I am neither to remain ignorant of you and merely press upon you my individuality, nor am I to lose track of myself, to lose myself, in you. Neither selfishness nor selflessness can contribute to real knowledge. Both are in reference to self. The degree of understanding that must be part of ethical knowing has nothing to do with self at all, neither negatively nor positively, but it predicates a singularity of being and we who do the knowing keep in mind that both we ourselves and the being we know are individual and unique. On the basis of that understanding then a body of knowledge can come about and communality can succeed. This is what is meant by "making the two one". It does not mean that the knower and the known, upon knowledge, are any the less singular. On the contrary, their singularity has been augmented due to the achievement of a common unity, or community based on a body of knowledge.

In the light of this albeit rather sketchy paradigm of ethical knowledge we can make out what happens when we, for example, look at something without seeing it. First of all, two single beings, each with its singularity, are not recognized. Instead there is a confusion of roles. My organ of knowledge cannot function because I do not predicate singularity but I try to predict an outcome. I do not augment my singularity but I get caught up in speculations. I do not end up with a body of knowledge but I profess a mass of information data.

Modern knowledge plays off objectivity and subjectivity against each other, so that whatever is known cannot be said to be, in so many words, but it must first be immersed in some ideal ground or distinguished on the basis of popularity. Even arcane or esoteric modern knowledge refers itself to popularity, but negatively, like selflessness to self. The loose change (or debt) left over after every modern scientific transaction is invested in future knowledge, so that one seems forever to be getting closer to 'knowing everything' without ever completely knowing a single 'thing'. However we can live comfortably only with what we completely know. Hence modern man's eternal discomfort.

*

Our organ of knowledge is the heart.

Ethical knowledge, we said, predicates the singularity of the knowable and the knower. We should not give any other name to what we intend to know, such as an object, because that makes our relation to it problematic.

We can think of our organs as themselves perfect and we can imagine them as single towards our soul and double towards the world. Organs such as our senses illustrate this by existing as two eyes but one inner faculty of sight, sometimes called the inner eye; which goes for our ears, nose (two nostrils), taste (tongue and palate) and touch (least obvious, but here we have fingers versus thumbs and then two hands partly for touching). In the case of our brain and genitals this outward double form is hidden in the former and divided between the sexes in the latter.

Though being in themselves perfect, these organs are not necessarily ours. What we have to ask ourselves now is how

24

can we <u>help</u> someone else, who is committed to the extinction of some organ, reverse that process, so that the attachment between being as thing and organ as mechanism is broken in favour of a rational relationship between an organ free for action and beings free in themselves. We cannot make that happen or cause it to come about of course, but we can appeal on behalf of rationality. We can do something possibly to make the free organic relationship to beings more appealing than the attachment of mechanism to thing.

This is where <u>art</u> comes in. The purpose of art is to extend to someone who is mechanically attached to things an invitation to free relationship to beings. The difficulty lies of course in making this invitation somehow comprehensible to the one who is mechanistically attached.

For someone to be able to extend such an invitation, he must be capable of organic relationship, but it is not necessary that all his organs should be free. This would be a nonsensical demand. A singular human being is born with a number of organs and can then add on to these many more. How this works will eventually be made plain. It suffices that at least one or two of our organs are in truth our own for the need for <u>creative expression</u> to awaken in us and to challenge our <u>fantasy</u>. The need and the challenge coincide. It is up to us now to meet this challenge and to satisfy the need.

The question that concerns us in this present work is: Do we try to rise to that challenge of fantasy unethically or do we do it ethically? Do we try to satisfy the need for creative expression unethically or do we do it ethically?

The telling element here is that we can try to do the one or else actually do the other. If we try the former we will never succeed but we will forever seem to be getting closer to success. In fact the need becomes less critical and the challenge less pronounced. We seem to be getting closer to the goal when in truth we are merely less eager to run the race.

But let's first look at how we can meet the challenge of fantasy ethically and how we can satisfy the need for creative expression ethically.

Our perception of the need or of the challenge is of the essence. It I am gifted with an organically knowing heart, that does not mean that on account of that I am now not prone to vainglory or liable to a forceful will. I am all the same at liberty to make a fool of myself in term of knowledge, in other words to translate the <u>need</u> into a <u>prerogative</u> and the <u>challenge</u> into a <u>provocation</u>. Why would I do this? For no reason at all. It suffices that I do not do the other. And what is the other?

In order to really satisfy a need I have to give up my right to the satisfaction of it, just as in order to really meet a challenge I have to trust that I have what it takes to do so.

*

So these are the ethical moves I have to make in the face of this need and challenge. In my own case, say, if I am gifted with a knowing heart, then within myself I will always be aware, and often painfully, of the immense discrepancy between mechanical attachment and organic relationship. I will deplore my proneness to self-justification and I will hate my unwillingness to trust precisely because I know in my heart that I have what it takes to come up with sound knowledge, whereas the next person may not know what he or she is doing and cannot be bothered.

I get plenty of practice in myself therefore in dealing with a proneness to attachment and changing it into relationship. I have to learn to identify the need and the challenge all in order to begin to invest my talent and to – ingest my gift. Once I have identified the need for creative expression half hidden by

26

the temptation to translate this into a prerogative – which is as far as modern man goes – I still have to make the thoroughly ethical move of giving up my right to the satisfaction of this need. If I do not make this thoroughly ethical move I become constricted in the modern dilemma of trying to do unethically, or at best half-ethically, what can only be done ethically. The same goes once I have identified the challenge of fantasy, half obscured by the temptation to provocation – again a modern limit: I still have to make the thoroughgoing ethical move of coming up with the trust that I have what it takes to meet that challenge.

The need for creative expression and the challenge of fantasy need to be more closely described if we are to have any success in identifying them.

The need for creative expression first becomes noticeable as a pressure that seems to curtail our liberty of emotion. We complain of emotional dullness, of a lack of spirit, of feelings akin to boredom and despondency. We would gladly admit we are in need – we need one thing or another; that would be our immediate expression of our self, and it would not be creative. The temptation to blame someone, or our circumstances, to blame or accuse anyone or anything for that matter, testifies to the right we have to the satisfaction of our need and to our willingness to insist on that right. We are liable to do this for one another, to explain an expressed complaint in terms of "that is because of this or of that". "You are feeling bored because you have nothing on our mind", for example. Or: "You are depressed because you have nothing to do." Always in such cases something like blame is involved, and the so-called explanation which is supposed to help really builds on a <u>right to satisfaction</u>.

We can take it for granted that any need for creative expression is always accompanied by a judgment of prior right, in the sense of: "It is not just, that I should be in this needy state. I have done nothing wrong so I am deserving of satisfaction, not of neediness." "Of course you are," our friends tell us. "Life is unfair." But our true friend says: "Give up your right, your prerogative to an uninterrupted state of satisfaction. Your need is not for satisfaction but for creative expression."

Not until this prerogative is dropped can the need become clearly identifiable as a need for creative expression. Not until then can it be perceived.

And then right away, of course, creative expression takes place. The organic relationship commences with abrogation of all prerogative to satisfaction. Where our heart is involved, we automatically then speak from the heart. The invitation we extend to someone whose heart is mechanically attached will be such a 'speaking from the heart', even as we can tell of that other one's temptation to pre-empt satisfaction and to have noting to do with organic relationship.

*

Before we speak of the challenge of fantasy which is really part and parcel of the change from proneness-to-mechanical attachment to organic relationship, we should perhaps emphasize that the right to the satisfaction of this need for creative expression is not a supposed right but an actual right. Unless we have that fairly and squarely in our mind we will get the wrong notion of what it means, and of what is involved, in giving such a right up. We are ourselves giving something up – and when we invite someone else to prefer organic being to mechanistic attachment we are asking that person to give something up – that is actually possessed and can be proven to be possessed. No argument to the contrary can ever be won. And logic will always be on the side of the one who is right and who has the right. Neither will the cowardly stance of: "I know you are right but that's all you are!" have any useful or good effect. Someone who knows fine well that he has the right to the satisfaction of this basic need is going to have to be shown in so many dimensions that something better is available. Challenge his right and he/she will insist all the harder. And if you yourself are not fully persuaded of the beauty and truth of organic relationship and perhaps you are only mouthing some creed, then you have no business even talking to someone about a change of that sort because first of all you must tend to yourself. The modern mixture of hypocrisy and presumptuousness, of weakness and cowardice, world-wide, is a force to be reckoned with for all of us and we should never underestimate how much we tend to be swayed – to be tried – by addictive half-measures and half-truths, even to the point of raising these up to the level of the super-spiritual.

When we have a right to something, such as to our identity or to our modern point of view, then we take a stand on some particular law or set of laws; we adhere to some particular idea or complex of ideas. Looking far enough afield, in history and on the earth, we can see those who pledge their faith in some particular angel or hierarchy of angels. All these fidelities, to laws, ideas or angels, give us the right, and rights, to behave, legitimately, ideally or angelically. What I am concerned with mainly here is the interpretation and justification of and for their behaviour offered by those who have these rights and under duress are willing to swear by them – and quite rightly so. It won't do for anyone who thinks he knows better to suggest that such individuals haven't the right to swear by their rights, and by the rightness of them. And the suggestion that laws, ideas and angels pertain to the individual and not to the person or to persons does not guarantee that anyone's eyes are opened either. I mean opened all the way. The modern squint is after all also a moral squint. We moderns have our own sense of worth invested in our rights and in a commitment to our rights to an extent and degree that would astonish us if we knew it. We have our rights, our idols and our certainties and nothing, absolutely nothing can shake them. The worst that can happen to us is that we are proven wrong by circumstances, that our idols show cracks, that our certainties become bloodless. As soon as that begins to happen, even right at the start, we invent a morality, quickly, to bolster our system, as a bulwark against the wrong, the bad and evil, to buttress our self.

What kind of a morality is that? It even thinks of itself as an ethic. Really there is nothing puzzling about it. When I know I am right I am happy with that and I need no morality to improve my lot. Alone on the island of my individuality among a crowd of the like-minded I have nothing to fear. I know that the sun rises for me and I crow my approval. Then, when it sets, I admonish it. I remind myself that it needs me as much as I need it, and on that thought my perfectly reasonable hope is grounded.

No, I need no morality; not yet. How often has modern man in so many of his guises not yearned for that paradise on his individual island among the like-minded and away for all time from the morality and ethics he has had to invent to safeguard his angelic and rightfully ideal edifice! It is at best a system that allows him to linger, to malinger. It holds out the promise of successful provocation and the promise of a temporary respite.

Not until my rightness is challenged by another rightness do I need to invent that foredoomed morality, that universal ethic based on ego and cold fear. I have managed to get everyone under the dominion of my angel, I have conquered all the tribes, subdued their princes, married their women until my harem is bursting at the seams, but now I grow tired – and the enemy knocks, so the time has come to prepare the moral curse for the head of the adversary. Time for the recipe of behaviour, the lists of do's and don'ts to guide my society, the identification of the common enemy and the supply of weapons in terms of opinion, creed, persuasion and conviction to keep him at bay, perhaps to destroy him for all time, to regain that nirvana where all are of the same opinion as to what is right, ideal and pure.

*

When we take our stand on what is right, ideal and pure, we eventually have to produce standards of righteousness, idealism and purity, and then it must seem only prudent to raise these standards to the level of sanctions, ordinances and credentials. The spirit that is poured into these standards to thus inflate them is suspect to say the least.

However, to coin the paradox of all paradoxes, once we have the right to see through these standards of morality – we give it up. Better yet: Not until we have given up our right to the satisfaction of the need for creative expression can we really see clearly what these rights and moral standards amount to – and then it would not occur to us any longer to be provocative, as I have been in the previous section, though artfully. Then it must be all too plain to us how the fearful and arrogant ego would not be entertained by anyone if he knew the true benefits of creative expression and of organic being.

*

And while we are in the habit of insisting on our right to satisfaction, we do not, of course, perceive that need as a need for creative expression. Rather we feel the need to be justified. That is more or less what we assume will satisfy us. That is our prerogative. And we have no notion what it is that challenges us except we are sure our righteousness is being challenged. What can we know of fantasy while our ambition is the legitimate pursuit of justifiable ends? Very little is known of fantasy in any case. We should never assume, for example, even at the best of times, that fantasy has a predictable content. All we can predict is that fantasy will, at a time we cannot know, appeal to us for recognition.

31

We know that the beings in our vicinity affect us; we have spoken a great deal about that affection and how we neither can, nor should wish to, escape from it, not even in death. We have come to the point in the development of our insight now where we can grasp the verifiable essence of that affection as <u>evidential of actual life</u>. We do not mean fantasy now as something misapprehended or as a thing totally and even studiously ignored but as an acceptable influence. We know ourselves in the presence of that which <u>needs to be received</u>.

*

In trying to appeal now, or rather in actually appealing, to someone who knows nothing of organic relationship, our way of approach – our art – must take into account such a one's very ability merely to receive prejudicially, by insisting on the right to the satisfaction of a misconceived need.

We ourselves, who have gradually worked our way forward here, can now understand how that right to satisfaction is both invented, out of nothing as it were, and then even calculated, to block and negate the influx of actual life which needs to be received. We can appreciate the tremendous difference between the negative attitude and the positive receptivity, especially since the negative attitude is supported by a morality that not only sanctions it but raises it up as a standard of dutiful performance and honour. Meanwhile the person we mean may have very little if any actual experience of life. No wonder so many of us despair when it comes to bridging that gap. And yet that is our reason for being here, so the sooner we knuckle down to discovering the most effective art in the face of <u>exclusive self-righteousness</u> the better.

By all means let us as usual begin by discovering in ourselves all the inherited hindrances and bad habits due to which we inhibit the influence of actual life because we suppose we are 'being surrounded'. For none of us can deny that we do

32

have experience of this, of being hemmed in, pressurized, inhibited and even handicapped, physically, mentally, spiritually. We know fine well what it means to run away from the obligation to exist, from the ethical duty, finally, to ourselves and to our fellow human beings. How often are we not convinced that some self-indulgence will liberate us from the at times extreme boredom of moral constancy or the sheer nothingness of ethical responsibility.

But moral <u>constancy and ethical responsibility</u> are the one central ingredient of the art that makes a good and useful difference. To continue when we no longer feel like it, to begin when we cannot see a reason for beginning, to stop when we are driven beyond the parameters of wisdom and common sense, these are rudiments of behaviour within the confines of this life-art.

*

We have said that if someone who is committed to his rights is going to be persuaded that he can improve on that, he is going to have to be shown. He will not give up his right to the satisfaction of any need for creative expression just because we say to him that he has misconstrued that need and that he will therefore never be fully satisfied or fulfilled if he goes about it that way. Unless he gets some evidence of a result of <u>creative expression</u> he will continue to misconceive that need as a need for justification, thus actively blocking out fantasy.

Now that we know that beings affect us in a way that is evidential of actual life we should no longer be surprised by all the trouble human beings and people take to guard themselves against it. Life is bad enough for us, while we are half alive, because it reminds us of being half dead, and who wants to be reminded of that! The very suggestion is outrageous. But worse is to come. This life is actual. That means the effect of it instils in us – is an instillation in us of – pure motivation. We are being urged to act. This is terrible! It would be tolerable perhaps if at the same time we were shown how to act and what or whom to act upon. However all we are given is this urge – which soon becomes an urgency.

But the risk is not as great as it seems. Fantasy is not this actual life itself but verifiable evidence of it. And on that account it is acceptable for us – or at least for those of us who are willing to give up our right to immediate or eventual satisfaction. We have evidence of actual life and we may verify it. Why should we bother?

Our own satisfaction depends on it. No one can have life unless he is willing to share it. Verifiable evidence of life is available to us from the beings around us. Those who know this can take the next step, of showing life, of demonstrating the reality of it. This is a very important step to take because the number of those who know that life is on offer is small. And not all those who know take advantage of it. They lack the ethical prerequisites for the next step. The tendency is always to shrink into ourselves and to take any new life we have received in with us, away from communal consumption. You could then say that once again 'we have had our reward'. For the new life to thrive it must be shared. And we are speaking of the very beginnings of that here. We have identified fantasy. We referred to it first as a human faculty but shortly afterwards we knew it as something akin to a spirit, tolerant of distinction from ourselves. We were not confused by this because we were 'right away' able to accept, that fantasy is 'neither from us, nor not from us, but both'. Whatever we say about fantasy, if it is to be correct it must also be demonstrated. We help ourselves to remember this by recognizing that <u>fantasy is concrete</u>. With fantasy we are into the realm of growth and we cannot know anything of growth unless we ourselves in the meantime grow. This must be anathema for us while we insist on states or planes of being, being committed, in other words, to lifelessness. The logic of lifelessness crucifies every attempt to bring life into the realm of being. We can all take it for granted that we have done this often enough to wish not to be reminded of it. That is why we spoke of the reminder as a challenge, a challenge of fantasy, if we but knew it, and all too often both experienced and acted out (shown) as provocation.

<u>The acting out and showing of new life</u>, by comparison, is what we mean by art, specifically by <u>ethic art</u>.

It would seem that we have equally to <u>abandon</u> ourselves here to a process as to supply a <u>structure</u>. That which was not in our heart is to come into our heart. Our knowledge is to become organic. We are to grow along with that which would grow through us. This art is work. But let us not worry about too much of a difference between art and work in any case. We are more concerned with what the two have in common. Art is a work and work is an art. New life is the common denominator. We have arrived at the growing tip where the affection that comes to us from beings is reciprocated human-affectionately by us. It is the green bud where the earth juices make contact with light and atmosphere.

Suddenly we have evidence of new life. This evidence is a mixture of sensations, sentiments, thoughts and opinions, moods and dispositions, of feelings, passions and emotions, of pictures and images, of desires, urges and drives. They may be pleasant or unpleasant, convenient or inconvenient, seemingly acceptable or unacceptable. They are neither true nor false, real nor unreal, neither good nor bad, neither beautiful nor ugly. Remember our first experience is not new life but evidence of it. The evidence must be sifted, ordered, tested and established or organically rooted, and all this is what we mean by <u>verification</u>. There are countless numbers of ingenious ways of verifying such evidence of new life, so that once again our singularity, our uniqueness and individuality, comes into play.

My experience is a plethora of evidence. My task is to verify this evidence. But – I must set myself this task. The evidence does not bring along with it any need of verification. No one points the finger and says to me: This is not yet life but the evidence it has been able to give of itself because of your knowledgeable heart, so now you must bring your singular human being to bear on it. It is the voice of ethics that says this, not the voice of new-life experience. And what the voice of ethics tells us we must commit to memory so well that at last we have it by heart.

But how often does it not happen that just as we are about to set ourselves this task of verification, we tire or else take a piece of that evidence for the actual goods. Why are we so reluctant to come to the fore as soon as the onus is on us to supply a structure? And what sort of a structure is it that is ethically demanded of us? (We have said that we equally have to abandon ourselves to the process and to supply a structure, so we have regard to the latter first.)

There is a very fine line between criticism and a critique. A critique takes courage and character. Criticism simply means a letting ourselves go, letting ourselves drift or hang, while new life-evidence plays over us. It is the 'passing away' of the cup not as merciful spirit wishes but as we wish in our self, in other words, a rejection of it.

It is verification after the manner of a critique that we are after. It is discernment in reference to the truth. It is a single structure that encompasses all of our evidential experience of actual life at that moment.

We must draw on our singularity.

*

Creative expression: meeting the challenge of fantasy not provocatively but with (self-abandonment and) a <u>structure</u> – this is the direction in which we have to apply ourselves now.

In our heart we know as never before of the very particular affect the beings around us have on us. We have learned to identify that affection as evidence of actual life.

We had to come to terms with some rather uncomfortable home truths about our own so-called identity before we could identify that evidence of actual life, and now we know it as particular, and therefore as material. Material evidence of actual life is what we have – as the raw-material, so to speak, for our heart-knowledge.

Right away we have to point to a difference here between knowing and knowing that ... or about ... There is an appreciable difference between knowing Paris and knowing that Paris is a city, is the capital of France. The former is greater than the latter and includes it. Heart-knowledge includes intellectual knowledge and there we have the beginning of the structure we are looking for. It depends on this appreciable difference between heart knowledge and head knowledge. As usual, we must be aware of there being two so that we can make them one. We know there was a time when they were not two, and the division was then often a painful process, where the heart and the head seemed to be at war, but now we can look back on that time as fortuitous and formative. We can appreciate what went on and also what does go on at such times. We can ease the process for others because we know of its good purpose and of the real reason for it, which is the ability, eventually, to structure the particular evidence of actual life from beings in the world and from world in general. There is the heart-knowledge of any particular being as such and this involves the head-knowledge of it as being somehow, somewhere, sometime etc. a being among other beings in the world

– that is to say, among the infinite number of beings to which we refer as world, (not *the* world).

We can see the role played by appreciation. You might say that we can appreciate the importance of appreciation.

*

Particular, material evidence of actual life: in order to have it for ourselves we have to make it available – we have to make that life, not the evidence, available also for others. We have to verify the evidence, which means that we have to structure it, and this in turn implies an appreciation of the difference between heart knowledge and head knowledge and the bringing of the two together as one.

The communal realm: whatever has meaning and substance here – whatever is structured here – is available for all of us. This difference between 'all of us' and 'some of us' has to be appreciated again. The verifiable evidence of actual life is available only to some of us. Some of us are 'chosen', or destined, or gifted – to have what it takes for such verification. It would be irresponsible to suggest that this service – and it is a service – can be supplied by all. Nor would that make sense. Just as we are all born individually imperfect so that we may seek our perfection in personal community, so are we all singular, i.e. individual and unique, when it comes to our reason for being here, which includes our function, our task, the contribution we can make, and so on. Considerations of morality allow us to stipulate singularity for 'all of us', even though we know that at any given time the number of those who are functionally aware of their singularity is never as great as it might be. This means that those who have managed to break through to a recognition of their singularity hold themselves morally responsible for all those others who are also individually imperfect but they have not yet managed that. They hold themselves accountable for them. They are counted. 'All of us' are individually imperfect and 'all of us' may discover and come to terms with this marvellous singularity of existential purpose that lets us at least guess at, if not profoundly plumb, our meaning and worth as individual human beings. _ But not all of us can verify the evidence of actual life. Only 'some of us' are ever able to do that. But then of course it always only takes a few to do that. Those few of us who do it, do it after all for all of us.

Again we divine in this arrangement not only now the higher purpose and aim of communality but even the structure of community. Those few who verify the evidence of actual life, know that they can be understood by those many who have broken through to their singularity, and both the few and the many are here for all of us, including those who are still entangled in their imperfections and searching for their singularity.

This has nothing to do with social hierarchy. It is throughout organic. Knowledge of it is organic knowledge. Levels and strata do not come into it. From the most insightful point of view we might eventually speak of the dead, of slaves, of servants and of friends, but those terms are so charged with social reference and misapplication throughout history and tradition that for the time being we will express what we mean in other terms.

*

We cannot make heart knowledge and head knowledge one, in the way that the former includes and also implies the latter, if we are not aware of that organic growth process to which we have referred, because what is required if we are truly to grow is that we at once abandon ourselves to that process and supply a structure for it and, if we are really to grow, that we act out and show the new life for which we have verified the evidence or of which we have verified evidence thanks to those who have done that for us.

Heart knowledge, full heart knowledge, is not definitive. This probably presents the greatest difficulty for most of us, because we are so accustomed to the modern notion of the eternal, admirable artefact. We suppose that once something has been found out, it has become a permanent piece of meaningful furniture in the public realm. Just as a house should eventually be fully furnished, so we suppose that the public realm, to which all have access, must eventually be sufficiently replete with established facts so that any further knowledge will be unnecessary and irrelevant. So one hears, for the example, the foremost proponents of 'theoretical physics' voice the opinion that in a few years just possibly, given the present astonishing rate of progress, one will know all there is to know and all that needs to be known in that department.

This shows nothing so clearly as how alien such 'knowledge' is to life. If we suppose we live because we are born and have not yet died, then we are equally liable to think of knowledge as something we might do or not do in addition to living, and that the chief reason for knowing and knowledge in any case is to still the urge for it or to satisfy the desire for it, to which we have the right. Presumably, according to this very prevalent modern attitude, a day will come when children will be in the enviable position of having at their finger tips, in some data repository, all the answers to every possible question they might come up with, so that at the age of ten, and then in the next decade, at the age of nineteen, after more progress, no more questions will have to be asked. And of course while knowledge is assumed to possess a final validity, one can only suppose that any persistent dissatisfaction in that department must be met with increasingly greater masses of definitive knowledge. Usually however the dissatisfaction surfaces symptomatically in such a way that no link with the business of knowing and knowledge can be detected, which is a kind of a mercy, otherwise every new shoot of green hopefulness would persistently be smashed with the same blows of the hammer.

But if true knowledge is not definitive and valid for all time, does that mean that it is valid for only a time? First of all we have to take on board that knowing is a part of living and that knowledge is part and parcel of life. From the modern point of view, this is incomprehensible because life means survival and knowledge is mechanistic. In a contemporary light therefore, validity has nothing to do with knowledge but only viability. Contemporary knowledge, which is heart knowledge and head knowledge as one, is not definitive but viable. We cannot know from one minute to the next what it is we need to know, nor is this a drawback, except that it seems to be a misfortune from the point of view of a modern death-orientation. As we grow, we gain in capacity for life and as we live more we know more. Also as we know more we live more, but the two are contemporary. Not until knowledge is rooted in our heart can we actually live, for one another, and not until we truly live can we know what it means to know. Outside the organic growth process one will always then demand to 'know': "Alright then, how does it all start? Which comes first?" but this is the typical modern manufacturer and mass-producer's question.

Self-abandonment and abandonment of oneself amount to the same if we have in mind the contemporary growth process of our knowing heart. The image of the river of life has often proved suitable in this context. While we run along the bank of the river equating life with a keeping up with the stream, we may be part of the human race, 'progressing' in the sense of speeding up, but we do not live. Not until we step into the stream and abandon ourselves to the flow can we live and then we have peace and a rest that is formidable.

Once we know of the growth process we can abandon ourselves to it – even as we supply a structure to the verifiable,

41

material evidence we have of the actual life consistent with our relationship as natural-affectionate human beings with other beings. We cannot say anything helpful or worthwhile about any of this unless we participate in what we describe or do what we advise. Our appreciation of the difference between intellection (head knowledge) and apperception (heart knowledge) – and above all of course of the nature of this difference – is crucial, so that our abandonment of ourselves will not be an inebriation but structured, just as this self-abandonment to the growth process is essential so that any structure we come up with will not be self-important and irrelevant. Neither do we want a self-sustaining system, for example, nor stagnant self-immolation.

*

The art through which we verify evidence of life is at once patient and constructive. The patience is due to our self-abandonment and the construction is due to a critique that overcomes and so to speak 'sidelines' criticism. The particular material for this art comes to us from created beings which affect us, as concrete evidence of actual life. A part of our task is to identify such evidence correctly as world-original and not to confuse it with self-original stuff. Such self-original stuff is really non-existent and baseless, so there is no reason to disprove it except coincidentally as we always and again return to an apperceptive critique of world material, patiently constructed.

This primary task of proper identification of our material as world material and not selfish stuff takes time. Finally it is we ourselves who grow, not some part of us. It is the commonwealth of reality that is to gain through us a further dimension and we through it our effective humanity. The difference between our affectiveness as beings and our effectiveness as communal, ethical beings, which we promised to clarify several pages ago, becomes abundantly clear now. Patient constructiveness and constructive patience are the essence of this effectiveness. We make something available for others which otherwise they cannot have. What we make available is actual life. Our work is necessary so that actual life may be gained by many, ourselves included. We recall what we said about a few, about many and about all.

Our work is not modern but contemporary. One of our main ethical contributions is that our work is not modern but contemporary. We live in the world of today and beings speak to us each day afresh. It is up to us to remain alert to the fact that actual life is available and that it can be accessed. Not only do we have access to it but it has access to us, so if we do not make room for it we run out of space and if we do not make time for it we run out of patience. We lead stressful non-lives in a non-dimensional world and our very condition bears testimony, albeit negatively, to the fact that actual life is available.

*

Why is it so important for us to realize that our feelings, opinions, mental pictures, sentiments, moods, etc. do not originate in ourselves? Why is the truth so crucial? Why can we not afford to ignore that reality is orderly and that we can have insight into that order?

If we suppose that the world is an inert mass – an assemblage at best – of static things with which we can do as we please, we learn nothing at all of our humanity because we leave it unaccessed. The notion of the world as something we read into the void is not much better. Although it saves us the aftermath of those errors that pile up guilt and shame as we manipulate wilfully and unconsciously things as though they were real, it nonetheless denies us entrance to that commonwealth of reality in which alone we can successful thrive. But the missed opportunity is not the only source of pain. The regret at having in some way missed the boat of life is only one side of the story. The other side is the condemnation and punishment for which we make ourselves responsible as we reject the reality of being and beings both created and uncreated. Our pain becomes meaningless if we fail to learn the merciful reason for it. And the suffering of meaningful pain, rather than its cowardly or angry rejection, takes us along the path towards new life, just as we become accessible to the life that appeals to us for acceptance if we learn some of the moves that coincide with the commonwealth of reality that must eventually affect all of us, to our undoubted advantage if we know that, but apparently to our detriment and destruction if we remain ignorant of it and do not come to meet it halfway.

*

Our first impulse usually seems to be to refer our inward experiences to themselves. We notice we are depressed, in a depression, in a despairing sort of mood. So we think about this unpleasant state. What could it be? What does it amount to? What might have caused it? Above all, how can we get rid of it and somehow substitute for it a state of elation? Elation would be pleasant, but depression is unpleasant. How do we know that elation is pleasant? We can recall being elated. It has happened to us in the past that our depression has turned into elation. It happened, but we cannot see any reason why we should not be able to make it happen. So we struggle. We strive. We throw ourselves into various postures and bring on a variety of sensations, to blot out, to mask, to ignore and forget the unpleasant depression, assuming all the while that as soon as the depression is gone, the elation, which must be its opposite, cannot help but appear for us. We apply leverage to our inner being. How are you? Depressed! So push down on the depression and up will come the elation. The law of mechanics must hold. If at first you do not get the expected results, try harder.

However this is a futile exercise. We are stuck in quicksand and we are trying to help ourselves out in terms of sand.

44

A modern attempt to deal with this 'self-defeating predicament' is to set up a hierarchy of values and virtues, a systematic creed if you like, and to tackle the unpleasant state by referring it not to itself now but to this system of definitive knowledge. Hope, for example, is laudable. Hope holds a position quite high in rank. Therefore, in any case of depression, try to hope. Pin your hope to something: to a better life, to cheerful attitudes, to advantageous circumstances – to elation? You owe it to our fellow man to overcome your depression, so there you have a moral duty in hope. I will preach hope to you until you not only feel depressed but guilty to boot. You are letting the side down if you don't hope. The characteristic element in all this is that I blame you for being depressed and hold out to you this system of morals while guarding myself carefully against infection from your unpleasant state. I make no attempt to carry your burden, or at least to help you carry it. I know nothing of actual compassion. I have plenty of advice for you but my chief interest is my own survival. When it comes right down to it, in my modern superiority I know nothing of actual life. Your depressive failure reminds me of this, so the best I can do is refer to the moral system for advice, on my own account this time, and there I am informed that when in doubt, espouse certainty, or a particular faith. So I do my best under the circumstances. The moral system allows me at least to be popular and fashionable and to belong to a group. I will then try to make you join our group. If you don't, you have no one but yourself to blame.

*

So much for the modern morality. My inward being is referred to a conceptual configuration of standards which is considered to be valid for all. I must convince myself of this universal validity or I walk around with a bad conscience. But as soon as I have convinced myself, I behave hypocritically. It's unavoidable. Either the bad conscience or the bad faith. The only alternative is inebriation. I abandon myself to sensation. Modern

45

art comes into its own here. It makes our inebriation its task and we judge it the way we judge wines. It has to take our minds off the bad conscience and off the bad faith but at the same time we want it to taste good and not give us too much of a hangover. More refined senses require amore refined art. Depraved senses enjoy getting drunk.

The dissatisfaction with modern morality and modern art often stems from the lack of argument against debauchery and the demonic. Finally one cannot see how any available morality is able to save one from those two that can be frightening. The possibility of the total destruction of one's soul and the total annihilation of oneself stares one in the face with the result of absolute terror and total horror. When that happened to me I screamed like an animal caught in a trap. I felt that I was literally being driven out of my mind. It was the closest thing to a rebirth I had ever come across and happily I had someone with me who stood by me for a time. I believe that the contemporary spirit had entered my soul. My soul had asserted itself. Understandably at the time I was confused. However, in spite of the panic and the distress, which came over me in several waves, I had the distinct impression, off and on, that something worthwhile was happening to me.

Today I can relate that contemporary spirit not only to the traumatic experience to which I have alluded but also to the previous states of bad conscience, bad faith and inebriation. I can see why, if even then that contemporary spirit was trying to get through to me, I should have found the modern morality lacking. I can even 'divine', if you like, why that morality would have done me the particular disservices that it did, because today I am somewhat acquainted with my singular nature and with some of my specific capacities for personality, and those were at that time severely distorted, inhibited and checked.

46

Now the contemporary spirit is in the world. Because it is in the world, the world is infinite, i.e. world without end. At one time the world was finite. At that time one feared with reason the end of the world, because that end implied the distinct possibility of a human catastrophe. Nowadays one fears without reason not the end of the world but the contemporary spirit. One fears, while one is caught up in modernity, the one who should be welcomed with open arms. And those who reject that spirit in a modern fashion usually assume in one way or another that they do not. It is the half truth of the modern approach to life and reality, to nature and humanity, that makes it so insidious.

It is mostly our unwillingness to hand over quite openly our inner being to the being of the world which contains and is informed by this contemporary spirit that closes to us the doors of human natural growth and universal change. We get stuck in ruts of defensive behaviour. We perform cruelties towards one another in the interest of our complicated self-protectionist schemes. The subtleties of our superstitious thinking and of our timid feeling are so vast, are such jungles of energy and despair, that our condition may well be likened to that of the Peruvian monk, who neither by air nor by water could make his way to the refectory and he died in an insane rage because it did not occur to him to walk through the court yard.

*

With the advent of the contemporary spirit, whom we may call <u>the light of the world</u>, we have arrived, in our book, where we may now cross over into that realm or field of research where we may respond with human-natural affection to the affect those beings have on us which we call not elemental beings, not mineral, vegetal or animal beings, but <u>human beings</u>.

Keep in mind that so far we have not so much been interested in discovering or establishing how to behave ethically towards

47

plants and animals, etc. as in mapping the terrain of ethics itself, of morality and ethics, so that those of us who then take the trouble of familiarizing themselves with that terrain may become more ethically human beings, capable of more ethical behaviour and action towards all beings – one feels inclined to add: first and foremost to human beings, but the nature of ethics is such that no rivalry is really possible between various beings when it comes to their claims on our attention. If ever we feel torn as to which way our loyalties lie, so that it seems to us that in order to behave ethically towards a human being we must behave unethically towards an animal, for example, then the fault lies with our grasp of ethics, with our assessment of our ethical capacity. Our ethicality does not involve us in <u>conflicts of loyalty</u> to beings but it solves those conflicts. Our first and only response in the face of such a conflict must always involve our assumption of our error of insight or else our cheerful acceptance of a further insight – with respect to our ethicality; the two, as we know, amount to the same.

Our primary concern so far has been to find out what it means to be ethical, to behave ethically and to act ethically. Wherever in the history of human habitation on the earth we come across attempts to behave and <u>act</u> ethically without <u>being</u> ethical, there the problems have soon mounted up and the embarrassment of a gap between promises made and promises kept, between theory and practice, between word and deed, has not been long in opening and widening. The temptations of definitive knowledge, of getting it right once and for all time, has misled us, not only in that direction but also into its opposite, which is total despair over the very idea of doing good. Time and again our collective lament has been: If we cannot <u>be</u> good, what is the point of trying to <u>do</u> good! And this lament has commonly arrived, as one would expect, in the wake of a period of: Since I am good, whatever I do must also be good! Those are traditionally the ups and downs not only of our individual ethicality but equally of the collective moral persuasion. The foredoomed desire or will to be good alternates at the head of the historic agenda with the failure to behave and act ethically with any real consequence of conviction. Similarly the neglect over really being ethical can never be compensated by special efforts at good doing and right action.

The suggestion that a human being can be ethical but not good and indeed, beyond that, the statement that a human being by definition is ethical, is bound to bring the colour of enquiry into or cheeks. Being creatures of flesh and blood, we are liable to suspect ourselves of irreverence if we cannot to some degree justify our existence on the earth. However at the same time we are spiritual beings and therefore feel intuitively inclined to take our presence, wherever we find ourselves, for granted.

With respect to none other than human beings does the fact of creation and of being present a problem. When we agree that humanity is the essence of being and that all that is is essentially human we not only point to the fundamental communality of all beings but we identify at the same time that radical difference between human beings and all other beings.

In the light of the world now – if I may put it that way even at this early stage of our process into this present terrain – an animal is, being an animal, and thus it participates in humanity just as humanity participates in it. The being of that animal guarantees its humanity just as humanity guarantees its being. but that does not make that animal a human being. What makes us human beings is not only that we are, along with all other beings, but 'that we are that we are'. What is involved in our case is being to the second power. A being is human; a human being is human again. Not only are we human beings but we have human being[i], and that is the same as saying that we have

---

[i] This coincides with the fact that not only do we live but we also have life.

the contemporary spirit and that we not only exist in the light of day, as do all beings, but we live in the light of the world.

*

Human beings affect us in ways other beings do not – this is important to keep in mind. Are we, for example, affected by human beings that have long since departed from the earth? What role does memory play in the way we relate to others of our own kind? And do we not always wait for someone, to come to our assistance? – to work things out finally so that they will never be problematic again? Or is that perhaps due to an insufficient response of affection on our part and are we not fully empowered in fact to relate to one another with perfect fidelity and the highest possible sense of honour?

My ethical response to you – this I have never taken fully on board – does not depend on whether you like me or not. If we ask ourselves, you and I, how we are alike in an case, we will not come to any immediate conclusions, first and foremost because my own growth and development depends initially on my singularity of being, on my individuality and uniqueness. Now the roots of ethics reach right down into that singularity of being and it would not do for us to ignore that. If we did, we would soon find ourselves in that all too familiar state of extinction, and of trying to correct and reverse that extinction by means of morality. But an extinct morality cannot help us out of extinction. And <u>true morality</u> does not depend on whether you and I like each other – and on how we are alike. It rather springs fully fledged from the fact that we are different, and from our not being indifferent to this. If I blame you for being different from me and if you are indifferent to my being different from you we have on our hands the nicest little recipe for mutual destruction. And yet we need nothing more at the start than a fundamental structure to our being so that we may come into our inheritance as stewards of the earth and effective members of the commonwealth of reality. Certainly we are no longer going to pretend that such a structure is achievable unethically. And yet the desire to be liked by others is so rooted in ourselves – as is, by the way, the reaction of animosity to not being liked – that we have to look far afield before we discover a strong and dependable example of ethical originality.

It is precisely such an example that we need, however. Where the instinct for survival, not life, is not strong, there is nothing of life-value to be hoped for. But where the instinct for survival is strong and where there is hope of life, how is a human being to break free from that dependence on the species which dictates a group-morality and from that indebtedness to mankind of which the highest possible ethical achievement is altruism and philanthropy? The human race is no more a receptacle of virtuous motives than the individual heart is a guaranteed source of good. And if we want examples of failure we need look not further than at all those attempts, throughout history and nowadays, to do good from out of the instinct for survival. Either that instinct is strong, and morality remains self-serving, or service of fellow man is undertaken, and then a weakness of individuality either eventually sets in or is predicated from the beginning.

*

We can be ethical but we cannot be good. If we are ethical, and to the extent that we are ethical, we are human beings. So it's possible for me to be not only a human being, but also more of a human being.

This is important, that we make a clear distinction between humanity and human being. It is important mainly for the following reason. On one hand we may suppose it's enough for us to be born to be human beings. This is clearly not the case. We are born as beings, and therefore, since humanity is the essence of being, we are, upon birth, like all beings, human in that sense. But we are not yet human beings. This sounds so absurd to our modern ears that very few will be able to accept it. Only those with a rational commitment to life and therefore to ethical being and doing will be able to accept it. But that's a start. Those who are in the habit of mistaking beings for things and who are bound to include themselves in that mistake, see only their right to a certain identity and unless they spur one another on to impossible ideals they break down. Their usual retort is: "Sure, if we are not all human beings even from birth, by definition, then it must be perfectly alright for us to maltreat and murder each other;" with the implication of meaning that it's "perfectly alright" to maltreat and murder those beings that are not human beings. Their protest reveals their state of underdevelopment. From the rational point of view, it appears that they have no true notion of being at all but they only know things. From the rational point of view, it soon becomes obvious that all beings are to be approached with human natural affection, that they are to be treated respectfully, with consideration and care. And this rational point of view is precisely so crucial because we, among all beings, are the only ones born not only with a capacity for being human beings but also at risk of losing even our humanity, our essential being. For no beings other than ourselves does the danger exist of voluntary perversion and depravity. By this I mean simply the annihilation of our essence, of our essential being – of our humanity. I fully agree that the use of the term 'humanity' in this context and with this meaning is highly unusual and unavoidably controversial but I see no better way of bringing out clearly and in the best interest of our ethical progress as human being our need for the care we are to take of all created beings and life-forms, not only of those we like at the moment. I am not entertaining myself by juggling with metaphysical concepts but I am trying as best I can to convey the knowledge and understanding of which I am capable while at the same time demonstrating in exemplary fashion what I deem worthwhile and essential for us to do.

*

A any given moment – this is what it comes down to – we are at liberty to be human beings and progress or else not to be human beings and regress. We are at liberty to be free or to be in chains. No one and nothing can take that liberty from us. In a very real sense we may at any time choose freedom or enslavement, regeneration or degeneration, human nature or perversity. I can think of no better news than this at a time when we fear we may be trapped forever.

To be fair, hardly anyone, probably, chooses entrapment and regression. It is rather a case, surely, of our not choosing freedom, and therefore we are trapped. No matter how often someone 'sets us free', unless we actually ourselves choose freedom, we degenerate. Those who seem to us to decide on a course foredoomed to disaster do so not because they hate life but because they mistake life for something else and something else for life. They expect salvation from little pleasures or real growth from indulgence in vice. We may fault them for ignoring their best interests but not for desiring the undesirable or for choosing their own extinction. Even the suicide wants rid of a burden and not of life; it is just that he mistakes his life for the burden.

So we speak of 'them' and of their mistakes, implying that we know better. Well, we may know better than some. More down to earth – we may at the moment know better than some but tomorrow they may know better than we do. I have an idea and I may try to inspire you but perhaps you will have none of it. Was it a good idea? Did I present it to you with sufficient clarity? Would it have helped you if you had taken my point, assuming that you did not, or could not, or would not?

In the absence of ideas now, I am always affected by you, by your presence in my vicinity, whether I realize it or not and whether I admit it or not. This affection is on the level of – and now I have to make a special effort: can it be on the level of humanity alone and not of human being? You as you are at the moment are either a human being or else problematic in your very humanity, regressive and degenerating in one way or another. You are either ethically committed or unethically at loose ends.

Now any other being clearly affects us in the one way, to which we may respond or not. A being is never a thing; we only suppose it is a thing when we mistake it. But what about you and me? I am either a human being or – a thing? Have we not agreed that unless I make the ethical decision to be a human being and all that is implied by that I cannot even vouch for the essence of my being, for my humanity? If we human beings are the only beings at liberty to forfeit their essential being, their humanity, what about the affect we have on the human beings in our vicinity, or on any beings for that matter, if suddenly we begin to degenerate and to regress?

*

These questions touch on what, specifically, pertains to our experience of one another. There is no need to speak to someone in order to come under his affective influence. It suffices that he enters my room, that I read a letter from him, that I contemplate his works. He has designed and built the house I live in, planned the routes I travel, discovered the electricity that presently lights my table. All that we mean by society, by culture and civilization, not only present but past too, can and does affect me, and what counts more than any identification by me of particular instances of this is that I rouse myself to a <u>generously affectionate response</u>. And here we stand in the presence of a puzzling truth. Our response is not to be geared to the type or style of affect we encounter. Whether it stems from human being <u>structured</u> upon humanity or from degenerate and regressive phenomena, what matters is that we respond with natural affection and that we make no attempt even to judge whether we find ourselves in the affective presence of the one or the other. The suggestion is not that we should somehow insist on being naïve, which is impossible in any case. Of course we are bound to notice that here someone is attempting to pull the wool over our eyes, then here is someone who honestly strives to enter into acquaintanceship with us by offering what is best in him and hoping for what is best in us to be offered to him in turn, and then yet another one sums up for us with practicality a handful of our perplexities and just manages to shed light on them from his more experienced soul. As we notice this, so we are advised to let it be. Are matters truly as we suppose them to be? Have we erred in our estimation of kind or degree? Are we merely projecting our self into external objective beings so as to justify a prejudice or to sustain a pleasure? Since we have no intention to pronounce on what affects us – as indeed we should not – and since we can see no reason for describing more or less accurately what we deem to be the case – and indeed we could not if we tried – only one thing is left, and that is the condemnation or admiration in our heart of hearts, and this we must studiously avoid, though time and again we repeat the folly, until we learn that such <u>unreasonable condemnation and admiration</u> comes upon us unsolicited and can only be avoided if we make a habit of generous affection, and can only be uprooted, once it has become a bad habit in us, if we learn to insist with sufficient vehemence on <u>generous affection</u> in all cases instead.

A good habit of generous human-natural affection in all cases and on all occasions is to be acquired by us here as a wise policy, precisely because we are smart enough to know that not all that glitters is gold. Gullibility, inexperience, a foolish idealism, are no recommendation. The starry-eyed optimist is only a step away from a rage or a resentment. And the critic, with his fine discernments between what is worthy and what is worthless in his eyes, is ripe for many an unpleasant surprise, not because he was wrong but because with all this rightness he had no defence against the evil in his heart.

It is this, the evil in the human heart, that is either taken account of by us in the design of our conduct or else it plays us false. It may even devour us. And the best way to take account of it is to be perfectly aware that it exists while at the same time refraining from entering into traffic with it, which can be managed if we commit ourselves to generous human-natural affection.

The generosity is the crucial element in this. Not that we recommend a miserliness in our affectionate approach to other beings, but that in the case of human beings a special effort, or helping, of generosity is ethically appropriate. In the absence of it we insist we see but we are blind.

This generosity is powerful.

*

It is the generosity, the powerful desire to help, that allows us to override the evil in our hearts. We know how difficult it is to really help and not to be waylaid by external signs of having helped. When a man asks us for a loaf of bread and we have one, we give it to him. This is easy. Even here it would be silly to try to establish first of all whether he really needed it. When someone asks us for help we give it. We are glad of the opportunity. But what if everyone has more than enough bread?

How do we override the evil in our hearts in a land of plenty? Is that a sensible question? Are we really in danger of succumbing to unnatural drives and supernatural forces unless we can find a 'good cause'?

It would seem to come down to a realistic appraisal of where exactly help is needed. We can take it for granted that our 'generous impulses' are signs that somewhere, somehow, our help is needed. The difficulty lies in matching need with supply. This seems to be an almost absurd shortcoming of our times. In the same individual abound generous impulses and helplessness. And when that individual looks around, he sees an abundance of bread and a lack of humanity. He looks elsewhere and sees a lack of bread but no way to supply any. Is it the old predicament, he asks himself, of the times being out of joint?

Imagine yourself entering a country rife with starvation. You have brought along sacks full of food. You are eager to give it away to any who want it but none come to ask. They see what you brought but do not recognize it as food. You eat some of it in front of them. They continue to starve. Some bring money because they want to buy your food but you know that even if you accepted their worthless currency in exchange for food, they would not eat it themselves but only insist on selling it again and it would spoil and not be eaten. This is like a nightmare. They have forgotten how to ask. They have lost the habit of eating. They lack the ability to accept help.

How does that make you feel? Is your first reaction not one of condemnation?

And yet, this too is you. If you yourself knew how much is available and how little you ask, you would be astonished. Even at this very moment do you not feel impoverished? Of course you would like to feel good, about yourself and the world. But you suspect that somehow more is to be achieved. Or you know in our heart that you will not be happy with yourself until you really learn how to do good and then do it. And perhaps this is a lifetime's occupation! Do your circumstances not continually change? You meet someone new almost every day. Once again you are stumped by the problem of real communication, of honourable conduct.

Honourable conduct indeed seems to be high on the list. With every new human being a different set of rules seems to apply. You can be charming with one person but then, afterwards, you wonder did you really do more than just flatter your vanity. The next one you meet behaves gruffly, makes you feel small and worthless. You shy away from confrontation. Afterwards you suspect you should have stood up for yourself. But how can you be sure? The next day you have to speak in front of a group of people. You carefully prepare what you are going to say. But then, at the time, it comes out without conviction not like last time, when you hoped you would be able to be spontaneous and then you blurted out improprieties and made a fool of yourself.

You wouldn't mind, if at least you could be sure that you were getting ahead, that you were learning something, above all that your existence and behaviour on the earth made a good difference.

However the very concept of goodness is in doubt. Sometimes you wonder have you still not advanced from the time when you depended on the approval of your peers. You identify 'the good' as a social benefit and you get even more confused. One man's standards constitute another man's downfall. In society we all want to rush towards our happiness or make do with at least a minimum of convenience. The social evil impresses us all too clearly with its insistence on the collective contribution from a conventional point of view. We are not impressed by the many wonders of scientific-technological progress. What use to us is immediate telecommunication to the stars while we are incapable of personal compassion? How can we possibly get enthusiastic about immense data manipulation while we remain ignorant about our own worth?

*

So far, instead of judgment, condemnation and admiration, and the evil from our hearts, we have advocated discernment and a powerfully generous affection.

In the interest of <u>discernment</u> now we need to distinguish between those who are ethically predisposed and those who are not. Our discernment will be clear only to the extent that we come up with an overall generous affection. In the absence of such generosity we will be swayed by what we like and dislike. We want our discernment to be clear because our conduct depends on it, and we want our conduct to be as appropriate as possible. Appropriate conduct is proportionate to clarity of discernment.

Those who are ethically predisposed we call human beings. Those who are not, we call people. The onus is therefore on what we mean by ethical predisposition. In truth this is one of the most difficult meanings to express because we tend to relate it to judgment and law rather than to generosity and human natural affection. People are not in the least interested in doing good, but we in turn are not in the least interested in pointing this out to them. People are not worse or better than human beings. Some human beings are at some times better or worse than others and I may be better of worse now than I was yesterday, but this business of better or worse still has nothing to do with our ethical human being or with anyone's judgment of ourselves. We are going to have a hard time extricating ourselves from a judgmental morality, which has become a part of the very language we use. The logical sequence of events as we conventionally know it is 'good, better, best', and for some the best is never quite good enough. In reality however the good is not comparative. An action, behaviour or conduct, is either good or not. Judgment does not come into it but discernment. You cannot point to a law in order to decide on what is good.

Now, if we ask what is meant by an ethical predisposition, we can understand that from the point of view of popular judgmental morality nothing like that really exists, while from the point of view of rationality, generously affectionate moral discernment is necessary in someone and from someone if an ethical predisposition is to be detected in someone else. Once detected, the predisposition becomes a disposition. The yeast has been activated.

We are right to call it a yeast, because once the ethical predisposition has been discerned and detected it gradually spreads throughout the entire human being until all members are affected.

In people no such ethical predisposition can be detected, but a generous affection brings forth in them, if we persevere somewhat, an obedience to law, which is nothing to be scoffed at. In fact people become quite tractable if human beings behave towards them with generous affection because they are able to sense that generosity of spirit. The power of the generosity makes a distinct impression on them and so they allow themselves to be guided and led in the name of the good, even though they can never do good.

*

The difference between moral judgment and moral discernment is crucial and well worth some specific attention.

Morality, remember, refers to an individual person's perception of the good and to a great extent it encompasses what we mean by foundation and preparation. When that individual person begins to interact with other beings and with the world then, on the basis of that foundation and in line with that moral preparation, we extend the meaning of moral to ethical. We know well enough how an attempt at good doing in the world that is not based on a sound individual morality is doomed. Hence, 'ethical' includes and involves the moral.

When asking about the difference between judgment and discernment in the context of ethics, we do well to look first at morality therefore.

Moral judgment implies a knowledge of law and an insight into practice. The purpose of such judgment is the conformity of practice to law. This is fine as far as it goes. We become aware of a difficulty as soon as we begin to speak of the good. The good does not conform to law. Laws, rather, are themselves greater or lesser forms of the good. It would evidently be absurd to suggest that the good should conform to its own forms. Neither does it make sense to speak of the good as somehow above or beyond the law.

A great deal is said and written about 'laws' and 'the law' in total or partial ignorance of the good, so we sometimes need to take pains to extricate ourselves from false patterns of thinking and feeling.

The good is willing to lend itself as law to those who wish to learn how to do good. However those who then misconceive of law as an end in itself rather than as a means to good action and behaviour find themselves entangled in 'laws' and constricted by 'the law'. So on our way to the good we are bound to proceed lawfully, but as soon as we loose sight of our goal, 'the law' begins to lord it over us and we use 'laws' to lord it over one another. This is basically the difference between law, on the way to the good, where law is the helping hand the good extends to us, and 'the law' and 'laws', where we ignore that helping hand and the one extending it, but as we realize how our troubles and problems pile up, we try to use the good which we sense in law both in order to attain to bad ends and also to prevent the consequences of such behaviour. Laws and the law are therefore, strictly speaking, respectively misapplications and a misconception of law.

*

Moral judgments are to bring about a conformity of practice to law and to laws. In the first case we must admit that law, which is the good extending itself towards us, does not require conformity because it is not formal. Law is not a form of the good but the good itself, however impersonal. It is we ourselves who are to obey rather than causing our practical behaviour to be like this or like that while we ourselves remain unmoved and untouched. If we ourselves obey, we are lawful. We do not obey 'the law' but we are lawful and obedient. To be obedient for the sake of the good, the good being personal, this is what it means to be lawful.

Strictly speaking there is no such thing as the law. Or, more specifically, the law is 'the thing itself', and we have made the mistake of pretending that we can invent it.

In the second case, conformity to laws is bound to be unfortunate. It is correct that laws are forms of the good, but if we now were to do what we do according to such laws, how would we ever arrive at the personal good? Laws are important inasmuch as they prevent us from falling away from the good once we have experienced it. Prior to any experience of the good, laws cannot play a vital role in our life. Not only do they prevent us from falling away from the good once we have experienced it, but they also keep us up to the cooperative mark once we have begun to grow in the good.

Finally then we can say that moral judgment attempts to conform practice to law, to the law or to laws. We have discerned that law does not suit conformity of practice but ourselves on the way to the good, that laws are not there for us to accord with but they safeguard and expedite our practice, and that 'the law' is really a free invention of ours when we try to standard-ize the impersonal good as the final and only good, so that the fall away from the personal good is sanctioned while growth in the personal good is for all practical purposes outlawed.

Discernment, not moral judgment, is therefore what we need as we strive to be lawful on the way to the personal good. As our skill of discernment improves, we become less likely to make moral judgments and we are less likely to be upset by anyone who subjects us to moral judgment. Our discernment of moral judgment frees us from any need to object to it, and, of course, we override our own tendency to make moral judg-ments by practicing discernment.

*

Moral discernment, then, does not refer us to the law or to laws but it conducts us to the truth and helps us to make our conduct more truthful. Moral discernment teaches. A simpli-fied scenario allows us to imagine a teacher who approaches a group of pupils overall with generous human-natural affection while at the same time, by way of moral discernment, trans-forming, in one or two cases, an ethical predisposition into an ethical disposition. The essence of the teaching faculty is moral discernment, therefore, and where moral judgment is involved, neither do people become tractable nor do human beings come to ethical awareness.

*

We are not only affected by human beings but also by peo-ple, and for that reason our human-natural affection must be generous, otherwise we run into trouble. The generosity, in combination with moral discernment, not only sees us through but in addition it wins us friends. By friends I simply mean other human beings with an ethical disposition.

*

Moral discernment, like all ethical attainments, needs to be practiced before it becomes, at long last, a good habit. Moral judgment will then no longer be a tendency for us.

Once we are ethically disposed, so that this growth principle, this yeast, as we have called it, has been activated in us, we become for a while in turns infuriated and dismayed by the rareness of human being around us. For a long time, as we attempt to relate to others what seems to be going on within us, we come up against puzzlement, rejection and persecution. Why, we ask ourselves, when we have discovered this well-spring of human being in ourselves, can we not now be happy and have an easy time of it? Why are we not universally valued and admired? The opposite seems to be the case. From among a thousand who seek the treasure, one finds it, and right away he is set upon by the others or – completely ignored. He cannot keep quiet about what he has found for his joy runs over, but his message is not appreciated. The main reason for this misunderstanding is that he speaks, as it were, a different language. Why, they want to know, could he not have arrived at his destination and still remained one of 'us'? Suddenly he speaks to us in words that eat into our flesh.

Being is not the same as human being. Human being as such is always at first separated out, for the one into whom the yeast has been introduced is being utterly changed. Not that his attributes are changed while he remains the same. He himself discovers that he is not after all his own master, and that if he would be a whole being he must allow himself to be shaped even as he participates in the shaping. It is this business of being, as it were, at the mercy of circumstances that suddenly looms so large and is so hard to accept. Not that he is more at the mercy of circumstances now than he ever was, but at one time he was able to delude himself about this because there was nothing within him available that allowed him to make a contribution. He is now in the possession of a creative potency and most of those around him timidly shun him because they hate the unfamiliar or they aggressively seek him out to harm him because subconsciously they sense he has what they need while at the same time they resent his freedom, his independence from social standards and traditional conventions.

He will be wise therefore to learn as soon as possible the ins and outs of this new reality into which he has been moved and been placed. Pressures he experiences from without he must accept as somehow beneficial for his growth in human being. If he is still prone to moral judgment, this does him much harm. Of course it is always most difficult to refrain from moral judgment when we are being morally judged ourselves.[i]

What counts most of all is that he should know what he is doing in the light of his natural development, for he can take it for granted that those who have no such natural development do not know what they are doing. He can draw benefit for himself from their behaviour towards him and he may know that his own wise behaviour does after all offer them a way out of their predicament. He is saved from vainglory by insight into the 'nature of his nature' as it were. He is not the prime mover of his fate. He is more than that and better than that in terms of modesty, humility and repentance.

*

How can we say that the good is <u>personal</u>?

Much of the insight into ethics that we achieve specifically due to our affectionate response to human beings hinges on what we mean by personality. How is personhood conferred? How dos it come into being?

---

[i] Hence the saying of Jesus: 'Judge not that ye be not judged.' In other words: Don't judge so that you won't be judged, but judge righteously. We criticise too because we are afraid of being criticized.

Usually when we wish to learn about what it means to be personal we make a comparison to the individual and then quickly come to the conclusion that individuality would develop into personality, or, more relevantly, that we as individual human beings, once we have become conscious of our individuality, would then like to become personally effective. As soon as our own house is in order, we want to open it to guests. If we don't, the order goes stale.

But right away we have an explanation too for that worrying phenomenon which is so-called personality, out on its own with no individuality to back it up. Someone who is not individually in order cannot be personally intact; he is not ready to be a person.

This readiness for personality is worth mentioning. Even at any given moment, if it occurs to us that we might be able to make a personal contribution, we do well first to check on the roots of our individuality, to make sure they are strong enough to support us. Personal communication, behaviour and action, expose us to mistakable dangers and it involves calculable risks, so we might decide that before we launch ourselves out onto the open waves we ought to make sure we are seaworthy.

But then what is so special about personality? Actually we see very little of it. Most of the time we find ourselves in the company of individuals, who refuse to develop as persons, and of individualists, who insist on their right to reject personality, and in the vicinity of personalities, who have a fake personality conferred upon them in the absence of any true individuality. An individual, also an individualist, has no personality, no viable link to others, while a personality, as that word is usually applied, is devoid of individuality. We talk to the individual but he does not recognize us as another human being. We talk to the personality but no one is at home.

That 'viable link to others' gives us a clue as to the essence of personality, its purpose and function. We as individual human beings are in the possession of our souls, of the uncreated being that manifests and presents for each one of us separately merciful good spirit, and it is the wish equally of that spirit and of ourselves to become communally active and effective in the world.

*

How often do we not break our heads wondering how we will manage. We imagine the goal of our desires and we seem, to ourselves, within grasping distance of total satisfaction. We can feel in our bones the perfection of a task, the mastery of an ambition, yet the crowning glory is beyond us. We come so close so often and fail so miserably, as often, that we begin to question what motivates us in the first place. A basic ingredient seems to be missing. The 'how' of our endeavour leaves us in the lurch just when we seem to need it most. Not that we lose our way but that suddenly it appears for all the world as if we had been on the wrong way all along.

Now whatever we begin from the beginning in the acknowledgment of merciful spirit cannot go wrong and will continue throughout our awareness of that spirit to its predestined end.

Just as our own destiny is personal, so is the essence of all our achievements. As I am at the moment, assuming I am a human being, this has been my destiny up to now and the person I am at this moment has been foreshadowed in merciful spirit form the beginning. When it comes to my achievements and accomplishments now, these are reflections of how I am at the moment and they communicate to all the world my personal connectedness to that same merciful spirit to which I am beholden.

*

How wonderful, really, that when we seem most fully ourselves, most thoroughly at home in ourselves, we are actively expressing merciful good spirit. Our most selfless achievements return us completely to ourselves and nothing is real for us finally except that we grow. We grow real and we are real while we grow. This notion of growth needs to be updated. It confers upon ourselves the personhood we long for. It is not enough for us to participate in humanity and still not enough to have human being but we finally want to be human beings, each one select. Indeed one can understand why some of us would be tempted to rest in their participation in human being; compared to popularity, this is like having arrived after a traumatic journey. But suddenly the joy and that sense of being special fades, precisely because we had not stretched out for human being. We persevere and learn what it means to accumulate in ourselves an organic potentiality, which is the power to do good, called human being, and once again we are so overwhelmed with gratitude that we want to glory in our state – and others around us let us know in one way or another that we have not yet begun to invest our power and to share our portion of the common wealth. We call it the commonwealth of reality because the wealth, the human being, each one of us accumulates is to be held in common by all of us, and to that end our personality comes into being.

I am a person as soon as I deliver my human being into the hands of my fellow human being. I am a person while I do that. My human being is the wealth I have accumulated even as I grow and work.

What is my work? It is ethical personality in action. Is it surprising that so many modes of being converge at this point of our human natural affection for the human beings that unavoidably affect us?

Finally people have no affect on us except inasmuch as we ourselves at that moment are popular. Here is where our moral discernment comes into its own. What does it mean when a human being has become popular? Does it not signify a gross misappropriation of select human being?

*

It seems that in order to be able to appreciate human being and human beings properly and fully we have to compare them to popularity and people. I apologize in advance for the misunderstanding this terminology seems to invite.

A human being can become popular, can be infected by popularity. Once we have our soul we are still liable to the ritualistic muse. We may have imbibed the waters from the stream of eternal consciousness but as soon as we are admired for it, how often do we not stoop to the muddy puddles of the deferential vanities. Or we glide along the surface of what we know to be the truth while paying lip-service to the shallow immoralities of convention.

Human being is a power, not an act. A human being is someone who translates that power into action. People are not in the possession of this very specific growth principle which we mean by human being. I am not labouring under the delusion that newspapers will ever use the terms 'people' and 'popular' in just this way. My concern is with human being and on behalf of human beings. The generosity we extend to people prevents us from becoming popular ourselves. There is a kind of bigotry and sectarianism into which human beings slide vis-à-vis people which does all of us a disservice. We slip into this error not because we do something wrong, loosely speaking, but because we fail to do something right. Strictly speaking, we fail to do something good. The generosity we equally extend towards human beings and people allows us to appreciate both, for what they are and for what they are not. As soon as we fail in this generosity we begin to make moral judgments, demanding from people that they should be human beings and blaming them because they are not, which is manifestly absurd, and

69

misconstruing in ourselves what it means to be human, which is a shame. I know that whenever I do this it helps me immensely to be ashamed.

The popular reaction to express human being is predictable. Eventually we fail to wonder at it. But our own reaction to a human-spiritual growth stimulus is equally predictable, and eventually we cease from wonder here too. What we need are properly trained rational responses to all such reactions, whether they reflect on our lack of generosity or on our lack of humility.

In the interest of comparing human being with popularity, I would hold this generosity and this humility side by side. There is the generosity equally towards those who can and those who can not see. Then there is the humility in the face of the human-natural spirit in the world. Both of these are equally crucial.

Let's deal with the humility first. Those who insist on definitive knowledge cannot come up with it, not for the lack of trying but because their epistemological bias prevents it. Phrases such as "we always have to be willing to learn" do not contribute much in themselves but at least they point in the right direction. The law of unavoidable reaction is another case in point. Finally what matters is that we grasp the essence of this humility and make a good habit of it.

Can we do it directly or do we have to wait for ourselves to react unfortunately once again to some growth stimulus for which we were not ready so that we may learn humility by contradicting our arrogance?

Both are equally possible to us as human beings. Personality however is the necessary ingredient. If I, in person, am committed to the search for a principle of humility, being fed up to the teeth with the obstructionist shenanigans of my unconscious self in the face of the human-natural spirit in the world, I will definitely succeed. On any impersonal basis I haven't a hope.

And immediately the other side of the equation pops into view. All my attempts at personality will eventually fail unless I at least combine them with such a search for a principle of humility, and best if I combine personality with humility itself.

We can see how in all such instances as the present one can, if careless, stray into a closed door policy, where A requires B and B requires A, so that one can never get hold of either. This is the fallacy of so-called orthodoxy. The priests hide the keys and will not themselves enter. In the present case all that means is that we have to strive for personality and humility at one and the same time.

*

Our darkest hour is always the one when we cannot for the life of us make any headway in the world around us. Meanwhile avenues of perception are closed. Then we may <u>behold</u> the material earth, the starry universe and the cloudy sky. This activity of beholding is the root position of our human personality. We may call it activity and position at once because we cannot relax into it as into a dream but we continually achieve a relaxation. Avenues of perception are closed only until we establish such positions of acknowledgment. It is the human-natural spirit in the world that desires to draw itself to our attention and our so-called 'darkest hour' signifies as much to us.

What is this human-natural spirit of the world? Or indeed who is it? The need for personality on our part becomes more and more obvious. Accustomed as we are to things in our environment and to the cold indifference of the lot of them, we are bound to experience it as an intrusion that a person should enter our environment and that we, as a consequence, should either be forced to march in step with him, ignorant of the event, or choose to live in community with him, grateful for the opportunity.

There is a common difficulty that plagues our ethical will at this point. Even all ethicality aside, if it is our will that has become accustomed to impressing itself on the world, and if suddenly now a spirit will is to return the impression, we are bound to be offended. The pride of our will, even under the periodic duress of privation, frustration and outright failure, is such that it defines for us our own personality wherever we attempt to bring it into being.

A wilful personality however is a curse. This curse is operational even more effectively where we disguise this wilfulness disingenuously as obligingness.

Conversely, wherever we take up with the human-natural spirit of the world, not being offended in it, we are then on a collision course with those who give themselves directly or indirectly over to wilful personality. No wonder most of us would much rather enjoy a temporary reprieve from offensiveness by working our wilful personality than work for permanent joy at the risk of being offended or causing offence.

What are some of the ways now, more explicitly, in which this human-natural spirit in the world seems to offend us? Ethical conduct in the world depends on realistic insight here. More often than not we begin with wilful personality just so as to be able to begin at all, towards some goal, and the first offence then is our inability to keep going. Problems crop up in our path, difficulties arise as if to spite us, and we are at liberty to insist on our wilful personality or to give up. We are not at liberty to cooperate with the human-natural spirit in the world until we have acknowledged its presence – his presence – for us. His presence for us must be acknowledged by us, and in the absence of that acknowledgment we will either resent being frustrated in our progress, our wilfully personal approach, or we will feel unworthy and look for someone or something to blame for our lack of persistence in that wilfulness after having thrown in the towel.

So this spirit seems to offend us by impressing himself on ourselves in person and not on our body or mind or spirit of flesh or soul. From our rational point of view here at the moment we can right away understand the reason for the offense and we can appreciate the nature of it. While my personality is wilful and not humble I cannot bear the contact of that spirit because I lack points of reference in common with it. Therefore I strike back or hide. I have no sign of the presence of this spirit because he appeals directly to me in person, and if I am not humble in person, the appeal occurs to me as offensive. The offence is a sign, if you like, that this spirit appealed to me, in the past, but it is also a sign of the fact that I was then not humble in person.

So this is one way this spirit seems to offend us, in that it manages to slip past all our own offences and defences, all of which are of course wilfully personal in origin. We are convinced that our offences and defences are perfectly honourable, and the fact that the are undeniably personal should, we suppose and feel, guarantee our inviolability and our invulnerability. The thing about personality that encourages us in this error is that it connects us primarily with other beings. In the case of wilful personality the crucial secondary connection with our own being is sacrificed, so that we only seem to ourselves invulnerable when in truth we are not. The connection with other beings must therefore gradually become an association with other things, and the true personality of the spirit we mean must appear to undermine us. The truth of the matter is, of course, that we are not being undermined but we have become hollow. The increasing shallowness and hollowness of ourselves as wilful persons coincides with an increasing vulnerability of offensiveness in ourselves. We feel we are being offended and we become offensive.

But what is humility? How can we become humbly personal instead of wilfully personal?

*

The belligerence that resides in those of us who do not take kindly to injustice affords us a major clue to the essentials of a humility that does not involve self-abasement and self-sacrifice. We would gladly have it known that we slept through the war but not that we idled or procrastinated. Any critical perusal of our inward motivations should end in defeat rather than in a discovery of unworthy moods. We have indeed arrived at a point well beyond victory if our joy at an inner and eternal peace outweighs any need for justification, whoever should be questioning our right to do or undergo.

The issue of war is not the same as the impending fury of it. Can we disguise what goes on in our breast at those times when all hell threatens to break loose and we feel driven to the end of our endurance? Can we claim to have relevant insight then into what we should do in the interest of the good or are we much more likely, perhaps, to delude ourselves as to the true nature of our own best interest, while renown beckons and the fear of opprobrium hounds us?

The looming catastrophe that throws our senses into confusion is frequently, as we know, a fruit of our cowardly invention. The courage we suppose we must, and often do, come up with to face such a catastrophe is therefore of a stamp that defies analysis unless we come to some sort of an arrangement within ourselves as to the terms of its original circumstance.

We cannot even begin to encompass the true nature of real humility until we have come into the clear about where we stand in relation to our present hopes and expectations. Do we

74

know what it means to be informed of good spirit, to be well inspired? Have we grasped the significance of the human-natural spirit in the world? To the materialist within us, who adheres, by definition, to the evidence of appearances, all such talk of 'a human-natural spirit in the world' smacks of blasphemy. Our materialist believes in a God who has cast aspersion on the world, on this world of disparate things for all of which somehow connections and relations must be fabricated. The god who has come into the world, as guarantor of all such connections and relations once again as from the beginning, is shrugged off by him as irrelevant or attacked as anathema. And we must not forget that he does believe in this materialist God of his.

Though he believes in Him, how can he hold Him? This is his problem. The materialist God, Who is really an exacerbated version of god, cannot be held, neither responsible nor in high regard. Eventually He must be blamed for what our materialist cannot squeeze out of Him. And when He is blamed He withdraws. This is His right of course. But then He becomes by definition inscrutable. Our materialist has defined Him and when He refused to live up to that definition the definition was altered. And so on. To the inscrutability will then have to be added an historic incalculability and a moral unpredictability.

The god who exists in the world and who is not only that he is but also so that we may be, makes no demands on us and promises us only a radical happiness, or blessedness. This human-natural spirit in the world will not hold still for analysis if thereby we hope to bring him within the confines of materialism. To those who would apprehend him, he must occur as a mystery. To those who know him as guide, friend and master he occurs as guide, friend and master.

*

The one we would know as the human-natural spirit in the world is active on our behalf in a way we cannot appreciate except in perfect humility and in the absence of all wilful personality. However since our first reaction is always wilful personality, we can be sure of the road to perfect humility by contradicting that mood-ridden determination of our self. We may contradict it equally in our thinking and in our feeling, it should not matter to us which comes first.

We notice all onsets of wilful personality by the way we become implicated interpersonally. That is to say we identify an injury or a deleterious state of affairs and right away we broadcast our opinion in favour of one or the other side of a developing dispute, urging a decision or willing a judgment. Little does it occur to us that our own original failure to suppress our cowardly motivations has brought us into that strange context of ideas and counter-ideas where no peace is possible and no true understanding is achieved.

Humility takes courage, we may be sure of that. Even the beginnings of humility in ourselves bring us into a zone of effectiveness where others are bound to experience this as a challenge, if not as an insult. Others are offended by our humility of feeling or thought before we know it and we must trust that their offensiveness cannot hurt us because of the human-natural spirit in the world. They are in reality not offended by us but by that spirit and there we must allow it to rest instead of attempting to take upon ourselves a justification we cannot with the best of wills sustain.

As I write at this moment in perfect humility, I am able to sustain with perfect equanimity the various upheavals of mood and temperament that flare up in me naturally from one moment to the next. And when I do get a moment of external peace too, I do not relax but I work all the same on this state of humility, which is really the only state worthy of the name.

A political state operates towards a state of humility.

What I just now described in my own case as upheavals of mood and temperament incidental to my state of humility – this is what I mean by a political state. Rationality proves its worth here again. From a state of humility a political state can be perfectly appreciated, but it rests on no grounds of its own whereupon policy may be founded.

Ethics in politics rests on the foundation of states of humility. Individual human beings are in such states – never speak of such a thing as the sum-total of them because that is an absurdity.

Personality in its approach to the world avails itself of policy. I myself, as soon as I bring my personality into focus in relation to other human beings, avail myself of policies. There is the one single policy of love out of which all policies grow, like the branches out of the trunk of a tree.

And how is love a policy? It comes into being as soon as we approach another human being ethically, with good will and good intention, and then it reveals to us its means and modes. We do not love except in one way or another, so we need these means and modes, which are however revealed to us under contemporary circumstances by love itself as the policy of policies which is the central platform of our ethical approach to other human beings.

This 'central platform' of love as policy is reminiscent of our state of humility. Other than supported by a state of humility, love as policy makes no sense and is neither conceivable nor effective. The very constitution of love is forever under scrutiny because we carry within ourselves our own materialist contradiction of which we at times are so proud that neither love nor life can find a foothold in us and we wither by the wayside. If only we could come up with a much more descriptive representation of such a state of humility, so that others might imitate and copy it for the good of us all, but really nothing is to be gained in that direction because our humility must advertise itself on its own ground by way of personality and love as policy. In our humility we hold our god and he holds us. This is the final crown of our achievement. From here radiates all the good we can do under any circumstances. From here too we can appreciate most fully what is expected from us by all other created beings. Our exposure to the inhuman and popular is balanced by our capacity for love as policy based on a state of humility for which we ourselves in our freedom are responsible.

*

The achievement of a state of humility by us in ourselves is best implemented in relation to other created beings and most effectively in relation to other human beings. We seem to have a choice whenever we meet another human being. It is a choice in terms of power. We are at liberty to opt for power <u>over</u> that human being, and indeed a great many pleasures present themselves right away as coincidental to such a choice. The power over another human being affords us the greatest satisfaction egocentrically imaginable, so no wonder that we make every effort imaginable to morally sanitize and ethically sanction every effort we find ourselves making in that direction. We find ourselves making such efforts, the process is pleasurable but at the same time there is the nagging doubt that comes along with all egocentricity in a human being, and the suspicion that we may be on the wrong track entirely. We know by now from our rational point of view that such doubt and suspicion testifies to the agency, in our being, of merciful spirit, but while we labour under the influence of those little pleasures that come along with power over other beings, especially over human beings, we become less rational and we decide to justify – to sanitize and sanction – the various attitudes and opinions with which we have begun to identify as they have come to happen to us. Often we call them ideas, these notions that come along on the back of an egocentric pleasure-drive in the direction of power over beings, especially over human beings. A morality and an ethic based on such an error is of course worthless or worse.

The question now is, in recognition of such error, do we deny ourselves that pleasure and do we sacrifice the sense of power to which our ego would accustom us? Does it get us anywhere, this <u>self-denial and self-sacrifice</u>? Can it in fact be pursued in any real sense and on its own basis? In other words, are self-denial and self-sacrifice enough? Indeed, are they in themselves even possible?

The alternative to power <u>over</u> another being is power <u>for</u> another being. We are equally at liberty to pursue one or the other. The only difference really is that we will never <u>find</u> ourselves exercising power for another being. If it happens, then it is power over, or superpower. If pleasures are involved, then once again it is superpower. In the case of power <u>for</u> someone, we will actually have to have made that choice right from the beginning, because no pleasures are available to lead us into it.

Our intention to be powerful <u>for</u> other beings, especially for other human beings, brings along with it a state of humility. However this is an intention we all too often mistake, such as when we find ourselves being powerful over some, or someone, allegedly on behalf of others. Here once again we try to indulge in the pleasures of egocentricity as we justify them in terms of chivalry, altruism, charity, etc. when in fact the chivalry, altruism and charity we envision are bogus.

The test is: Are we able to <u>contradict</u> ourselves even as we deem ourselves to be powerful. There are so many ways in which we lord it over others. And those others do not always mind being lorded over. They even invite it and enjoy it afterwards. And usually those who try to prevent us from lording it over others in one department are motivated by their own tendency to do so in another, or perhaps even in the same department. We have to take the reins in our own hands and devise a method by which we can decide for ourselves that the time has come for us to change.

If I am able to negate my power, then it must have been power <u>over</u>. However by way of such negation I have right away opened myself to the powerful human-natural spirit in the world. By way of such negation I remove whatever at that moment inhibits or excludes my state of humility. And right away I am personally effective. I cannot be in a state of humility without at the same time being personally effective. And this personal effectiveness, not the humility, will occupy the centre of my attention.

*

In a state of humility, whatever we do is well done. Of course it may be important for us not to do as such but simply to be. Simply being is sometimes most difficult. Our wilful personality desires to assert itself and we may end up with quite a struggle on our hands. What helps us then especially is if we have in mind that the human natural spirit in the world is most significantly then on our side and much more than being present is actually acting on our behalf.

For remember that this human-natural spirit in the world is the ethical necessity per se. But for him we would not be horrified by the prospects of our unethical being and doing; and that very horror of course causes us to abjure the very notion of such a spirit, while the suggestion of the existence of that very being, of that uncreated spirit-being, is anathema to us. The touch burns us. We shrink back in dismay.

It would seem advisable to negate in ourselves as much and as often as we can all the power that can be negated, so that the only power able to flourish and thrive as personal being and action is power on behalf of others rather than power over others. We must understand how it happens that we mistake egocentric power for the power to do good, when we tell ourselves that by lording it over some we give benefit to others. Therefore we learn to apply the test of negation. Therefore we learn to insist in ourselves on a state of humility.

It should be possible to demonstrate that conduct other than on the ethical basis of a state of humility is not conduct at all but to some extent adultery or promiscuity. <u>Behaviour and conduct</u> would have to be compared to <u>passion and action</u> and to doing and work. Doing and work also could be divided as <u>being and doing</u>, <u>rest and work</u>. Whenever and while we are in a state of humility we know what we do, and at such times our knowledge penetrates each time to the heart of the matter where 'I and the world' are correctly appreciated as two in one.

Take <u>behaviour and conduct</u>. By whom or by what are we to be guided in each? Evidently the onus is on ourselves to come up with the principles that will keep us on the move and see us through difficulties. But principles invariably end by being moralized. We heed them not because they enable and empower us but because yesterday they were heeded and not to heed them would make us unfit for Society. (I capitalize idols.)

To behave and to conduct ourselves on the basis of principles is therefore a risky business because such a great investment of the discerning capacity is needful. Given that capacity, why not opt right away for that principle of all principles, which is a state of humility? Why not indeed? Because so much will have to be flung overboard. Are the eyes of Society not upon us constantly? How dare we let go of a fashion except for the more fashionable! The alternative to the latest civility is always the barbarian. Were a man to think and feel for himself, were a woman to trust her deepest instincts – well, admittedly in addition to being more of a woman and a man, could they not incur the wrath of vested moral interest? Once I have established in myself a good habit or two – and very likely that suffices! – shall I now impose these on all those around me and judge their loyalty by the adherence they demonstrate?

Except for that state of humility we cannot imagine how we might still cope if we left the beaten track of timid tradition. And yet not a forthright step may be taken except in departure from it. This latter fact, baldly stated, is known to some who equate such departure with a conquest of an ideal. But a state of humility is not an ideal and the path to it is not by revolution. Neither the fearful nor the stiff-necked may enter.

But we can cope very well if first we learn to behave ourselves within the confines of our own <u>moral integrity</u>, and then our conduct in the world will be aptly licensed. Moral integrity? Where am I to look for principles and guidelines? I will not be content, I know this ahead of time, except with something from the definition of human being itself. As soon as I negate whatever power in me can be negated, I also contradict my leaning to impotence. That has not yet been mentioned. This <u>negating spirit</u> seems finally to have discovered its appropriate application. And no wonder that we were able to round the matter out on this present instance, since our conduct and behaviour characteristically veer away from their human-natural source not through superpower but on account of impotence. We make do with kinds and types of behaviour, with modes and fashions of conduct, when we might search in ourselves for the singular application and the original response. However both impotence and super-power get in the way of it and have to be removed.

*

82

Moral integrity is unsustainable except on the basis of humility, and we know now that we arrive at such a state of humility not by being humble but by negating all power in ourselves that is negatable, which implies the negation of impotence.

Now even as humility is really inseparable from this spirit or act of negation, so is moral integrity inseparable from behaviour and conduct. No one has moral integrity who does not behave in one way or another or who does not conduct himself under given circumstances. Moral integrity presupposes, therefore, an environment, and, more to the point, our awareness of our environment and of the fact that – we live. Our sensibility of our neighbourhood is crucial here. We need to keep in mind that we exist in a vicinity, that created beings surround us and that a finite portion of the infinite world concerns me in particular. Moral integrity dictates, we might say, that it matters to us where, at any given time, we are. Remaining alert to the fact that we live, in other words, is at first a task we have to set ourselves. In any case we cannot really say that we live unless we behave and conduct ourselves within a certain appreciation of our surroundings, and in order to be able to do that, we must of course be awake, which means awake to our surroundings. If the world as an infinite being is a mere concept to us and not a live reality we are incapable of behaviour and conduct and we have no moral integrity.

Being awake to our circumstances and surroundings implies rationality too of course. We cannot be awake to the world as to a collection of things. Behaviour and conduct is among beings and our thinking and reasoning must be taking account of affection, of mutual affection, and not just of a mass of trivia such as can be mechanically stored in any case.

The fact that we live, once we have begun to live, is bound to impress us, reflectively. A certain kind of awareness of ourselves as in affectionate interaction with the beings in our vicinity actually arises out of our achieved state of humility and returns to it, magnifying it. One is reminded of sun flares. Out of our state of humility we become aware of ourselves as truly living and this awareness makes us more humble. The power we have increases.

The ethical power, this power on behalf of others for the good of us all is described here as behaviour and conduct. Later we will come to terms with it as action and passion, as being and doing and as rest and work. Forget about definitive knowledge and accustom yourself to knowledge that is live.

Ethical power as behaviour and conduct has to be maintained. We don't just have it, suddenly, and there it is, for all time. As human beings we are the stewards of our power. We have to maintain our state of humility, and if in addition to this we can see to our moral integrity, so much the better. But really this integrity is implied by what we mean by a state of humility. We learn more about such states if we contemplate what we mean by moral integrity. That we might possibly be morally whole and in a way that cannot be diminished or harmed, this is surely good news, especially once we have admitted to ourselves, after sufficient painful experience, that the power over other beings we automatically come up with, the unethical power, cannot stand and endure so that we have to make a career out of negating and contradicting incessant opposition to it, like those who must defend their reputation and secure their money and bolster their ego or lose it – and then they lose it anyway. The negation and contradiction is misapplied by them. It is misapplied by us, through misconduct and misbehaviour, unless we negate our unethical power, our self, and contradict our impotence, our lack of self.

Moral integrity, then, is what we have when we know that we cannot be harmed or diminished in our ethical, powerful effectiveness and when we know, in addition, that this integrity

84

depends both on our maintenance of our state of humility <u>and</u> on the human-natural spirit in the world which responds in personal freedom to our ready state of humility.

We do well to become intellectually secure in our understanding here. The state of humility is entirely up to us. We depend on no one and nothing else for our ability to negate our selfish power. What is not up to us, and what we cannot cause and effect, is that which renders us ethically powerful. If we say that a state of humility never remains unempowered, as we may say from faith, from human-natural faith, then this does not imply that the human-natural spirit in the world is an impersonal force or a material quantity <u>over</u> which we have power. We do not know the human-natural spirit in the world if we ignore his personal freedom, and this freedom implies of course a being at liberty from our unethical influence. If, for the sake of useful reminder, we call him the merciful, human-natural spirit in the world, we emphasize the fact that his personal freedom like all freedom, implies his being for our sake and on our behalf, and of course through us his being for the sake and on behalf of all created beings, since human beings are the stewards of creation.

*

What does perhaps still need to be emphasized here, always in awareness of our modern semi-existence, is that behaviour and conduct in reality are ethically powerful. Behaviour and conduct in Society by comparison are always more or less in accordance with rules and regulations and therefore based on fear or motivated by greed and other forms of selfishness. Ethically powerful, or live, behaviour and conduct are not according to traditional and calculated manners and means for the purpose of predicted goals and ends, neither is moral integrity culturally embedded in any such tradition. From the modern point of view, no merciful, human-natural spirit exists in the world. Modern man at best waits for it to enter the world, or to enter it again. Modern behaviour and conduct therefore strikes one as a kind of insanity. Imagine the following:

A: Ah, good morning, pardon me for having entered your house but the door was open. I did send several letters to let you know I was coming. Are you only just up?

F: The noise of you in here woke me. I find that appalling, that you walk in here without even knocking. The door was locked and bolted. How did you get in? I am awaiting a very important personage today and I warn you, unless you immediately leave I shall call the police.

A: I assure you the door was open to me, and I am the one you invited, the one you expect. Look, I brought you a box of chocolates.

F: I must get the house tidied for my visitor and you are in the way. I have planned all these preparations so I really have no time to talk, whoever you are and however you got in here. Leave at once, please.

A: You see me and you talk to me but you refuse to recognize me. Why will you not believe that I am the very person who introduced himself to you by letter and over the telephone? We have time now to get to know each other, face to face.

F: Are you mad? Do you not understand my English? I said out! ...

... and so on.

*

Now we will look at <u>passion and action</u> in the same light.

Where our ethical behaviour and conduct include an awareness of our immediate and live environment and at the same time of our moral integrity, so that the two are known by us to be by definition that which becomes one through our ethical and powerful behaviour and conduct, so do our action and passion imply a discernment of that live environment and also of our moral integrity, and such discernment becomes relevant as soon as we accept the responsibility for our own organic growth. Along with greater perception, for example, comes an increased capacity for action and passion while a higher and more variable sensibility triggers off in us a renewed moral compulsion to effect beneficial change in the world.

So the first thought in relation to action and passion cautions us that moral discernment (not moral judgement) and organic growth (not mental or physical growth) go hand in hand. We know from our own unfortunate experience how destructive action and passion on the basis of moral judgment becomes, simply because moral judgment amounts to conceit, where I demand of others what I should be doing myself and where I see faults in others that really exist in myself. Looking at it from the other side, we know from similar bad experience that due to inorganic growth we usually are forced to take two steps backward for every step we take ahead, and the backward steps often are taken on terrain we cannot readily associate with the context in which we took the step forward. So we associate an apparent increase of authority with some malady such as a viral infection. Moral discernment and organic growth go hand in hand, since both arise from a state of humility, but moral judgment and inorganic growth are out of joint, hence the adultery and the promiscuity. Inorganic growth is because of wilful power, of power over, or superpower, as we have called it, where the merciful human-natural spirit-being in the world is ignored or ignorantly rejected – or insanely misconceived. A more descriptive term for inorganic growth would be extinct growth. Because superpower was not negated in the interest of a state of humility and consequent ethical power, an actual spirit of negation develops and pulls down that extinct growth – and us, inasmuch as we are committed to such 'progress'.

*

The most rudimentary description of action and passion is that in the case of passion we allow ourselves to be moved by the merciful human-natural spirit-being in the world, taking care only to make as much allowance as possible, while in the case of action we give evidence of our organic growth, taking care only to adapt that evidence to our human environment.

Technically, we grow because we are moved by that one un-created being in the world. But in order to be moved by him we must allow him to move us, passionately. This is not as simple as it sounds. This being is merciful and we, by comparison, may be quite the opposite and contrary, namely <u>vengeful</u> and <u>vindictive</u>. We lay claim to what we deem is ours by right and the role that justice plays in our lives is usually one-sided. We cannot be trusted with real growth because we aim at extinction. While we make a habit of claiming our just reward, there is no room in us for any organic benefit, so that the most merciful act of the uncreated being in his world is really that he withholds himself from us while we insist on justice. If he did not, we would get what we really deserve, which would not be pleasant and most confusing to us, as can actually happen at times when we drive our idiotic bargain too hard.

The trick for us therefore is to learn how to be passionately merciful and mercifully passionate, so that there will indeed be room in us for movement under the influence of the merci-ful one.

So how can we learn to be merciful when we would much rather be vindictive?

The best time to learn this is when we are being dealt with vengefully or unjustly. Really in our minds the two usually oc-

88

cur as one. Not only do we accuse someone else but we also accuse circumstances. Our most inward motivations are concerned here. Learning mercy is probably the most difficult task many of us have faced and we are bristling with defence mechanisms and plans of attack that are programmed into our flesh through early training. It depends on us now that we become wise to these, that we begin to notice them and to admit to ourselves that they exist. It is not enough to agree that: Oh yes, no doubt we are full of badness; and then to leave it at that. Actual identification has to be made of specific instances of vengefulness so that we can say: Yes, now is the time for me to be merciful instead. And at that very moment we ourselves are given the wherewithal for being just that.

*

The more we know about what goes on in us at such critical times, when we might be changing over from vengefulness to mercy, the better. We should look at it from several sides, because when we are, so to speak, under attack, we have to depend on insurances that are ready in place. Mercy, after all, is not just the absence of vengefulness. When we try to repress our vindictive moods and we do nothing else, we fail miserably. So it is bound to help us if we have in our minds some configuration of behaviour and conduct that will not be entirely wiped out under attack.

But all such insurance policies are best acquired at such times as when we possess a measure of equanimity. If our policy is love, we will get many small opportunities for practicing mercy, since the loving we do sets off in others a variety of resistances which they frequently express as accusations of injustice. Do we not all of us requite our god's love with stiff-necked abuse?

So this would be one way for us to learn mercy and to get into the habit of it, in that we deal mercifully with many small instances of rebuff to our love. Certainly forgiveness is part of it. But still we should look for the merciful action, for something we actually do to infiltrate the other person's system of fight or flight. It is a relief for someone who is expecting to be attacked not to be attacked but the merciful act must somehow remind that other person that his survival tactics are themselves a resistance to life and a rejection of life, for survival is not life, and as soon as survival becomes our priority, life escapes us and we begin to kill one another. This killing goes on then especially in the realm of spirit, so that we no longer seek good spirit nor are we accessible to it.

Of course we cannot argue anyone out of his survival-priority stance. People insist on survival at any cost and nothing will shift them. But a single act of mercy can work wonders because of its extraordinary capacity for overriding the entire survival context and highlighting instead that which moves survival issues into the secondary position.

We need to discern between survival and life therefore, so that we can understand why our survival cannot succeed if we know nothing of life. When people use the word 'life' they mean survival and the world 'life' is so often misused that one feels one ought to avoid it altogether. Just as we must <u>negate</u> our egotistic will to power 'over', the <u>will to overpower</u>, so that real power, and the wish to <u>empower</u>, can thrive in a state of humility, so we must <u>transcend</u> our <u>survival instinct</u>, so that our survival rather than looming absurdly as our reason for being, becomes that which we do not neglect while we concentrate on issues of life. The possibility of such a transcendence depends of course every time on our having available to us that to which we transcend. If we are to leap across a brook, the other side must at least be in sight. Attempts to spiritualistic transcendence end in drowning. Mercy is either an everyday down-to-earth practice or the most horrid of hypocritical conceits.

Concentrate on issues of life – what are issues of life? What is life when it takes priority over survival? Elsewhere we have thought of it as a gift or as a reward for certain kinds of preparation. Viewing life now as the goal of a merciful transcendence of survival instinct, moves it into the forefront of our deliberations on ethical action and passion. To have life in this case means to be sensible of our solidarity with all other life-forms and to be sensitive to their organic appeal to us.

*

He who lives survives in any case but he who survives does not necessarily live. Strictly speaking, no one who does not live really survives, but we have to take into consideration our popular misconceptions to do with survival here. Sometimes we say we "have to survive", but this is about as true as saying: "you have to eat". The meaning presumably is: You have to eat to survive. But this holds no water either, because no one can survive indefinitely. We survive shocks to our system, public shame and private grief – meaning we get through, we are not destroyed by it. No complications set in until we discern life from survival, and then we can understand survival from the vantage point of life, but not the other way around.

Issues of life really must begin for us with such discernment. Transcendence of 'mere survival', as we might also call it, most commonly arises out of a recognition such as: "There must be more to life than this!", where 'this' is 'the rat race', 'the dog-eat-dog existence', 'the hand to mouth existence', but also quite ordinarily: 'the social round'. After such a recognition, the negation of the overpowering survival-instinct must be next on the list and a state of humility is passionate. Passion implies that we are undergoing influence of the uncreated being in the world. We can imagine how a passionate negation of self is much more effective. In the case of passion, then, we have actual help from that uncreated being, in our endeavour to negate self. And because of this help, issues of life become obvious to us and we may act. It means we do not act from ego or self, but we ourselves as humble human beings act, in concert with such issues of life. Action therefore presupposes passion, while passion is also active. Issues of life are not revealed to us while we are entangled in mere survival issues. But any premature action is to be avoided. The meaning of transcendence therefore must include a previous revelation of issues of life, so that if once again we are entangled in mere survival issues, we may aim for *eventual* life issues while none are revealed to us at the moment. We can work our way out of another tight corner because we have the memory of human-natural experience, but we cannot do it if we have no such memory vouchsafed us, such as from childhood or from some adult inspiration. Knowing this, we do not demand the impossible from others. However we know that when we act passionately as humble human beings in concert with certain life issues, such action lets others in on a secret, as it were. It gives them an opportunity to experience their essential human nature, which experience in turn may urge them to come to the fervent supposition that 'there must be more to life than this!'

Real action inspires. This writing I am doing is real action and perhaps it will inspire you. However the spirit of real action is human-natural, and while we cannot say that it in itself is good, we can say that it is beneficial. Our action in concert and cooperation with it is good. If we understand this, we will also be much better able to be merciful to one another. If your good action inspires me, that only means that I am now in touch for a time with my own human nature. This is a lot, but it is up to me now what I do with it. I can invest it or waste it. Would you let out your vengefulness on me for not investing? Would you judge me as unworthy for not rising to the occasion this time when I might very well do so next time and when my wastefulness has not cost you anything in any case? And besides, how did you come by your very first experience of your beneficial human nature in the world? Did you wrest it egotistically from stone? Did you force your maker to pay heed?

*

Before we go on to 'being and doing' and 'rest and work' let us enquire of that human-natural spirit in the world how we should behave and conduct ourselves so as to be inwardly prepared for its outward effect on us. The fact that this spirit is contemporary, lets us know from the beginning that we too must rise to the contemporary realm of existence, from where time past, present and future are no longer meaningful as psychic valences. This effect on our perception of time is the salient one. In effect we are able to perceive time rather than being forced by circumstances to picture it and then to mistake those pictures for reality. Past time is related, future time is predicted and present time is told and, if we but knew it, in the telling, relating and predicting, the contemporary human-natural spirit is approximated, apprehended and approached but never lived. We cling to time present, past and future whenever we fear we will lose that proximity, little realizing it is the foretaste we refuse to exchange for the actual experience.

Once we have begun to live the contemporary spirit, our attitude towards time has changed and what we mean by time is no longer the same thing. The role that is played by history is changed. If now we perform an act of thought, we are limited automatically to practical, down-to-earth considerations which may be described as concrete. Concrete history, therefore, radiates out from ourselves to those in our vicinity, to our communal circumstances as they immediately touch on our lives and on the lives of those with whom we communicate. Concrete history relates what goes on and what is the case in spiritual proximity to our own spirit. The notion of time we acquire now presupposes in us the ability to discern our own spirit too, just as we are able to discern our body, mind, soul and flesh. We know that the merciful spirit and the contemporary spirit are all in one, while the latter, like we ourselves, is in the world. We may discern our spirit and also the contemporary spirit immediately but the merciful spirit is perceivable only through the medium of the contemporary spirit. Time in its turn, though we rarely know this, is a merciful invention which cannot be immediately known. Our discernment of the contemporary spirit is essential if we want to take concrete time. And really if it is to be meaningful what we do when we take our time, then the time we take must be concrete.

*

We can compare the effect of the contemporary spirit on our human nature to its effect on our spirit.

Once I know who I am, and that I am someone, I accept the responsibility for my human nature and my spirit becomes the functional extension of myself. This much is required of me if I am to become a fully ethical human being.

Now the effect of the contemporary spirit on my human nature is such that I become aware of myself as real in time and space. This reality does not allow me to separate time from space. I am at liberty however to tamper with the effect of the contemporary spirit on my human nature, to falsify it and to misinterpret it. What happens then is that I become spiritually unsound. My distortion of my human nature shows up as a malaise of my spirit.

What we need to keep in mind here is that the human-natural spirit contemporary *with us* in the world, due to the fact that it is in the world, guarantees *me* this oneness of my nature and my spirit. The worst thing that can happen to me is that as I become spiritually active I lose touch with my nature, or that I am no longer spiritually responsible for my nature. Due to the contemporary spirit, this cannot happen without my knowing about it right away. Either it draws my attention to my nature or to my spirit, letting me know that my intervention is required.

How then should I intervene? What is it I can do and how can I go about it?

The crucial point here is that I am able to detect in myself problems that are too difficult for me alone to solve. In other words I can become sensitive to needs and shortcomings that not only draw to my attention my own wrongs which I can right again, or to the failings of others which I myself can remedy. I can become human-naturally sensitive to areas of misfortune and misachievement for the improvement of which I am forced to confess myself and my own means painfully inadequate. Put more succinctly, I end up with burdens I cannot pick up and carry. This seems on the surface dreadfully unjust. All the same it continues that we break down under loads which we cannot relate to ourselves, to our needs and requirements as we see them. The demands of ethics seem to surpass our capabilities. Morality makes similarly exorbitant demands. Whether the anxiety has to do with ourselves alone or with our responsibility for others, we are in the grip of it and cannot come to grips with it. The corrosive influence touches on our very capacity for intelligently suffering pain and initiating beneficial change. We are seriously afraid of being 'wiped out' by the evil in the world and by the evil in ourselves. How can we possibly stand up to anything of such superhuman destructiveness!

The answer of course lies in that uncreated being, the contemporary spirit, which is human-natural and in the world. Not only does it, by its being in the same world with us, unavoidably point out to us, in terms of our nature and our spirit, where we come short and where we fail in relation to the commonwealth of reality, but it also makes itself available to us as the one necessary remedy. I say it makes itself available. We ourselves have to avail ourselves of it. We have to learn how to approach this spirit, how to be ready for it (for him), how to read the signs of its proximity and how to fight our way through our own self-caused obstructions.

The commonwealth of reality is upon us, with this there can be no argument. It is not something we can wait for. Waiting for it does not bring it any closer nor is it a future thing. The commonwealth of reality exists here and now in concrete time. Whether or not we fit in and how well we fit in, that is our business. When we do fit in, we are fully functioning human beings. Metaphoric expressions such as 'fitting in' should not confuse us. Both our spirit and our nature are required in unison if we are to make reasonable sense of the commonwealth of reality. We cannot imagine it in terms of our nature alone, nor can we conceive of it exclusively in spiritual fashion. All attempts to do one or the other merely give evidence of our lack of solidarity with the contemporary spirit who is in charge of this commonwealth.

Knowing this is crucial. Unless we are informed and aware of the facts we haven't a hope of getting our act together in the contemporary spirit both human and divine, natural and spiritual, created being and uncreated being are not mutually exclusive nor at variance but one. This at first is bound to confound to the extent of our dependence on categories in our feeling, imagining and thinking. Mere survival makes us cling to such categories but in terms of life we must be ready to view them as stepping stones and to lay them aside when the time is ripe.

The commonwealth of reality and the contemporary spirit are finally worth it. We have come to our final rest now in contemplation of constant change. We are moved exquisitely to the limits of our capacity by the one we love and honour and respect. The one who has made all this possible for us by suffering our shortcomings through for us has become the mainstay for our worship.

And it is worship with which we now face the reality that previously merely astounded us. We add something to this reality. We add ourselves.

*

As soon as we worship in reality, everything becomes meaningful for us. To worship in reality really means to render reality meaningful. At any given moment I am free to ask myself why I should not continue to be as I am now. Wherever and however I am, what need is there ever for a change of appearances? When we worship reality we rest. We are, we live and we rest. We have no ideas, no wishes or desires, no motivations or drives, no appetites, no emotions, moods or thoughts. Not that we keep these out or away from us, so that we might rest, but they stay away because we worship. And we cannot say that worship is a combination of other activities because this is precisely what makes worship in reality unique, that it combines in itself all our faculties, uniting them in a single, lively art.

So by way of this worship we achieve for ourselves a universal point of reference. It affords us an ethical balance by which we can measure our commitment and the intensity of it. Since it is at once natural and spiritual we can probe our nature and apply our spirit from here, from this worshipful point of reference, without distorting the truth. And now, too, whenever we speak of nature other than our own nature, or of spirit other than our own spirit, we may be sure that we ourselves are not excluded from the equation. Any interest we take in nature *separate* from our own nature is <u>vanity</u>, and anything we have to do with spirit *exclusive* of our own spirit is <u>conceit</u>.

But vanity and conceit are the two main enemies of an ethical human being. Once again discernment is crucial in order to

97

come to trips with these. The discernment of our own nature as distinct from human nature, of our own spirit as distinct from the merciful spirit, as the particular from the general, eludes all but a few, whose task it is then to bring this discernment home to the many, though never to 'all'.

Why should we bother? Why make this supreme effort of discernment when the seemingly comfortable alternative of the mass media and the herd instinct are always so near at hand? Even when the commonwealth of reality was near at hand, it was precisely the mass media and the herd instinct in their then still embryonic form that flew in the face of it, albeit counter-productively helping to highlight the contemporary human spirit and perfected human nature. Now the mass media and the herd instinct are near at hand and those who espouse them are legion as ever, while many are capable of conquering their vanity and doing down their conceit, though they must accept and welcome those who are capable of the requisite discernment.

My <u>own nature</u> is always in ferment. It is human natural for me to seethe with excitement, to linger within sight of my goal, to be ravished by beauty and to rise to the challenge of the erotic. It is equally human-natural for me to dither on the edge of a decision, to rush into friendship, to dream of imaginary states of being and to be furious in the face of defeat. All this, as it occurs to me here and now, is human-natural for me, but not necessarily for you. Even when I say that my own nature is always in ferment, this is the way I myself just then expressed it, and you yourself must keep that in mind when you hear me describe what is human-natural for me. If my description is truthful – or let us say: to the extent that it is truthful – you yourself, if you welcome me, will be uplifted by it and edified. Not that you critically approach my description and expression but that you welcome me, that is what counts. I am able to discern my own human nature from human nature in general and it concerns my welfare that I do not pass on, vainly, as my own that which is not my own. As soon as I give in to vanity, I am cut off from my soul. However by truthfully giving you access to my own human nature, quite independently of what it does for you if you welcome me, I open myself to the gift of personal life.

Now human nature as such, in general, is the same for all of us and we may pride ourselves on its generation within us at all times. What we must be careful not to do is to imagine that this human nature is somehow separable from human spirit. In general these two are one, as the contemporary and human natural spirit in person. It is only in the particular, when it is my spirit or your spirit, my nature or your nature, that nature and spirit exist for us each in itself.

My <u>own spirit</u> always urges me to action. It is human spiritual for me to impress myself on the world, to court the companionship of other beings, to achieve certain goals and to alter the appearance of things. It is equally human spiritual for me to interfere with the creative process, to create problems to be solved, to imitate life forms and to speculate about the so-called mysteries of the universe. If you were now to re-enact your own spirit for me you would do it in your own way, but once again, as in the case of our natures, to the extent that we do it truthfully, we make it possible for someone else, who welcomes us, to be energized and enlivened.

I have access to my nature and to my spirit separately, just as you do to yours. This access however is limited. When I notice for example how my spirit urges me to action and how I am energetic and enlivened every time I enact my spirit for others, I am liable to confuse that sense of energy and liveliness with life itself and to make it my overall goal. I mix up my human spirituality with life, mistaking the one for the other, and as a consequence I either pervert my human spirit or forfeit it altogether, due to conceit.

The same goes for my human nature. If I become attached to that sense of fervour and ferment and, once again, mistake that sense of personal life for life itself, I will pervert or forfeit my human nature, due to vanity.

In both cases then it is brought home to me soon enough that my particular human nature and spirit are not in themselves fully mine after all, mine in the sense that I cannot lose them or be separated from them. They are mine inasmuch as I alone have access to them but not in that they are part and parcel of my being.

All our misfortunes and tragedies can be seen and understood as the result of vanity and conceit, when we become attached to our particular human nature or addicted to our separate human spirit. Of course we can commit ourselves to a social morality and to a worldly ethic for a while so as to pretend to one another that vanity and conceit are not a problem. We can even convince our own selves in terms of esoteric and occult indulgences as to the real state of our affairs. Eventually however we break down under the pressure and are forced to admit defeat.

*

We see a foreshadowing of the contemporary spirit-being in the fact that our nature is accessible to us just as we are accessible to spirit. Once again, it is not truly <u>our</u> nature and spirit. Only while we cooperate naturally or spiritually towards an acknowledgment of the contemporary spirit-being, readily moved to action and not loath to bear up under the ferment of our nature, can we really and truly progress.

However we are ashamed of the one we need to make contact with life and we are offended by his approach. In 'my' nature he speaks of himself as the one who once lived and was killed but today we may enter the commonwealth of reality on account of him. In 'my' spirit he realizes himself as the one who must be before we can be and therefore before I can be.

We can see here how all this once again needs to be thought through. I who am fully persuaded that my satisfaction in life depends on the good I do, suddenly come face to face with the realization that in order to do good I must rely on another being who has done <u>me</u> good. Am I not after all then to be the original source of benevolence and advantage? Must I play second fiddle to another, who once lived, and today he is with us in reality?

*

Let us work for the time being with this model of 'our' nature and 'our' spirit. We may delude ourselves into assuming, or even presuming, that they are ours when in fact they are not, or they may in truth be ours, as soon as the contemporary spirit/being and the commonwealth of reality become our chief interest and even the goal of our various achievements. We have noted how wrong we can go when we try to unify 'our' nature and 'our' spirit independently from the contemporary spirit/being and the commonwealth of reality, because then, for one, we cannot ever have the full satisfaction we crave, and for another, in addition to our not having the essential and necessary benefit of that personal spirit/being, we mistake the great good of that reality for a stressful pressure, for a cause of misery, misfortune and disease, when in truth quite the reverse is the case and we are merely drawing the unfortunate consequences of our error.

So this is how we can go wrong. We can also go badly wrong, but this is how we simply go wrong. We erect institutions, come up with systems, methods and techniques, we invest energy and talent in enterprises, in the works of culture and civilization, we govern ourselves and our fellow citizens and countrymen by way of such methods and for the sake of goals that are themselves invented out of the fear of scandal and out of a scandalous fear. When we diagnose this fear we still come up with causes that are not true but are geared to protect us from that same scandal, from the shame and offence that blinds us and amounts at times to cataclysmic reaction, even on a world-side scale.

All these works are wrong. We can identify them simply as wrong works. If we want to do good work, we must be able to identify wrong works. There are also bad works, when we go badly wrong, but these we mean now are simply wrong, and when we perform them we are forever preoccupied with 'getting things right'. It is not an ancient, but a modern preoccupation. We never succeed in getting anything perfectly right but eventually we tire of the attempt and learn to compromise. Usually what we more or less admittedly combine with such wrong work, especially once we begin to tire but also during periods of zeal, is a hope and longing for release from such frustrating activity and for some agent, more or less personal, who will somehow save us all this trouble. The terrible irony is that by way of our wrong work we actually close ourselves off to the one who is more than ready to release and save us but cannot until our work at least becomes right. Right works prepare the way for him, so that eventually we may even do good work, in cooperation with him, but wrong work excludes us from him and from the commonwealth of reality, so in that case any longing at the same time for some eventual saviour in the future is at worst absurd and at best yet another indication of how in spite of all our wrongdoing this spirit/being all the same still exists for us, though we have become attached to his mirror image or shadow.

*

The bad work, in comparison to the wrong work, shows that no attempt has been made to unify 'our' nature and 'our' spirit but that we simply relied on that nature as though it were really ours, when in fact there is nothing in it of spirit, or we strove solely in 'our' spirit as though it really were ours, when in fact it is devoid of all nature.

But the nature that is really ours is united with our spirit in that contemporary spirit/being we continue to mention in the full knowledge of our incapacity to name it while we are still ashamed of it or offended by it and while it presents a scandal to us. Bad work is scandalous in that we do it shamefully or offensively in the face of that being. He has a name but it has a face, and this face is experienced by us traumatically. We are definitely injured in our pride and in our worthlessness as seekers after mere nature or pure spirit. Our merely natural pride teaches us to focus on all that we can point out to one another and it is a bad teacher indeed who insists on a sign before accepting the real. Our purely spiritual worthlessness teaches us to be happy with abstractions, with formality and consciousness and it too is a bad teacher, because love takes no foothold and appears only to the one who pre-tends and in-tends to love.

Such bad works demonstrate the need for practical love and for faith. Out of a revulsion against bad works we seek faith and love. Even our own bad works appal us and we hunger and thirst for the reality that eludes us on every side. In our extremity what happens is that the contemporary spirit/being is able to lodge in us a seed of mercy.

Until then, while we were involved in wrong works and bad works, we knew nothing of such mercy, and even now we cannot recognize this seed for what it will one day amount to. We only know that we have experienced a release from bondage to bad works and wrong works. We are no longer scandalized, no longer ashamed of, or offended by, the contemporary spirit/being and may begin to reflect on our state and condition of being somehow singled out. Even though we may not yet be able to do much, we are certainly not able to join with those who do wrong or bad work, and so for a while we must seem like out-casts, though of course it is we who have taken a foothold in the commonwealth of reality while those who do wrong and bad works keep themselves out.

*

Now we can continue with our discussion of <u>being and doing</u>. We decided earlier to compare this to behaviour and conduct and to rest and work.

In a state of humility we certainly are, as certain as we possibly can be. If we wish to differentiate this being from doing we simply need to remember. This remembering prevents us from doing ourselves harm. Doing could be described as outward being. As soon as I move my hand to achieve some end, my foot to gain ground, I break out of an aesthetic circumference and commit myself to some other being. As soon as I am for another being, I do.

Why is it then that we can be wicked but not good? We must come out of ourselves in order to <u>do</u> good. While we are in ourselves we may be happy or sad, disappointed or satisfied, and all this depends both on our state and on how we are being affected. The only state of being that allows us to rest in ourselves is the state of humility, and that is after all not really a state of being, since we cannot 'be humbly' any more than we can be good. At the moment I am perfectly content, but no sooner do I say so than I remember what that means and I do make my mind up. A state of humility is brought about by my negating all my negatable power, including my impotence. This negation is work. Can I rest in that state of humility? Certainly I can. Does resting mean I do nothing? Not at all. Rest and work are really one and the same. Being and doing are not.

Memory prevents us from doing ourselves harm. How is it that we do ourselves harm? By trespassing on the terrain of an-

104

other being. Criticism, for example, is such a trespass. We suppose we are right and another is wrong, that is fine, but then we expose that other one to our egotistical power. We try to make him admit he is wrong. In this we do ourselves harm because we destroy our moral integrity. Doing is outward being, but criticism is outside being. While we are outside ourselves we are not ourselves. We cannot be outward ourselves, the language does not allow it. So whatever we do, let us remember the one who guarantees our being – our own being by his. If he were not we would not be. If he were not we are not.

*

It must seem peculiar to insist on memory when we set out to do something. This is probably so because all too frequently we do to forget. Our doing is a flight from uncomfortable premonitions, about ourselves or the world. Also, forgetful doing fascinates. We become implicated in mindless preoccupations and a mere change in appearances seems to reward us for our efforts. As soon as we cease from this doing we are faced with our own, as a consequence deplorable, being and feel obligated to throw ourselves back into doing, if for no other reason than so as not to have to be.

Of course when we associate being with discomfort we try to avoid it. When we notice ourselves rushing into doing to avoid being we do well to ask ourselves – not what it might possibly be we try to avoid and what might be causing us the discomfort (or shame, or guilt, or downright terror) but rather what we can do to establish ourselves in comfortable being. It must be a kind of remedial doing. If we accept, that doing is outward being, then we would have to take into account – that this remedial doing cannot stem from our flawed being. Memory is this specific remedial deed and it must be a memory with content. We must remember the one who was so that he might be forever. Who was this? We speak of the contemporary human-natural and merciful spirit-being as though we knew what we were talking about but also we know that so far we have not given it its name. In a sense we are sidling into this crab-fashion. The remedial doing that is to save us once and for all time from harmful doing so that we might do good rather than harm is really a case of remembering the one who was the first to give his life so that he and we might live. What we need to countenance here is not a sacrificial giving but a merciful giving. If we say that he died so that we might live, this invites an interpretation of what he did as a sacrificial act, and that does not get us very far, because it does not allow us to view this being as the contemporary light of the world. It makes us feel indebted and it makes us wish to repay this debt, so we end up futilely trying to repeat something when we might be taking advantage of it having been done. If he has died so that we might live, it must now be up to us to die so that he might live. This is the sacrificial interpretation, involving an indebtedness that can never be acquitted. Moreover it involves an equation of the giving of one's life and of dying.

*

If I have killed someone, that does not mean that he died for me. Of course it is quite understandable that if I have killed someone I should try my best to lie about it and to pretend I did not.

To give one's life or to lay down one's life, even to submit to being killed, if one does that for that very specific reason of life for oneself and for others, then this is the sort of remedial doing that can only be explained from the point of view of that new, gained life, in comparison to which then the life which one gives or lays down should really be given a different name. The new or eternal life is not just another name for vitality. Often enough in the past we have distinguished between, on one hand, vitality, survival instinct, the will to overpower, and on the other hand the new life or eternal life. Now when it comes

106

to giving one's life so that another might have it – quite independently now of what one might gain oneself by this – one cannot give of any new or eternal life until one has given all of one's survival vitality, because while one clings to the latter one closes oneself off to the former. If one is convinced now that one wants the latter and not the former, then from one point of view it amounts to the same whether one voluntarily lays it down right away (whatever that means) or else lets go of it when others want to take it. Needless to say the eternal life cannot be taken away. And of course if one were killed[i] and if one right to the end did not cling to that survival vitality, then one would certainly demonstrate in the most effective way what one was doing.

*

There is one reason for differentiating between the life that can be lost and the life that can not be lost, but there is another reason for not doing so. While I am attached to my psychic affections and affectations, that is all I know and often all I want to know of life, and the more someone, or circumstances, would separate me from it, the more I cling to it. Of course I want to live, that is fundamental, but I make an equally fundamental mistake about what it amounts to, to live, and how to 'acquire' this commodity called life. If I am told I have to let go of something I palpably experience in order to gain something I know only from hearsay, then the palpable something, even if not entirely pleasant, is preferable to that comparable 'nothing'. So it would always be best if I could have some indication of 'the real life' before I let go of what is described to me by some as comparatively second-rate. I ask for a sign. But then I am told this is impossible, because 'the real life' cannot be indicated in terms of the ephemeral substitute. Of course this makes sense, but it still leaves me adrift. I don't insist that

---

[i] That is to say, if one's psychic life were taken away or destroyed.

107

you too would still hesitate, but I in my personal individuality am perplexed and I waver. A sick bird in the hand might be better than the ghost of a bird in the bush.

However the more I hear about this real and eternal life, especially from those who cheerfully and generously live it, the more I feel obliged in my own interest to pursue the matter.

What interests me especially is the gap that almost invariably opens between my doing and my being when I begin to do. I seem to be one sort of being while I am and another sort of being while I do. It seems to me I should be able to do as I wish and as I see fit; after all I am an adult. However time and again I do much and accomplish little except frustration and stress. My doing seems somehow unhinged from myself. I get involved in a lot of business, which takes my mind off my self for a while, which does at the time seem like a good idea, but to be honest what meanwhile happens is that a backlog of interior dilemmas piles up which increasingly insist on my undivided intention. So I cut myself off from all that hectic outside business and activity and I concentrate on what I think of as my being; on leisure time, rest, meditation and contemplation, recollection and what all else. For a time I breathe easy. All this 'therapy' is doing me a lot of good. I feel ready to do again. For a while I seem to be doing quite well. I feel reluctant to throw myself into my customary activities with the usual vigour, which is a bit of a shame, but is a bit of timidity a high price to pay for a bit more peace? The peace is relative. The activity is compromised. Am I ahead?

Instead let us return to the possibility of that <u>memory link</u> between doing and being. Let me, for the moment at least, remember the one who is said to have given his life so that we might live. Let us extend that: he gave his life so that he and we might live. Let us correct that: he gave his life so that he would live and so that we might live. Let us explain: he gave his life not in the sense that he died but in the sense that he submitted to being killed, and let us not entirely ignore that we probably do some of that killing every day. That sounds absurd. He was killed nearly two-thousand years ago, so what has that to do with us nowadays? What is this killing we supposedly do on a daily basis that compares to, or even imitates, the killing that took place then? A state of humility is of the essence here if we are to break through that absurdity. What I have to keep in mind is what I do to myself when I kill in that way. What did they do to themselves when they killed him then and what do we do to ourselves when we overpower one another, when we put one another down rather than empowering one another? What do we do to ourselves when our survival takes the place of or living, when we insist on our rights and assume that we alone know?

*

The desire to assert ourselves in the face of evil is strong in us. And what we first call evil is whatever seems to thwart our individual development and growth. This is not surprising. We can say quite simply and see quite clearly that if there were no evil we would all walk around in isolation, totally ignorant of one another and of the world. Due to evil, which you can imagine any way you like, this unique individuality of ours is questioned, is cast into doubt, is interrupted. In the interest of our individuality we then defend ourselves, and these defence mechanisms are really the first actual evidence we have of evil. We try to return to our previous state of 'innocence' as we call it, as we were prior to any such defence, but even this attempt is a kind of defence against the same evil. What we blithely call our innocence is nothing more than ignorance of evil, and ignorance is never a recommendation. All the same, our initial notions of the good, namely goodness, are nothing more than ignorance, and we might as well be honest about it. Our struggle to return to that state of ignorance is itself evil.

*

When we think about it this way, we realize that what we initially sense as evil is not evil at all but a merciful reminder of our individual tendency to remain alone. There is a big difference between what is commonly sensed as evil, namely this timely reminder of the hell we automatically tend towards, and actual evil, which is our rejection of this reminder and our insistence on being little kings and queens in ourselves over a realm of our defensive and aggressive invention.

Is it sensible and helpful now to say that we are all originally evil because of this automatic wish to look after ourselves alone? Really it seems to me to make more helpful sense to call that evil which amounts to our rejection of mercy and our insensitivity to mercy. Prior to such rejection and ignoration, due to which we initially become culpable and subsequently remain guilty, what or how are we? There must be a 'prior' to this, because being precedes doing. Let's at least assume for the time being that in some way it does, even if only in our imagination.

A word that is sometimes used to describe this state is wickedness. But this too suggests a degree of evil, even though it may invite a discernment of 'natural evil' from intentional, practiced evil. A better solution of the problem would stem from a description of the prior state in terms of the condition which is urged upon us mercifully, so that we distinguish between initially being merciless, incontinent of mercy, and then being either merciful or wicked, depending on whether we reject the mercy that comes upon us or else practice it towards one another.

This is an important image then: In our merciless state, mercy (which still has to be described in detail) comes upon us and we either pass it on, so to speak, albeit after an initial awakening of sorts, and subsequently have the benefit of it, or

110

else we reject and ignore that mercy, call the effects of it evil and consequently become wicked and do evil.

What are the effects, what is the sensible evidence, of the merciful spirit on ourselves by which we may recognize it? Our vindictiveness and our vengefulness and our angry or timid reactions to supposed injustice are the sensible evidence of the merciful spirit's affection on ourselves. Our best option, therefore, as soon as we notice even the first traces of this in ourselves, is to behave mercifully and to practice mercy.

Revenge as recoil and backlash to mercy, to merciful affection of spirit – this is difficult to take on board. We are much more accustomed to think of revenge as a response, either laudable or reprehensible depending on our morality, to an evil or injustice. If we consider it to be reprehensible, then we feel we might try to forgive the injustice, but we do not call into question the existence of the injustice and, of course, our ability and right to judge. If, however, we acknowledge that our vengefulness and resentment is essentially a case of our flying in the face of merciful spirit and that we can remedy this deplorable situation by practicing mercy and being merciful, then we are going about all this in a much different way. At the beginning we refuse to judge and we confess that we cannot really say for sure ever whether someone has it in for us, much as it would give us pleasure to do so. Actually the judgment and the vengeance coincide, so that we get rid of the one along with the other. But we can find this incredibly difficult. A careful and detailed study of mercy is therefore very beneficial to our ethical being and for our ethical doing.

*

A vengeful state is a terrible hell to be in. Sometimes we exist in that hell for days before we realize what ails us. Our mental and physical health is destroyed by it. We dwell on injustices and secretly plan our revenge for them. They may even be injustices not to ourselves but to others. On behalf of our children, for example, we may go through periods of vindictiveness that tear us apart and alienate the very children whose plight we allegedly hope to remedy. One thing we frequently fail to recognize is that the vehemence of our approach is disproportionate to the dimensions of the problem.

*

If we are merciful now, then the merciful spirit, when next it approaches us, will find us accessible and amenable, so that we will not fly in the face of it, vengefully and vindictively. There may be quite a lapse between our merciful 'being and doing' and the next approach to us by merciful spirit, so once again we recognize the importance of memory. Merciful being and doing will fully succeed only if we understand this provision we make for ourselves with regard to the merciful spirit of god and mindful of the wickedness and evil we are bound to fall into if we mistake that spirit.

*

There is the mercy that approaches us, as merciful spirit, and there is the mercy we ourselves can come up with and project into our environment. In the case of ourselves being merciful, what is it we need to remember? (Our memory too must have a content.) Certainly we are not to remember our own personal history. That would not help us. But the modern age lies before us as all those years since the advent of the commonwealth of reality, and it is the sum total of all those years that forces a barrier to our memory. Modern history is a catalogue of more or less interesting evasions and avoidances of that reality and of the more or less dramatic catastrophes that attend such flights from reality. Whatever has happened and was done during those years, in other words the being and doing of human beings and people as perceived in retrospect, cannot bear any relation to that reality. This is extremely difficult to countenance. We carry in our minds a concept of history that intrudes into what we call the past. We pretend that the past is one reality and that the history of it, which we may choose or not choose to tell, is another. In fact the modern age as past time is that history.

When I set out to tell you what happened to me today and what I did today I can do so in an infinite number of ways. But surely, you say, you either ventured from our house or stayed in; you talked to a few people or read a book and it rained or it did not. You cannot get away from facts. And it must be a simple enough exercise to record those facts, then perhaps to study those records and draw conclusions about their affinity and proportion.

But surely that is not the essence of what we mean by history! Our modern history especially is to do duty as an intricate mirror of what we really were like. This is not memory but <u>recall</u>. What we recall is appearances. Jack fell into the well. King John took England to the brink of civil war. No, after all it seems that Jack was pushed and that King John was as much a tool of circumstances as those who were pleased or displeased to call themselves his subjects. Who can say with certainty? It was one or the other – or perhaps a third, and many more possibilities are equally likely. We recall and suppress as we please and as it suits us, so that our history is really much more a symptom of our physical condition than a record of our past behaviour.

Once we have become members of the commonwealth of reality, modern history vanishes before our gaze and what we remember is that reality itself. We remember it from the beginning and we remember all its parts. We know for example that this reality breaks in on history and makes a mockery of it to the extent that we cling to it as an aspect of our identity. In what land, in what year, indeed under which star sign were you born? This cannot possibly be remembered. A record of it may be kept and modern history is a record of all such appearances to hold between ourselves and reality.

*

That we hold this record between reality and ourselves, this is what is modern about it, and of course this purpose and intention helps to shape the record itself.

What we must ask is: What is our reason for keeping a record of the past? Do we want a story of ourselves as a collective entity, a story in which we can delight, that will draw us together in a quickening celebration of our common humanity in a living diversity or do we want to secure our position as surviving egotists in the face of the corroding and undermining influence of reality? If the former, then we must stop confusing accuracy with truth. And if the latter, then we will be glad to admit that reality into our historic processes, acknowledging our need for real history. It is not that our modern attitude to the past needs to be changed but that our modern perception of time needs to be revised, and of course this cannot be done in terms of modern life or of a modern disposition. Neither will an analysis of modernity get us ahead unless we see this as incidental to a build-up of a real historic 'mesh'.

Another important and related question might be: Do we who have a 'handle' on contemporary reality and the 'number' of modernity, owe it to the ancients to remember them? It sounds fanciful, but let's not be too quick to reject it. Our usual model of ancient, modern and/or contemporary will have to be adopted at least for the time being if we are to make sense of this. It is merciful being and doing that calls modernity into question in the first place.

If the ancients looked forward hopefully to the commonwealth of reality – and I posit here a single history for mankind

114

– then modernity as a commitment to the prevention of that reality must be seen as a betrayal of the ancients. Now when we say ancient, modern and/or contemporary, we admit that a direct transition from ancient to contemporary is possible. We are implying that since the advent of the commonwealth of reality under the hegemony of one being, the possibility of contemporary reality for human beings has always existed as it does today, even as did (and does) the liability to a modern popular delusion. This modern delusion supplies for itself a vision of time as historic past, present and future and notions of periodicity, of development, evolution and progress are avidly pressed into service to establish and maintain this vision. Even if the advent of true reality is admitted, the actual event of it is not, by those of a modern predisposition who have inherited the modern bias and invest their energies in its preservation. Now true reality is and always will be something that can be rejected – though not with impunity. While we reject it, it bears the characteristic of 'not yet' for us and at the same time we draw the actual physical consequences of that rejection. The modes and types and sorts of rejection are legion and not limited to any particular place of being. The typical modern notion of progress, towards what is assumed to be an improved state of affairs, depends on opposing one kind of rejection of reality with another. We need to acquit ourselves therefore of all commitments to such things as the present, the past and the future so far as memory is concerned and to commit our memory instead to the being, not the passage, of time. Time as a passing thing, measured by clocks and the calendar, will interest us only so far as it helps to regulate the smooth course of our affairs, and while we discern passing time from essential time it is no longer a mere thing but a regulative concept. Meanwhile the time we remember blossoms and bears fruit. It is only while the two are confused, in modern fashion, that time is bound to withdraw its being from us and to hide as a thing behind the faces of clocks.

What we are looking for therefore is an ethical memory of eternal time. On the surface it sounds impossible because we associate an impenetrable wall with the notion of eternity and a super-sophisticated bag of tricks with the notion of 'getting there'. We insist on waiting for it, on pushing it away in favour of the passage of modern time. Memory and recall then sit there like the sphinx, obstructing our own passage and challenging us with its riddle.

But eternity is simply the here and now with all its content of human relations. We gain insight into this meaning when we say to someone: "I will do" such and such, and then we ask ourselves, are we making a promise as to our future behaviour or are we describing what we are doing here and now? What we mean by our will, by or willing, is a stake. The difference between "I am doing it" and "I will do it" needs to be studied. Language usage has adopted will as an auxiliary of tense, but it is entirely up to us how we use that language. The human will as a forceful capacity or as appetition does not lend itself to appropriation as an ethical entity but pretends to exist somehow beyond or prior to good and evil. Our very apposition of such a thing as 'the human will' or as 'will', imagined as somehow separate from any act or performance of willing, has to be called into question because it lends itself all too readily to the type of transcendental speculation that quietly parades its suspect wares as 'the modern spirit'. Let's face it, it is itself the product of such speculation.

It makes more sense to speak of an ethical willingness, as the fruit of human growth. It is a willingness of which we become capable after much struggle with our various unfortunate propensities and after much practical application to that commonwealth of reality which is our constant and repeated aim. Like-

116

wise it is a willingness of which the effectiveness cannot be measured in space and time. Its effectiveness is eternal. Evidence of it cannot be referred to it. A narrower description of it would be eternal good willingness, and certainly nothing can be said or known about it except in relation to that search for reality. While we still toy with forces, with the urge to overpower and with magic, we cannot come into this ethical willingness, which has now arisen on our horizon as we come to terms with the true historic memory and with mercy.

*

What happens when that ethical willingness espouses memory? What if the ethical human being will remember? Will he stumble across all his misdeeds? Does that worry him and is that why he would rather recall modern history? Indeed as he remembers, this ethical human being with a will, he locates time upon time both the splendour of his blessings and the horror of his curses, but he passes them as one who is on a journey passes way-stations both pleasant and unpleasant without flinching or turning aside.

What if this ethical one now insists on remembering simply to remember? What will he remember? He cannot know ahead of time, he must simply proceed in the light of his ethical will. Vistas may open before him beyond his imagination, and these he treasures. It would be interesting to note the outcome of much of this remembering, where it is really the ethical will of the one who remembers that broadens the outlook and scope.

Is it not then the history of the human being that gradually comes to the fore? Would that not then be the beginning?

The ethical will of the one who remembers with a will returns us to the beginning of the commonwealth of reality in time and then supplies us with the chronicle of what one might call individual fates. This is most unexpected and one should not hesitate to compare it to unpredictable events. The temptation will arise to catalogue events themselves and to sidestep the demands of individual destinies, and then those events will themselves seem to be premeditated and before one knows one is back within a system of modern hesitation, prevarication and pretence.

The beginning of the commonwealth of reality in time is first of all summed up by the one who is ethical will in person and individual destiny as such. What we may know of this one depends entirely on our own ethical will to know and to remember him. And of course our approach and attitude must be personal. The slide into <u>modernity</u> and into representations of past, present and future is either due to a loss of personality, which in turn accounts for a distortion of destined individuality, so that the one who is actually here and now in power is at best present in ritual anticipation, or else it is due to a misappropriation or misconception of individuality, so that systematized opinion and dogma, or definitive knowledge, takes the place of reality, while an infinite marvellous world becomes dark or dangerous. A part of the '<u>modernist</u>' error is then that one awaits and beseeches one who will save from this dark and dangerous world – which world is really self-created. Similarly modernist is the hope that from within the modern time-scheme of past, present and future, an imaginary or ideal world may be invented, manufactured or progressed towards.

*

Philosophically we can tackle this via discernment of memory and recall. We also make use of the term 'recollection'. Our main aim all the while is of course to identify what we can do to initiate and assist our perception of reality as a commonwealth, which perception, as we now know, cannot succeed against a backdrop of time as past, present and future. Really we should speak of reality as <u>the</u> commonwealth. Also we need to keep in mind that this reality is personally engaged and anchored. We are not concerned with the world now, but with reality. By personal engagement I mean the following: We ourselves as personal human beings, no matter how far we have strayed from our loving relationship with all beings or how much we still need to work our way into such relationships, participate in this reality, and by way of our memory of the one who founded or established this reality, our participation becomes meaningful and appreciative and significant. Now when we speak of the one who 'established', in the past tense, this reality, this commonwealth, we adopt a modern historic point of view and find ourselves in the awkward position of having to explain and justify a tradition that takes/took us from a 'then' to a 'now'. We get caught up in arguments of authority, of interpretation, of degrees of orthodoxy and universality. We create problems for ourselves which drive us into a twilight corner where we have insufficient light for identifying solutions for problems of darkness.

If instead now we speak of the one who is, in his very being, the foundation of this reality and who lives in our personal behaviour and conduct, in our being and doing, our rest and work, then we need only ask: How can we get to know him and how can we know him well? All answers and responses to those questions are readily achieved by way of our ethical memory. From our own personal being we may address the personally rooted and organized commonwealth of reality; we may address and access it at its point of origin and inception by way of ethical memory. We cannot do this as individuals. I cannot do it for my own good only so as to gain power over you and others. I can only do it as a person, which is to say in communication and for the sake of a few, of several or many.

But memory is in any case a human faculty which operates from a contemporary point of view and we cripple it ourselves as soon as we ask it to serve our modern perception of time. Or let us say that time in tension, as past, present or future, should pertain exclusively to our everyday affairs, to the outside of the cup as it were, and it is our various efforts to remember such time that are characteristically modern. Time in tension is to be recalled, while reality, through its personal foundation and organization, is to be remembered.

Time in tension has always to do with how long it takes to do something or for something to happen. Something or other is always involved, and when we refer to our business and everyday affairs, we mean the extent to which we as mature human beings take on the task of re-cognizing things as beings, by taking responsibility for things and for some of those who espouse them. Cryptically, when 'something' appeals to me it looks to me for a recognition for its being. Remember that things are rally beings that are misconceived, misconstrued or just plain mistaken.

So what we recall, we recall for a purpose, and this purpose can generally be described as a recognition of things, of something or other, as beings. Recall leads to recognition, and precedes it. Beings have fled from us, have gone into obscurity because of our misbehaviour and misconduct and now we recall them for recognition. We have overpowered them, forced them out of existence by way of our own selfishness and egotism, and now this has occurred to us since we have come ethically of age and we are eager to do reparation and to mend.

*

No one, of course, can even understand the difference between beings and things, not to mention take the responsibility for things as mistaken beings, who has no notion of beings, such as exist in the commonwealth of reality. The memory of reality therefore is essential before we are able to recall time. We must attend to our being so that we do not misconstrue time. Modern time and times are such a misconstruction because we apply our proper human memory to wrong ends.

Now when we remember the one without whom reality is not the commonwealth, we do not recall his time on earth. Perhaps it would help our understanding if we knew that the commonwealth of reality cannot be recalled. Only that which has been in the past, or has happened or been done in the past, can be recalled.

When we remember reality, we begin by believing it. Our faith, our simple human faith, with which we are born and which can atrophy or be nurtured, tells us about reality, just as it tells us about truth. Faith is our faculty for truth and reality. If we are asked whether reality and truth are, from faith we say yes. But if we are asked what they are, we cannot answer from faith alone. However the being of truth and reality is of course fundamental and radical. As we exercise our faith, our believing, the being of truth and reality becomes more persuasive for us, but still we cannot say what it is. We might be forgiven, if our faith is strong, for wondering why anyone should want to know what it is, once he knows that it is, and there are indeed those who reject such knowledge, or if they do not actually reject it, they have quite enough with knowing that truth and reality are, so that their faith is sufficiently exercised in meditation, contemplation and recollection of that being. As a result they have a strong and reliable sense of true and real being of their own. It is strong in that it allows them to withstand with equanimity setbacks and misfortunes and it is reliable in that, once it has become habitual, it announces a need for further exercise of faith by turning into a sense of loss, which is unmistakable.

Calling meditation, contemplation and recollection all exercises of faith, for our present purpose, helps us discern these activities as lying outside the realm of temporality and recall. A tradition exists which can benefit from such discernment. And any amount of such exercise can only be of use to us if we should eventually decide to remember reality and the truth.

We will decide to do so as soon as we begin to take an interest in work and in works. From being and doing we pass on to work and rest. Now it occurs to us to ask: What is this reality and this truth which I believe?

And this is where the modern fallacy is most likely to occur. This is where modernity is always most likely to set in. As soon as we ask: What is truth? and What is reality? we become impatient with ourselves for not being able to answer right away. A tension sets in. We can sense that we will not be able to reply from faith alone and we momentarily doubt ourselves. We doubt our ability to fulfil a desire that has come over us. This is in fact the desire to work and the urge to work. In its very first stages it is the wish to communicate the being of truth and reality. We turn to the one next to us and speak of our faith-knowledge concerning truth and reality and – doubt sets in. This throws us into consternation. The wish to share is upon me, but as soon as I give, I find myself questioning the veracity and the soundness of my gift. So I shrink into myself and wonder what went wrong. After a period of quiet contemplation perhaps my certitude is mended but I am left with an appetite for work – which demands satisfaction.

The start of modernity is to view this as a dilemma which requires that I choose between contemplation and action; perhaps between inward and outward dedication. I will be modern to the extent that I feel I must either lead a life of action, in which case my faith is bound to be undermined, or else I must lead a life of inwardness, in which case I feel I may never quite feel sufficiently effective. It may well be the case that my natural predisposition will incline me one way or the other, but only after I have become modern – in deciding that human-natural faith and perfect work-satisfaction cannot go together and that I

122

cannot have both. Perhaps I will accommodate my faith to a faith, which will allow me to cope better with degrees of self-doubt. Perhaps I will decide that, after all, action in the world is bound to be a dirty business and I should not overly concern myself with results but concentrate on the process and on progress. I may try to get the work over and done with so that I can play my flute, and indeed to that end are supposedly eternal empires established. Or I may rattle off a few prayers so as to get back all the quicker to that adrenalin-rich job satisfaction, and indeed all religions will help me here.

Right from the start, then, modernity testifies to the incompatibility of individual believing and personal acting. We are modern inasmuch as we have not found a solution to the problem of doubt in the being of truth and reality once an appetite for action and work has set in. But that appetite, or will, is as central to our human being as the simple desire to tell a friend about a joyful experience. We believe that reality and truth are – indeed reality and truth have become – the content of our simple human natural faith, and now we see around us the desperate lack of such faith. No wonder there is awakened in us the urge to make our faith-knowledge more widely known. But as soon as we come out with what we know, it no longer seems to be what we knew.

What we might do now, to avoid modernity, is <u>remember truth and reality</u>. In that case no time would pass. In that case no problem exists that needs to be solved but cannot be solved. The dilemma is a mere semblance, the doubt is a call to memory, not to renewed faith-exercise or to heedless action. The truthful and real alternative to modernity is, simply, rest and work based on memory of truth and realty; and the more we remember these two, the more thoroughly do we understand them as our commonwealth.

*

Let me think a little more about what, in the context of our concern right now, it means to remember. When we remember, we do not try to have an effect on anything other than ourselves. What we do try to do is to bring ourselves into a different state of mind. And our reason for doing that in the case of memory is the <u>inhabitation of reality</u>. Why should memory be so crucial to that end?

Because we have forgotten reality. And by reality I still mean the personally managed commonwealth of reality. In what way have we forgotten it? In the modern sense. We have forgotten it in that we have let our sense of time as past, present and future obscure it. We have not managed to limit our sense of time in tension to the periphery of our experience but we have allowed it to take over our entire consciousness. This is a difficult teaching and I intend to approach it from various sides. First of all we need to realize that we cannot manage, and could not have managed, our sense of time in tension in terms of that time. It is what we do and how we are in eternal time – and of course it is finally that we are able to be and do – to work and rest – in eternal time, that causes the limitation, the peripheral limitation, of time in tension.

So a forgetting of reality, in terms of time now, is an ignoring of eternal time and a burgeoning or going wild, a growing rank, of time in tension.

The ancients, prior to modern cultures and civilizations, were often preoccupied with the high risks and dangers of a life based on time in tension, so that any confusion or obliteration of that overexposure was combined with a veneration of those who no longer existed there, in the hope of avoiding disasters and catastrophes both 'natural' and 'supernatural'. Worship of the dead, veneration of heroes and of heroic times etc., was to counterbalance the horror of outer space, of too much life, of estrangement from the earth. Empty space and endless time together were an aspect of horror and terror.

But time in tension was not known to the ancients. This is a modern phenomenon, which testifies in itself to the commonwealth of reality, which is not real for the ancients, but it is for the moderns. Time and again, as we explain this, we will have to step out of the peripheral sense of time in tension so as to highlight the process of memory and to challenge our own exclusive sense of time as in tension. It is not the ancients that have forgotten reality but the moderns. Without metaphor, please remember, we could not even bear the distinction between the two. We cannot forget except what we know, what we have and hold. We are born with the eternal word fresh on our lips and the 'process' of forgetting sets in. Right away the parental adult has the joyful task of helping us to remember.

Every culture and every civilization today testifies to this need to remember that which is but has been forgotten, namely the personally managed commonwealth of reality. Not that it has been forgotten and therefore it was, no, it is all the same, in spite of having been forgotten, and memory is the faculty we need. It is almost as if we needed to unearth this faculty itself, because we confuse it with recall and try to force it into the service of time in tension. The very fact of culture and civilization as distinct and separate is symptomatic of time-in-tension oversubscribed. Mention eternal time to the average citizen and you will not find a sympathetic ear. The culture that must be modern to be admirable is itself a flight from reality.

*

Our problem is, that we suppose we remember when we 'remember' the past. Actually what we do then is recall the past. However the fact remains that we would, subconsciously, like to remember. We would like to recapture something we possessed or knew in our childhood, perhaps only in the earliest days of it, so it is almost as if we were nagged by fate. The fate which is such a momentous force for the ancients and which should be replaced in us by our commonwealth of reality experience occurs in our lives as a fearful combination of aggression and self-doubt. So if we were alert to our real needs, this is the accidental predisposition to which we would look for the voluntary commencement of our real memory. We would have to identify in ourselves this typically modern 'hectic mood', from which we try to escape and which we try to appease in so many ways, and there where this mood is rooted we would have to remember faithfully. It must be done by faith, because we cannot possibly have a sensation, of it or for it.

So the memory through which we regain the personally managed commonwealth of reality commences faithfully as a voluntary work instead of any modern experience of hectic strain and stress.

*

When we say that we remember faithfully, we imply that we do not remember according to any sensation. This in itself will be a hurdle for many of us. But if we have forgotten reality, it is not very likely that our faith and our ability to believe are very strong. Probably faith, for us, means a faith, and believing is tantamount to credulity and blind trust. At the same time we know that an ethic based on faithless sensation either gets lost in utilitarianism or perverted as a myth. So the search for our human natural faith may be just as important for us as our memory of reality.

We cannot have a sensible memory of reality. Faith precedes sensation, in that our senses themselves are no use unless informed by faith. Because of the modern confusion of faith with 'a faith', modern man is faced with the choice of factitious knowledge or fictitious believing. The road back to faith once we have espoused a faith, is similar to the road back to reality.

126

Now if we were to rediscover our faith, we would hunger and thirst for reality and for an ethical approach to it and it might take some time before we learn to remember it. But once we have recovered our true memory, our faith is intact and we can concentrate on the reality that knows no bounds until we work. Work and rest can then be defined in terms of that reality. Through memory of it we begin to inhabit that commonwealth. Through our work, which usually involves some memory, we share our habitation with others. And when we rest, we simply inhabit that reality.

*

The question arises as to the content of memory. We say that we remember reality, or truth and reality, and by this we mean a personally managed commonwealth. But even there we have to check ourselves, because what we mean is not a, but the personally managed commonwealth. It is not one of several but the one. And it is here and now. This is beyond question. You have to decide now; is it here and now for you? I myself have to decide is it here and now for me. This 'for you' and 'for me' is important. Am I inhabiting this commonwealth? Even calling it this commonwealth causes a break in perception because in that way I remove myself by referring to what was mentioned earlier, as I write; or if I were speaking I would, if I said 'this', invite an objectivity of the whole, which is not possible. If we compare the commonwealth of reality to a house which we might inhabit, then we would have to keep in mind that we can never have a view from the outside. What we can have from the outside is at best a number of inhibition-experiences.

So each one of us has to remember, in order to inhabit what is always and everywhere inhabitable.

But is there a content to that memory of a non-sensible reality? Again the question is wrong. It is not a reality. It is not one among several. Is it in fact non-sensible? Just because we cannot sense it, does that make it non-sensible? Perhaps we need to be a bit more open-minded as to what we mean by sensation. As we noted earlier, if our senses are informed by faith, we see and hear, and know, differently from when they are not thus informed. We should not suppose that our inhabitation of reality leaves parts of us unchanged. Our senses are in fact overwhelmingly altered. Afterwards we are appalled at how much we had ignored. So let us not get into the bad habit of suggesting that reality is invisible, insensible, or unknowable. It may be unknowable by me with my present epistemological apparatus, but that merely means that I should begin to remember, faithfully. Remember what? That of which I know nothing? How absurd!

And yet this faculty of memory is such that its activity brings reality to my notice. Its activation by me is therefore in itself a step, by me, into that reality. It is a case of 'remember and know'. It is not a case of know and then remember what you know. Again the confusion with recall lies close at hand. This morning I drove to Holywood. I know that. What was it like? It rained a little. Huge puddles covered the streets. My son was in the car with me. We spoke very little. And so on. I might be able to recall enough to cover ten pages before I decide to stop. Would I be recalling correctly? Witnesses could be called. In the end it turns out that I had confused the day. Anyway, I did not recall what I knew, but more of what I recalled. When I said: "I know that," namely that I drove to Holywood this morning, I was wrong. I did not know it but recall it in the first place. And, as it turns out, I recalled it incorrectly. Memory of reality had very little to do with this. What I recalled then, was <u>that</u> knowledge? Not really. But how can I be certain?

As soon as I activate my faithful memory, on the other hand, I take a step into reality. Depending on where I am now, I may even be taking a further step into reality. As I continue to remember, my focus changes. I am no longer in time-in-tension but in eternal time. My vivid perception of this is a perfect delight to me. I know that what I do now could not be done by anyone else. The reality I begin to perceive informs my senses. Certainly I feel more real. I continue to remember. Of course I know that I remember reality and that 'this' reality is our personally managed commonwealth, but I do not make a thing of it. The being of it does not escape me, because my own being goes into the remembering I do. Also I work. I might be resting, but I work. You have the evidence of that in front of you. Directly as I remember reality, I tell you about it and this takes, above all, courage. I stand behind what I say, I back it up. I have no need to quarrel with anyone regarding the veracity of it. But you might be unfriendly. I am not only telling you the truth but I am giving you a sample of reality, of the personally managed commonwealth of it. The wealth is ours in common. Have you the faith to accept that? Are you prevented from accepting it because you hold to some particular faith? Or because you have thrown out faith along with all faiths?

An ethical work makes reality available to others; that is what is good about it. And reality is the apex of our achievement. To be real means the same as to inhabit reality; we should not suppose that we can be the one without doing the other. Even the dead have a claim to reality, in that they are really dead; however they have no knowledge of it.

This knowledge is a peculiar context for our real habitation. It means that we have learned some of the ins and outs of reality. It means that we know the one who ushers us into and leads us out of our place of work, metaphorically speaking; for our work is tied to specific applications. We always work in reference to how and where we just find ourselves and we make no special demands on our situation and conditions. How and wherever we are – this is our median locality, our optimum sphere of reference.

An ethical work is the greatest possible achievement. It begins within and has outward consequences. As we enter within to begin such a work, we are eminently grateful for being able to do so. Within the circumference of our true individuality we are able to make contact with the truth, even as we know why we desire to do so, namely so that the truth might be known in reality. Then we come out of ourselves, aware of the burden we bear.

Now we make contact with others, by choice. We decide to do so, because we know what we are about. The truth we touched is life to us and oh how we appreciate it now, now that we live, having gained the true assurance and certainty of our individual meaning and purpose. We feel we are on the earth for a reason. In terms of what we are able to achieve, we are indispensible and we know it. We have read the message in our heart and we have learned it, so that we can truly say we have life.

But now we are to lay down our life for others. If we cling to it we lose it. If we lay it down, if we make it available to another, only then do we really possess it. We may speak of life here as though it were a substantial quantity, because the quality of it surpasses all qualities. We must know what it is that tugs at our heartstrings in the company of others, when we cannot bear it that they should be ignorant of the truth just then. If they reject us, we know it is really the truth they reject and we may cheerfully persevere. Is the one who has made it possible for us to lay down our life and to pick it up again not with us just now as we do the same?

*

The outward consequences of an ethical work are everywhere to be seen but nowhere to be apprehended. What I mean by this is that we cannot point to them as we can to a pyramid that has been built or to a rocket that has landed on the moon.

What we see however is the merciful spirit at large upon the earth in one or another capacity. In this we experience our complete satisfaction. It is what people approve of and applaud that we shun, by comparison. The merciful father-spirit always remains anonymous. It does not like to be tied to one particular person. And where would it get us, if we slept on the job while others rocked us to sleep, with their applause and approval? Would it help us conquer the devil in our midst?

There are so many notions at large about how to come to the merciful spirit that we must not forget the one that involves combat with the unethical. The polemic spirit must needs be identified. However let it rattle and rage within your breast. Contain it. Know it, recognize it and contain it. You will not be changed to the good by that spirit if you prosper because of it, for the prosperity it brings is the seed of future destruction.

*

The <u>polemic spirit</u> rages within us as soon as we know what we want. Here is the thing we want and we are willing to fight for it; while the thing we do not want has never moved us so passionately. Why should we not be willing to overcome the one with the aid of the other? If we can picture so clearly the need to eradicate this alien opposition, what should prevent us from throwing ourselves violently into the fray? Or if not violently, then sneakily, calculating, after a mustering of forces and a build-up of resources?

Eventually we are bound to triumph.

And isn't it amazing how one thing leads to another! Our wish to triumph feeds on the opposition of the thing we hate. Of course we can shroud concurrent sentiment in virtue and honour and no one will then be in a better position than ourselves to appreciate the justice of our cause. All sense of measure and proportion must surely be superfluous – unless of course in harness to the end of our triumph. We would gladly see sense, but the enemy beckons, the enemy must be destroyed, how else can we prosper? Not that prior to that spirit's onslaught we were aware of an enemy or of any danger to ourselves. The two concur. At one and the same moment the enemy appears and we know we have always been at risk. Once and for all therefore let us rid ourselves of this eternal hindrance to our comfort.

From a rational point of view, we can tell that this enemy is indeed – if not eternal, then timeless.

Now a world of difference separates the eternal from the timeless. If only we had known this years ago when we set out on our journey to the successful life! But then there would not have been any reason for any journey. Today we might coldly speculate on the nature of the clock as a metaphor in comparison to the history of dreams, but these two, as it were, are complements of each other.

The timeless enemy – if we will not gracefully admit it, we are forced to confess eventually – is timelessness itself. Our task is to discover – and to recover – eternal being, and eternal being makes itself known to us in contemporary fashion.

This is the lesson to be learned by those who would more than triumph. Time is not the enemy, but timelessness. If instead of 'eternity' we always said 'eternal being', we would all the sooner extricate ourselves from that labyrinth of major and minor animosities wherein both our soul and our senses are so painfully and destructively constricted.

Eternity is a concept which is to help us eradicate the senselessness of time – once we have overloaded temporal things with vanity and cupidity so that we mistake the dress for the person, the appearance for that which appears. When the hollowness of the item in question dawns on us, right away a hankering for eternity takes hold of us, as if we could have the thing but devoid of appearance. Heedlessness turns to foolishness. The horse on which we gallop through the streets of our mind has never left the barn. Enamoured by things and counter-things and bewitched by the spirit that sets one against the other, we consign our being and the beings of the world to oblivion.

Of course the most difficult task of all is to let go of temporal things, if as yet we have no notion of temporary being as manifested by eternal being. Why should we let go when we have no guarantee of anything else worth holding?

This is where the polemic spirit captures our imagination, and our imagination, once captured, willingly serves that master – at the cost of its own destruction. The worst we can say of any man is that he has flailed his imagination to death in the service of the polemic spirit, to rid himself once and for all of the eternal enemy, namely timelessness.

But timelessness is itself a figment of our diseased or overwrought imagination, though in one sense we may see it as a cry for help from the hollow depths of divorced temporality. The longing we profess for the romantic dream testifies to our bondage to watches and clocks. Let him who has insight diagnose and aid. Let him who has true experience of eternal being give ethical evidence in time, so that those of us who are fettered by temporal things may gain the courage to break free.

*

So eternal being is what we must come to view as normality. And time in tension, i.e. time as past, present and future, is like the surface tension of that normality. Except that beyond that surface tension – nothing. Not space, not time – no being. When we think about eternal being, we must include temporary

133

being, and even as we do think about eternal being, by that very act do we participate in timely fashion.

To live eternally means also to live in time. We don't say that the trunk of a tree is only the heart-wood, ring upon seasonal ring, but we also mean the bark. Now some insist that the bark is dead, which is a dreadful and misleading oversimplification. Speak rather of a transformation, of a passage from one state into another, and of distinguishing borders, limits of discernment. Ask yourself, can eternal being make sense in the absence of temporal being; can a tree live if stripped of its bark?

From the point of view of eternal being, which subsumes temporarily, time can be fully understood, but not the other way around, for obvious reasons. The whole elucidates the part. But they speak of eternity as though it wiped out time, or came after it. Mind you, eternal being as a whole cannot be espoused by us while we cling to time as though it might be whole. So in that sense adoration of the part is threatened by proximity of the whole. Nearness of the good threatens the half bad and the quarter bad.

The ethical is a threat to the non-ethical. The truth is a threat to the lie. But let us not oversimplify. We are merely attempting to identify and plumb the meaning of the polemic spirit, of our tendency to war; the underlying purpose and origin of our incorrigible belligerence. We make war on ourselves, on one another, on nature and the on earth. We attack the one who sustains us, bite the hand that feeds us. We go to great lengths to justify our addiction to strife. It brings the thick blood into flux. It redresses injustice.

But let's face it, we make war because we know nothing of real peace. The only peace we know is a temporary cessation of strife. It is a peace without substance. It is built on nothing and nothing can be built upon it. The more we cling to it the more do we prepare the ground for the polemic spirit at loose ends.

*

Once we know real peace, substantial peace, any experience of strife is painful for us and we try to avoid it. We are however all the same open to the polemic spirit, susceptible to its tensions and liable to various types of addiction to it.

And the purpose of this spirit, its reason for being, is the victory of ethical being over unethical existence. But let's understand this aright. It is our own victory over the belligerence that rises in us in the face of the unethical that creates new ethical being. In a sense we are describing here the fundamental good deed.

Needless to say, in the grip of the polemic spirit we are not ethical – but we are capable of ethical action, otherwise that spirit, which is brought on by our confrontation with the unethical, such as unethical behaviour and conduct, could not have found fertile soil in us. Those who are not capable of ethical action are not beset by the polemic spirit.

This is an important piece of information then. It has immense bearing on how we interpret and of course deal with radical tension, stress and strife. It lets us appraise meaningfully what those do who declare war, advocate revolution and – counsel appeasement. They do not conquer the polemic spirit in themselves.

And here is the secret of that particular endeavour: we can conquer that spirit only if we do so for one another. Even the intention transports us onto the communal level of being, where life is gained.

In the grip of the polemic spirit we are unethical – but equally so in fear of it.

*

Several important elements of the ethical endeavour come together here. The confrontation of the ethical impulse and the unethical state is one. Another is the indicative rise of the polemic spirit. The third is the necessarily communal unmasking of the polemic spirit to reveal its true origin in the caring human heart.

The last of these three may seem the most complicated, because we have so much mentality invested in the sheer physicality and psychology of strife. We would like to remain above it all, to control it from the top down, and when we end by pitting force against force and fighting fire with fire we sometimes feel that the worst that happens to us is that we win. When we count the losses they outweigh the gains and the face we saved is unworthy of the soul we lost.

Neither in terms of physiology, which is a study of our body and mind as one, nor in terms of psychology, which is a study of our psyche, in the absence of our soul, are we able to understand strife in the way that will allow us to harness the strength of the caring human heart. Imagination is required, and a willingness to participate and to be moved. In other words it is from the point of departure of our soul, while we are not in the possession of our soul and not while our soul is possessed by the polemic spirit, that we must seek to make inroads, first of all on our own ingrained bad habits of aggressiveness and timidity. This is the beam in our eye that needs to be removed, and we mention both the appetite for strife and the fear of strife, since one can beget the other. If often enough we have been hurt in our soul because of strife visited upon us or by us, we are liable to become timid and cowardly. On the other hand and by the same token, if we have experienced timidity often enough in ourselves and others we are liable to become aggressive and abusive.

So the first step is to recognize the proximity of strife and the avoidance of strife, of war and appeasement, of aggressiveness and timidity, of the bully and the coward.

The next step would be to acknowledge how both of these really have in common an insufficient sense of <u>honour</u>. While I bully you or shrink from you, I do not sufficiently honour you. Can I honour you while you happen to shrink from me or while you are bullying me? This is the burning question which merits a careful and sensitive answer. How can I honour you, irrespective of your behaviour and conduct at that moment? What does it mean, in any case, to honour someone? Should we perhaps honour only those whom we have judged to be worthy of honour? Or ought we perhaps to honour especially those who stand in need of it? And is anyone more in need of being honoured than the one presently in the grip, positively or negatively, of the polemic spirit?

But how can I go about honouring you, even at the best and easiest of times?

*

The psychology of 'honour' limits human endeavour to the realm of what is allowed. The honourable thought is the one that does not interfere with the traditional body of rules. We bring dishonour on ourselves by presuming to stand above the traditions of our tribe. The collective consciousness is foremost in our mind, so that we operate on a level of mutual benefit that is ruled and regulated by the past and by our culturally acquired notions of the past. Our thinking moves in predetermined circles, our feeling remains accidental and of eternal reality freely embraced we know nothing.

In this case, honour is a protective measure of superstition. A false sense of wholeness, of health and sanity has been acquired and the honourable thing is to ensure the support and prolongation of it. The dishonourable thing is to question and thereby undermine these hardened assumptions.

Now while we cannot advance beyond honourable superstition, because once we move in those circles any such 'going beyond' implies dishonour, we can pay heed to those times when we feel betrayed or shamed. Probably this has to happen frequently before we begin to question some of our suppositions and assumptions. No one freely admits to superstition on any level of being; what is always required is disappointment or constraint. Through the experience of such disappointment or constraint one finds one's circumstances altered and one's disposition changed. Usually one resents this and strives to return to the status quo. This status quo is the original set of honourable superstitions. The fact that one feels dishonoured, shamed and betrayed is not readily associated with an improvement in circumstances and disposition; all the same, that is the case. Whatever or whoever has brought on the change is judged and rejected as subversive. In truth, nothing and no one has brought on or caused the change; it has simply come about, as one might have expected, as a collapse of superstition. All superstition, no matter how rigorously honoured and underpinned by promises and threats, by rewards and punishments, does, mercifully, in the end, reveal itself as unsound in one direction or another, and we either reap the consequences of our insistence on falsehood or else we diagnose the seeming dishonour as pain due to just correction, which pain can be beneficially suffered.

Even where we hope to gain honour superstitiously, we demonstrate all the same, though ineptly, by default, how honour and life are inextricably linked. The life we lead, in other words our behaviour and conduct, our being and doing, our acting and suffering, our work and rest, etc. either involves our taking into account the true wellbeing of others or else we forfeit our hold on that life. An honourable man desires my true

138

wellbeing, whether I know what he means by that or not, whether I am aware of that or not and whether I thank him for it or not. That honourable man knows in fact that the good he does me in secret is the real good and therefore also the most use to himself. However, all that being said, he is honourable specifically in that he equates the hold he has on life with his desire for my true wellbeing, and of course for your true wellbeing too. It is this desire, the desire for the true wellbeing of others, that brings honour into focus as a gift or blessing, which in turn then facilitates the doing of good.

*

The desire for the wellbeing of others is <u>love</u>. How often would we not much rather opt out of a living relationship than to love! When we offer our services and they are rejected, it is the ethical relationship that seems to break. We are not yet honourable, in the sense that we cannot yet gracefully cope with rejection; we cannot love unless we are liked in return. All the same we feel strongly that we should be able to do this. We sense that we ourselves are loved in this way, and if we do not sense it we believe it. We believe god loves us as our father and his love for us is not diminished if we reject him. We ourselves would like to be able to love like that. We would like to be ethically mature. What is it that gets in the way?

A contractual relationship runs counter to a loving relationship. A contract is based on law but love is god. Is it unlawful to be godly, or ungodly to be lawful? Surely it is our love of god that allows us to be lawful, while we cannot, through lawfulness, become godly. When the law of the land seems to demand one thing and god another, we find ourselves in a tragic situation. What are our priorities? The question of <u>ownership</u> rears its head. We would like to own god. And god seems to be quite willing to be owned – until it comes to the point of our being owned in return. That love and ownership, experienced within the same context, should prove problematic is no great news; very few of us are not painfully familiar with it. We cling to the thing we love, but a being will not be clung to. A being will not be forced into relation by contract. If by means of a contract we attempt to bind some being to ourselves, it is bound to appear to us as a thing and then we will blame it for no longer being.

So how can we find a way out of our predicament of being loved but not being able to love? of owning things but not being able to own beings? of desiring the wellbeing of others and not being liked for it?

How can we continue to be honourable while at the same time being dishonoured?

Finally it comes down to that. It is a shameful experience, to be dishonoured. Thoughts of revenge are never far. And yet, when we are dishonoured, are we not like god, who is everywhere dishonoured? Should we set ourselves above god and insist on at least a show of honour? Perhaps that is all it takes to stop us from being dissatisfied. We are happy enough to take on the burden of another as long as our efforts are publicly acknowledged. I find it very hard to face the fact that my private and my public life are separate in order to accommodate such a lack of strength. I know that a truly honourable man is not merely honourable in public and that his sense of honour is not limited to the experience of his society. He can be counted on to be equally honourable in private. In fact the distinction of private from public has little meaning for him. His god hears him more clearly in secret, but unless he testifies to his perception of the truth he soon loses ground.

*

How can I be owned by god? What does that mean and amount to? It means that the god I believe in also believes in

140

me. This is a live relationship. Some of us have that with god, so it should be documented. It amounts to a perfect knowledge of god. Those who have it know that nothing irrelevant can happen to them. They also understand every state they are in. This makes them the appropriate interpreters of the human condition at any given time and we do well to pay heed to their instruction.

*

God too can become for us a thing and no longer a being, and then we look to theology to arrange matters for us in such a way that this thing will make sense to us, and to the degree that this actually happens we are then damned. We erect barriers between ourselves and god by substantiating the thing we take for god. It would make real sense, by comparison, if we knew god as the being.

And humanity is the quintessence of god. Our ethical approach to god must be one of relationship. We cannot know ourselves as human beings unless we know god as the human being. Knowledge begins and ends in our knowledge of god who knows us as we know him. If we distinguish between knowledge and love we must associate freedom with knowledge and ownership with love. It is quite correct that some feel more at ease with knowledge while others feel more at home with love, though not everyone needs to distinguish the two.

*

Let us look forward therefore to the organisation of our thought and feeling in terms of our secret relationship with god. We know it as a relationship of love and knowledge, of ownership and compassion. An ethical work this is, this organization, for what we are saying, practically, is that we as creatures participate in our creator and our creator in us. All it

141

takes to turn this participation into organization is <u>conscious desire.</u>

But why should we bother? Is it not enough that we know ourselves to be loved by god as we love? What need is there for this secret organized relationship?

Some have need of it. It is the task of some, that they should build such a relationship, and then for them not to do so is an invitation to hardship. While they desire it, they are incapable of being otherwise occupied, and by this they know that their desire is right. If, during the course of their desire, they are given insights or arrive at perceptions, these they make available to the members of their community. Their community is made up of those who welcome those insights and perceptions.

Really, from their own point of view, there is nothing further to be desired once one desires this secret organic relationship with god. Does the possession of god not imply the possession of all else? Why would anyone want more? But also they wonder: How could anyone be happy with less? And there they need to remind themselves that not only is their task unusual but their gifts are extraordinary. If they did not exist, the world community could not be envisioned, not to mention realized. But that does not mean that all should be like they.

*

A fundamental ethical principle is the one that combines affection and <u>instruction.</u> Human-natural affection, as we know, is what allows us to know beings in themselves. As we come to know human and other beings, they become dear to us and then it can happen that perfectly normal circumstances seem to contribute to an interruption of the relationship and we wonder how we could possibly have incurred so much shame and guilt when our intentions were so pure.

The answer is that we are in need of instruction. This is a very definite need and we should not underestimate the seriousness of it. We are in need of instruction by the being itself, which is god. Each and every being, whether human or not, stands after all in some relation to god, to the being at all, the being itself or as such, or however we want to put it, and it is in this relationship that we must seek the instruction we need. Not that we should withdraw our affection from a being when we find that the relationship has been interrupted, but rather that we should concentrate on the inward relationship of that being with god.

*

One is tempted at times to judge that in the case of one or another person in our vicinity or ken no inward relationship with god exists. But even if it were so – and we are not wise to make such judgments – we could still concentrate on the possibility of such an inward relationship. We may not be able to bring it about, but that is not the point. Whatever did not work today may work tomorrow. The usefulness of our task as we seek, or seek to give, instruction depends entirely on our concentration of inward relationship with god.

We must view instruction within the larger and wider context of affection – of human-natural affection. We have identified the need for instruction as initially a breakdown of natural affection and now we are saying that our first step in responding to this need must be a concentration on inward relationship to the being, which is god.

Now this concentration on inward relationship with god will first of all blot out the grievous hurt that is bound to attend any interruption of the flow of affection. We experienced it as a flow and were perfectly happy with that. Such a perfect happiness leaves us wishing for nothing and we cannot see for the life of us why we should ever again have a sore trial in the world. When it stops we are doubly aggrieved: once because we are no longer happy and again because that perfection is no longer ours. Unhappiness twice over gnaws at our vitals and reminds us forcefully of just that – of our vitality, of the organic life we were born with, which one day we will have to return to the one who introduced us into the world. We call it our vitality and while we were perfectly happy in the enjoyment of that flow of natural affection we did lose track of it. Or is that a fair way of expressing it? Could we have kept track of it? Would we not, had we kept in mind our vitality and subsequently of course also our mortality, have sacrificed that very perfection in happiness which we prized at the time so highly? And then it would not have been a case of having the one while not letting go of the other but of having the other and losing the one. But we lost the one in any case – the beauty with which we were in love.

To be in love with beauty – to enjoy the perfect happiness of human-natural affection in flow: these two are the same. They are one and the same. What they are not is constant and sustainable.

Here we have come face to face with the predicament that besets all striving for ethical being in the absence of ethical doing. A typical misconstruction of the problem pits the angels against nature in a drama of conflict without end. A popular saying describes a person as being too heavenly good to be of any earthly use, and that makes some sense at least, because of the humour. But finally we confess our helplessness when confronted with the suggestion that the good must die while those who live cannot avoid being bad and ugly. From that premise begin all those who fall prey to what we might call the <u>romantic delusion</u>.

Let us call it the romantic ethic and be done with it.

And now let us discover what is wrong with it.

There is an attitude towards beauty and towards happiness that will not rhyme with life. We need to examine our innermost being to find how much of this attitude we hold, for it does not play into our everyday notions of what is pleasant and acceptable. It may develop into a secret rancour or bitterness, into a creeping weakness or malaise. And it does prevent our inward relationship with the good. It prevents it in that it makes it seem unattainable or magical. The consequences are both horrible and horrifying. If this inward relationship with the good is aimed at as something magical, with the attendant feelings, sentiments, imaginings and force-addictions; if it is aimed at or invited or sustained as such, where usually both pain and pleasure are after all accepted as being of secondary importance in comparison to what is mistaken for truth – then obviously the true inward relationship is forfeited and the human being turns into an organism.

So in one sense the romantic ethic is yet another case of building on sand. Where magic, or the love of magic, is involved however, the case becomes rather specific, and in a way that, so it seems, has to be looked at again and again, on the one hand because the possibilities of magic intrusion multiply endlessly and on the other hand because our integrity, our steadfastness of character, our constancy under trial is never so great but that we can afford to neglect opportunities for improvement and increase. And cleansing our being of all reliance on magic is tantamount to such increase, and helping one another in that interest amounts to the same, only more so.

And as a matter of fact magic is seeming improvement and increase but actual impairment and decrease. This we hope to demonstrate in the following pages.

*

Only those can speak of magic with impunity who have arrived at a ripeness of character. Then, and only by those, the organic burden of truth may be borne and not shrugged off in pursuit of vain imaginings. What do we mean by this organic burden of truth? The ethos of any particular set of circumstances depends on it.

All our organs obey us; they are not our organs, and not yet our organs, if they do not. This obedience is not to a spirit or to a soul but to a real human being. My organs, furthermore, do not obey my will but they obey me. The difference is frequently overlooked. You, before you bring your will into action and before you are, so to speak, willing to do something, are in shape for organically effective influence. How do you do what you do? I myself, if I see the appropriateness of such an influence, how do I bring my influence to bear – without any degree of willing or wishing?

We bear the organic truth with which we are burdened under a given set of circumstances. That alone suffices to bring about the resolution, to solve the problem, to ease the difficulty, to mitigate those very circumstances – to change fate into fortune.

A great deal is involved here because the matter in hand is so simple, while we have invariably become accustomed to the circuitous route over elaborate terrain in pursuit of anticipated results.

As we said, a certain ripeness of character is required before our organs may register such a circumstantially induced burden which is not right away delegated by us to the realm of wish or will. They are not our organs if we cannot bear it that they should come under the influence of circumstance. However, if they are our organs, then such a burden empowers us, and as we bear it – which we can only do for the sake of resolution, of easing, of healing and such-like – that comes about.

This all makes sense and works because truth is involved. We may not yet be conversant with truth as other than a match of appearances, but in that case we may all the same experience this burden and bear it, thereafter learning to appreciate truth for its own sake, rather than attempting to harness it, for calculated motives or preconceived ends.

Our organs are such as afford us aspects of the world. The world of beings remains a closed book to us until our organs become in truth our own, and only then are we able to sustain – to bear – the real nearness of other beings, rather than fleeing from them or rejecting them, as we insist on dealing exclusively with things.

*

All too often organs get confused with tools. Will-power turns into a tool what might otherwise be an organ. Our will is goal-oriented, and that is how it should be, and it avails itself of tools and devices, almost as if it were an intelligence in its own right. But our organs depend on ourselves. Between a tool and ourselves stands our will. The tool obeys our will. Only in this case obedience is hardly the right word. A tool is more of an extension of our will. And our will is more or less an extension of ourselves. We can differentiate between good will and egotistic will, depending on whether that willingness is an extension of ourselves or of our ego, but in both cases the extension is there, rather than an obedience.

It makes no sense merely to will; we must will something. However when our organs are involved, it does suffice simply to be, and then to bear whatever burden is placed upon us by circumstances.

So when we speak of the ethos of some particular environment or aspect of the world, of some set of circumstances we are involved in, or even of the community in which we find ourselves, we mean that which has coalesced for us due to the burdens of truth we have born organically. It is not the world

147

we have changed but the world we have suffered that forms our character, and quite often we know nothing of character precisely because we have been too busy changing the world ever to have been affected by any beings; in fact, if truth be told, beings do not even exist for us and therefore the ethos of any aspect of the world escapes us.

So we speak of 'the' world, as though it were finite. But we know that in truth the world is without end. An infinite number of beings make up the world. Their impinging upon us affords us the opportunity for character, for turning outward what we have gained and stored inwardly. What we have called a certain ripeness of character should perhaps be better called a ripeness for character, for it must be the available pathos of our being to which other beings become attracted. We then must be able to direct that attraction.

*

Pathos is an interesting term, especially in counterbalance to what we mean by ethos. From the point of view of this pathos we can learn to differentiate finally between 'the world', as finite, and 'world', as infinite. But 'the world', as finite, is also mythic, and it is in the interest of an appreciation of myth and of the mythic quality of certain beings, that we will try to come to terms with the meaning of pathos and of the pathic side of our nature.

Calling it the pathic 'side' of our nature itself reveals an approach that must be selective. We are very much aware here of how important these related insights will prove towards a better understanding of the so-called romantic ethic and the romantic fallacy, which will always be with us in one guise or another as potential disaster. We intend to concentrate especially on an analysis of the dubious benefit envisioned as something like a true society of individuals – in comparison, please take note, to a real community of persons. While one deems oneself capable

148

of achieving the former, and while a desire for it is – always artificially – sustained, the latter hasn't a chance of even appealing to us. This supposedly 'true society of individuals' is therefore a calamitous short-circuit. Nearly two-thousand years of a modern approach to 'the world' offer us a great number and variety of what must be called symptoms, all of which fit within this category of attempts at a true society of individuals.

Keep in mind that individuals are not persons, or, more hopefully stated, not yet persons. A person is also individual and can with profit speak of his individuality, but an individual is someone who knows nothing of personality because he makes a thing out of the difference between himself and others rather than investing that difference in the furtherance of personal community. We can make a more enlightening separation still between individuals and individualists, where the former make a thing out of their difference from others and the latter actually insist on that difference as a measure of their rightful identity. An individualist is therefore at an even further remove from personhood and personal community because he is actually involved in constructing a false edifice, with the implication that the building of any true edifice must occur to him as dangerous, sinister and destructive.

*

The pathic side of our nature determines how far we can go in the direction of ambition and achievement without incurring a diminution of human being, or just plain of being. What we mean by pathos may be typified as an illumination of soul or intensification of spirit but we are not yet aware of it, only conscious of our soul's reluctance to be illuminated and of our spirit's unwillingness to be intensified. We move into the realm of myth here, because technically our soul cannot be reluctant; it is we ourselves, as soul, who are reluctant, and equally our spirit cannot be unwilling or willing except insofar as we pretend it may do so and confer on it that power, which is then a mythic power. Technically it is we ourselves, as spirit, who are willing or unwilling. But prior to our awareness of what is really going on, there is unavoidably this consciousness of a reluctance of soul and of an unwillingness of spirit, and such consciousness, with its content of soul or spirit, is pathic.

Two elements are involved: spirit or soul that is mythic and consciousness that is not yet awareness. Reluctance and unwillingness are inextricably linked with both.

In our pathic state, and within this burdened consciousness, we know nothing of an eventual awareness. Once we do, we are ethically engaged or committed rather than pathically burdened. What we do know, however, is ourselves as affected. Something has come to lie upon us, to weigh us down; we feel dispirited and our soul is heavy. The notion that it is something, that something is involved that is responsible other than ourselves, arises automatically and no mental adjustment is required. "What is bothering you?" someone asks, and right away we have company, as we wonder what it might be, what might be the cause of it and possibly to blame. Then the mythic faculty, a measure of artifice, takes over and comforts us.

Now this mythic faculty, this measure of artifice, is important, because without it we would be exposed to trials and tribulations in a way that would soon wear us down and out.

Prior to the ethic awareness, the mythic comfort allows us to come to terms with our pathic state.

Why not substitute ethic awareness immediately for any pathic state? Why bother with pathos? Is the perception of a burdened, reluctant soul and of a depressed, unwilling spirit not simply an understandable mistake, which should be avoided, and if not avoided, then as quickly as possible rectified? After all, if it truly is our soul, then there is no need to look for an

150

agent that causes discomfort because it will suffice for us to carry the burden we chafe under. Equally, if it is really our spirit, then why not, as soon as a depression sets in, give in to it and experience the intensification of spirit? In other words, as soon as we notice a pathic state, or, more precisely, ourselves in a pathic state, why not immediately become ethical?

The problem is that it takes time to come to that realization. As soon as we are affected in spirit or soul, our entire being tends to concentrate on where this seems to take place. We become disoriented, we try to deal with the emergency with our usual faculties and with customary means, only to discover that we cannot succeed. This is hardly surprising, since our faculties and means themselves are to change and to undergo change. We are in discomfort, possibly in severe discomfort and we may be ready to grasp at straws.

*

This is where the need to be selective comes in. We must choose a particular item from among the plethora of mood-oriented feelings and emotions and 'do something with it'. There is no need initially to be more specific. What counts is not what is done to this or that mood- or myth-orientation but rather that something is done, that we do. This perspective by us on ourselves as doers is crucial. Finding or discovering that perspective can take a long time. During that time we are, unknown to ourselves, being affected by good spirit as order. But we, in comparison, are in disorder. Hence the pathic state.

We speak of a mood- or myth-orientation because, in comparison to the 'higher' order affecting us, which higher order is all-embracing, our pathic state amounts to a back and forth between myth and mood. Speaking of mood-swings in connection with such inner experience is therefore not entirely appropriate, since the 'swing' is not from mood to mood but from mood to myth, and unless we understand this right we cannot really help anyone in that state cope. We seek to 'put down our head' either in mood-states or under mythic conditions; we wish to come to rest in happiness, in grief, in peace, or else in someone's company, in some particular environment, or in subjection to some figure of authority, and this is perfectly understandable, because as yet, prior to having 'done', we have no indication whatsoever of the spiritual order affecting us except the symptoms of our rejection and unwillingness, which are depression, despair, a bad mood or an outright enemy.

Form the point of view of the spiritual order affecting the individual now, it must seem that this unwillingness and rejection of the ultimate good is in a sense perverse and therefore deplorable. However, from that same point of view and of necessity as participant in that spirit, one also realizes, having gone through the period of training, education and enlightenment, that the missing link which alone can connect the pathic state of fluctuation between mood- and myth-orientation with the order of good spirit is mercy, and the quality of mercy.

*

The swing from mood to myth and back again, and the failed attempts to find rest in either, can be diagnosed mercifully from without, by a person, but the individual in that pathic state sees the world and all beings, him- or herself included, either within some framework that is coloured by mood or else as mythic entities, and the astonishing part of this is that while he knows beings in a mood he is not conscious of myths, and while he knows beings mythically he is not conscious of moods. He himself (or she herself) is not astonished by this, because he is not aware of it. He is like someone who speaks French and just before he really feels at home in that language he suddenly begins in rudimentary German and cannot recall ever having spoken French.

Whatever mood he is in colours his vision of what happens to him, his perception of his environment. It may be a 'good' mood or a 'bad' mood, he may be pessimistic or optimistic, enthusiastic or despairing, what matters is that there is no hold, no reliable constant, no firm basis to anything.

And yet we who observe this individual are able to tell, from an ethic point of view, that he is in this pathic state and therefore – and this is of crucial importance – therefore ready for the step into the ethic. The human-natural pathos sets in, in one or another shape or form, no sooner than there is readiness for the first ethic step. Meanwhile the pathic individual knows nothing of the ethical so far as ethic action is concerned, but he does have a sense of the ethic reward, a more or less dim premonition of it, and this draws him on. What he vaguely perceives as the light at the end of a tunnel and what he longs for without really being able to put a name to it, is what sometimes, ironically, appears in letters on gravestones, namely eternal rest, rest in peace.

The reality of this eternal rest in peace is not his, not yet, and he may never have it unless he takes that ethic step, but meanwhile it plays into his moods and appeals to him as myth. Perhaps we should say it occurs to him as mood, and appeals to him as myth. It accommodates itself to him, and this is the beauty of it. It is willing to divide itself and either to occur as pleasure or appeal as beauty. We, from the point of vantage of ethical behaviour and intention, know it as one, as glory, or more specifically as the glory of god, but a pathic individual knows as yet nothing of this glory except the odd pleasurable or beautiful hint. At best any notion he has of real glory is one-sided. Neither pleasure nor beauty can be whole, as he is forced to find out again and again to his delusion or dismay.

*

So we can in a sense imagine the pathic individual as stretched out between pleasure and beauty, between moods and myths, while on the far horizon he has a glimpse now and again of the glory of god. While he seeks this glory in terms of beauty or on the basis of pleasure he must fail in ugliness or pain. He needs to be reminded that while his aim is correct, his means are wrong. And this pleasure and beauty is of course wrapped up for him with his moods and his myths. His moods give a content of sorts to his existence while his myths lend a framework or context of sorts to it. His desire or ambition is to rest in peace in the glory of god but his experience of reality is such that he tosses and turns on his bed and is thrown from one uncontrollable sensation to the other. Moments of steadiness are afforded by conflicts resolved with integrity but a moral dimension no sooner appears than it is shown up for its lack of actual effectiveness and once again disappointment reigns supreme. Out of the ashes of individual morality no ethic rises and to the compassionate onlooker the pathic state must seem like an exercise in futility where nothing short of drastic measures will brake the deadlock in which a self-defeating mentality finds itself.

*

Training, education and then, if possible, even enlightenment can help the pathic individual out of his unfortunate state, so that he has the opportunity for freedom as a person in community. But these three: training, education and enlightenment, must in themselves be ethical and administered from an ethic point of view.

The training helps an individual to differentiate between mood and moods, between myth and myths. He learns to identify moods, to recognize when he is in one, and then he is endowed with the religious impulse, with an impulse that is called religious because if he gives in to it, he becomes capable of creating for others the communal medium, simply by being.

The differentiation between mood and moods prepares the ground for the gift of the religious impulse – in good time. The training comes to an end with the advent of such an impulse. It is then possible for the individual to step out into some communal context and to participate in some interpersonal relationship.

Here we have to be careful with our definitions. The pathic state is unavoidable. Training is therefore of the essence. Even as children we end up in this pathic state, when our individuality so to speak overwhelms us, and we need to be trained by parental adults around us, preferably by our own natural parents. Usually we do better by calling that training our upbringing.

But right away it should be noted that with proper training or up-bringing no education is necessary. Education must come into it if the training does not bear the fruit of the religious impulse – or rather if the religious impulse, once available, is not taken hold of by the individual. Technically training must and does go on, in one way or another, by controlled and planned program or through circumstances, until the religious impulse is experienced. The pathic individual is bound to be taken aback by this, and in his dismay he may discover community with others. His training should really have included some anticipation of that bewildering experience, and if it was a truly parental training, then the child recognizes the communal mood soon enough on such an occasion and is willing in future to relinquish all other moods in favour of this one, which we cannot name otherwise but we must identify it by its source and end, which is community. This communal mood is not a good mood or a bad mood but mood as such, unstained by pleasure and untainted by pain.

Once we have been endowed with the religious impulse (really there is only the one) and we have decided, admittedly after a period of gestation such as must follow each and every organic impulse, to behave communally, we will no longer tolerate the formation of moods in ourselves, neither good nor bad, and we will, as mature adults, always turn our perplexity or bewilderment to communal behaviour, because more and more we recognize such disconcerting experience as an invitation every time to communality and we get into the good habit of acting on such invitations.

What we have to countenance however is that the religious impulse may occur, upon sufficient training, but the pathic individual does not necessarily pay heed. This is unfortunate. What happens now is that the individual builds up a degree of morbidity, which is actually a bad habit, and this, then, is where education has to come in. Education is to lead and guide the mortified individual out of his pathic state, by degrees, but because of the morbidity that has set in, which is like the pathic state ingrained due to non-recognition of the religious impulse, this education must take into account the inability and unwillingness of those individuals to rise to the occasion of the religious impulse, so that all depends on <u>an appropriate presentation of myth</u>. It must be appropriate in view of the fact that mortified individuals think and feel according to myths, and these myths must be educationally countenanced in such a way that a translation into myth will happen <u>almost unconsciously</u>. It is a cleansing process that goes on, and it amounts to a liberation of the understanding faculty so that <u>reason</u> may be seen and done.

*

What does it mean to think and feel according to myths? The mortified or morbid individuals, young or old, due to non-recognition of the available religious impulse, get into the way of thinking and feeling not for the sake of a greater reality and more abundant life, which is the innate purpose of those faculties, but so that they might perpetuate themselves, in their morbidity.

When we turn away from the religious impulse rather than embracing it and behaving communally, we usually do so because of the perplexity that cannot but precede such an impulse. Our training or upbringing has brought us to the point where we are able to sustain now – or rather we would be able to sustain now – the sort of change to our constitution that is necessary before we can become personally responsible and accountable to our community. But the aspect of the messenger who brings the message puts us off. An experience of bewilderment is part and parcel of that new impulse, that invitation to newness.

And the one single virtue that is guaranteed to bring us through this bewilderment and perplexity is patience.

Patience is not a case of ignoring the problem until it goes away. To be patient means to be in a most certain way, and since it is patience that will eventually see us through the fog that lies over us at the crucial culmination of our life training period, doesn't it make sense that it should be practiced even during the course of our training? It serves us well in the end if we have meanwhile learned to be patient.

Neither is patience merely a case of suspended interference. It could be described as human being in action. It is helpful for us to keep in mind, while we are patient, that not only are we allowing something to grow that needs to grow in its own sweet time but we are also supplying the nourishment for that growth. So we can speak in terms of offering and allocating our patience or impatiently withholding or withdrawing it.

*

What, again, does it mean, to think and feel according to myths? We reject that experience of dismay, of perplexity, and impatiently seek perpetuity in old ways and means, in old maters and issues. Why should our standard existence be interrupted? It could not have been a proper and useful training that brought us to this point because the sudden weariness took us not only by surprise but equally 'to the cleaners'. Now this pallor settles over all our points of view. A melancholy affects us and whatever we touch is infected with it. Boredom brings itself upon us as though it had a will of its own. The world is a settlement of fools and their back gardens boast great crops of sophistication. It may be time after all to appreciate some of the innocence we have lost. Let us compose a science to the tune of speed, mere matter and efficiency. Society will applaud. Not until now that this mood of rejection has coloured the world for us can we be interesting. Lo, we are interesting! A god would not think so but we ourselves think it and confirm one another in the prejudice. We have become self-conscious suddenly and why should we not enjoy it? Life is a necklace of moods worn by the dog who turns to his vomit. We have not come up with what it takes to push through to the communal mood and now, it appears, we are to be educated. God is all-merciful! How can one make oneself understood at times such as this except by expressing the fruits of an itinerant double-vision? One eye below and one above the surface of the pond. Before you know it you are caught up in reasons for your morbid existence that are nothing but demonstrations of panic. Of course you will never forget entirely that unknown 'glory of god' on the horizon, but now you are happy to make do with a virtual reflection of it. All the same, take your melancholy in hand and construct a theory of natural selection and survival of the fittest, that will be your myth of the day. Or instead, depending on taste and on who is impressed, argue for justification by faith, by deeds, by ingrained moralist ticks; but guard against the cynic chained to the gatepost because his bark gives the game away. Or lead a parade of liberal theologians to the third world, to the last world but one, if you like, then bounce your android witticisms off the stars and congratulate yourself on your communication skills. Another myth is born. Man progresses. The world is nearly saved, the truth nearly understood, nature nearly subjected, the universe nearly explained from beginning to end and even in your lifetime you shall rest on your couch of public esteem with nothing to do but push buttons.

*

<u>Myths are bad reasons at work.</u> They are bad reasons because they try to perpetuate morbid points of view instead of making room for good reason. Myth, by comparison, is good reason at work. The difference between good reason and bad reason<u>s</u> is our unwillingness to be educated. We do not like to be disentangled from our morbid old standards of thinking and feeling.

The communal mood is religious, just as the communal myth is reasonable.

Our training, or upbringing, should be all we need. If successful and consequent, it contains nothing unreasonable; neither is there any mortification nor does any morbidity set in. This should always be kept in mind, that education is necessary only because of a failure of upbringing. The religious, or messianic, impulse is really the same as the light of reason, except that the latter takes account of the morbid rejection of the call to community that has become habitual and ingrained.

*

In our day, education is the password for culture and we have to keep in mind now that this is not necessarily education at all unless its goal is the glory of god in personal community for individual human beings who have undergone mortification and who have not, for one reason or another, accepted the religious impulse, and they have not received it though it has been available for them, so that instead of knowing the communal mood they fall prey to a series of good or bad moods.

The mortification and the morbidity can be explained in terms of the various experiences of beauty and pleasure that are dominant and relative in any given society at any give time.

First of all we have to look at the separateness of beauty and pleasure as a unique situation and not necessarily as a real state of affairs. The main reason why any definition of beauty or of pleasure has always proved problematic is that the two do not separately exist, although of course a human being an get into a state where he falls in love with beauty or gets hooked on pleasure, which has dire consequences for his constitution.

It is not until we are in the possession of our <u>soul</u> that we realize that our body and our mind are not after all separate entities, so that pleasure for the body and beauty for the mind become falsified and are misapprehended to the extent and degree that the human mind and the human body become separately functional, in default of any soul. From the point of view of an intact constitution we are able to diagnose these partial perceptions of beauty and pleasure because we can compare them to an experience of the glory of god, which in itself depends on an interconnectedness of body and mind as soul – just as we cannot come unto the possession of our soul until we receive this glory into ourselves. The creator always longs for the creature, but the creature, specifically the human creature, does not always go to the bother of longing for the creator.

*

What good does it do us to explain the modern morbidity in terms of pleasure and beauty unhinged: can we rectify matters by altering our approach to beauty and pleasure? Should we try to be more ascetic and more aesthetic? Will tinkering with our errors achieve a perfection for us?

160

What we can do, in the twilight of our sensitivity to beauty and pleasure, is shift our gaze in every case and on ever occasion to what we have called here the glory of god. Would it be possible to give it another name? So many of us today are embarrassed by the word god because of the atrocities and improprieties perpetrated in the so-called name of god. Anyone interested in ethical behaviour and action in our day must always be ready to ask anyone who uses the word 'god': "What do you mean? Whom do you mean? Is it the Christian God? the god of Islam? the god of the humanist? of the plutocrat? of the professional victim?"

As for myself, I prefer to show what I mean and whom I mean through my work. Where the definitions of the head are one with the intentions of the heart, it soon becomes obvious whom and what we mean, whether we say god or not.

But the glory of god embraces a total experience by ourselves of our soul wrapped in the splendour of creation. It is also in his works that we know god and we as we live are one of his works. We as we live are the main part of his work. God is glorious in his works on behalf of ourselves as his creatures.

*

All the same, we can incorporate into our programs of education a reasonable approach of the glory of god, so that our one-sided, morbid attitudes to beauty and pleasure, our ascetic excesses and our aesthetic aberrations, become neutralized.

It is this reasonable approach to the glory of god that must inform our ethic education out of a morbid pathos. Both children and adults are in need of such education. Of primary importance is as accurate as possible an appraisal of the judgment under which those to be educated exist.

When we say that someone is under a judgment we refer to the misfortune he has brought on himself due to misbehaviour or negligence. An educator or teacher is able to gauge and estimate such misfortune. He is able to distance himself from his own pathic state sufficiently to take upon himself the judgment under which those he would educate must labour and then he has what it takes, as an educator or teacher, to guide the educatee or pupil out of his self-caused, self-imposed predicament. He knows his pupils from within and they recognize him as one who does not pile more judgment and condemnation on their shoulders but who points them to the way out of their misery.

Such a teacher of course has the glory of god as his own goal always and he knows the path of reason leading to that goal. He knows that to be reasonable means also to be loving and forgiving and that the power of reason is available to him only to the extent that he empowers those who look to him for guidance.

*

Reason is available to those who ask for it. Being becomes asking. Being becomes asking plus that for which one asks. I ask for reason and gradually get rid of my morbidity. I believe that reason is the glory of god in action, in reality, in time. Let us ask for reason now and see what happens. I believe that only good can come of it. If you believe that reason is the fuel for argument, then that is what you get when you ask for it. But reason is the glory of god in action and here we have it now. I am, at the moment, in that I ask for the reason I get. Of course I am an author, so naturally the reason I get manifests itself as the written word for me. I do not try to state a case logically at the moment nor do I try to argue for one kind of meaning or another. When I have nothing left to write, I do not hasten to think of some related topic nor do I spin out the past theme to make it yield more sense. My main and central motivation is to illustrate the presence of reason and to demonstrate its availability. Of course I may tire, and I do tire at the moment. But such a mood of fatigue cannot stop me from asking for reason.

162

It is I myself who would finally have to say: I am too tired to go on and this writing is tiring me out. In itself, a mood has no power over me. But we know how reason is to oust these moods, so it seems only reasonable that the culprit should present himself to me before leaving and give me one last chance to forsake reason in favour of, in the present case, tiredness.

The whole point of reason is to make up for the fact that we have not responded to the religious impulse. We may have talked religion, we may have attended religion, we may have been schooled in its rites and rituals, but we did not inwardly give ourselves to the universal life. We withheld ourselves. We may have had any of a great number of reasons for doing so, but it was just these reasons from which our entanglement in problems now stems. The reasons for which we rejected the religious impulse underpin our imprisonment. Naturally we are reluctant to admit this and to face up to it. What we know as reason and what we mean by that concept is really negating and negative throughout. We imagine it to be positive because for us the call to religion involved shame and guilt, and as soon as we sensed that, we mustered our forces to exclude the intruder. Something therefore ends up being called rational thought based on reason which is in truth a compilation of reasons called criticism. The religious impulse threw us into confusion and we were given a glimpse of ourselves in comparison to how we would be if we embraced universal love and justice in person. This comparison frightened us, gave us a taste of shame and guilt but we did not accept this shame and give it its due, neither did we confess the guilt and receive our reward for this, but we nervously shrugged off any complicity in our present state and started to produce reasons why we should do so. These reasons came to us quite naturally, though not human natural. They stemmed from bad nature. As we gave in to them, our nature went to that extent bad and consequently to that degree incapable of humanity. The guilt and the shame have not gone away. Our argument suppresses them. Together with the criticism and the bad nature, this amounts to our rampant morbidity.

If we notice this morbidity in ourselves and become aware of how we spread it by means of our behaviour and conduct, foremost in our conversation and social contact, we may well feel obliged to ask ourselves how we might change. The scruples we experience are a god-send. Momentarily we may hate ourselves and feel some relief. But more than a short-lived regret is required if we are to succeed in breaking out of the incarceration of our self-constructed armour against religion, against our human-natural longing for religion, for being whole.

*

What is this communal behaviour of which we become capable once we have accepted the religious impulse and the challenge to be whole human beings? Even our being itself becomes communal, so that when we are with others it suffices for us to be, albeit aware that we are, to be of benefit to others. Evidently something is alive in us that cuts across the individual divide. We do not expect to be openly recognized for the effect we have, but that makes no difference to us. In fact we may wish to avoid such recognition, for we know that the communal influence operates best in secret, which also means that what we ourselves get out of it, out of whatever goes on during such a time, does not depend on open recognition or gratitude from those who benefit. The truly ethical act, as we shall never tire of repeating, is of equal benefit to both the doer and the one done for. It is of actual benefit to the agent and of at least potential benefit to the one on whose behalf the agent acted. The latter must of course accept or receive what is being done for him. Only those who are incapable of religion will interject that a deed is either selfish or altruistic and that it cannot be unselfish if one is aware of one's own benefit ahead of time, so that the only unselfish act must be self-sacrificial. Such thinking testifies to the presence of moods and would remind us of Aristotle's notion of ethical virtue as halfway between extremes, such as generosity between extravagance and miserliness; whereas ethical generosity stems from the communal mood, of which extravagance and miserliness know nothing.

So what we must come to terms with is that communal being, communal behaviour and communal action spring directly from human-natural being, upon access by someone who is aware of it, and not from an individual human being. It is the access and the awareness by an individual person that makes the community available for a few, for several or for many.

*

But again, what is it that cuts across the individual divide, that urges us in the beginning to be discontent with our individualism and to search for a way out of private isolation or public deprivation, out of our pathic state so that we might have it itself and nothing besides?

How despondent we can become, when we feel pressed to answer that question and nothing occurs to us except trite definitions and empty phrases! How much better, how much more satisfying, if every time, instead of explaining ourselves, we can show what we mean, give examples of it, actually do what we were talking about and is this not precisely as it should be? <u>Any work on ethics must be ethical</u>. Being written, it must express the urgency and need for the good while showing at the same time how to attain to it. And if I as an individual cannot do myself alone any real good then it must be obvious and explained why this is so, and what can be done instead. If happiness cannot be the goal but must be a by-product, then this should be honestly admitted, otherwise we will add to the collective misery rather than showing a way out of it.

Some are given the task of expressing their hunger for morality; they awaken that hunger in others. But morality that does not flow into ethics can at best point individuals towards the establishment of a state. This is always a pathic state. Now the establishment of a pathic state is a mighty nuisance from one point of view, because it does seem for all the world to offer a haven of peace and rest, so that no further search should be necessary. From another point of view however such an established state does seem to prevent a total falling back into immorality, so that one feels it ought to be supported – but then one supports too the <u>moralist short-circuit</u> that prevents ethics. One supports the state in bad faith but hopes that with enough effort ethic community will somehow eventually come about.

But it will not. There is no line of progression from the moral state to an ethic community. Before the communal mood can be entertained, all commitment to moral pathos must be left aside. But so must any active interference with or rejection of that state be laid aside. While community cannot arise from society, ethics does all the same grow out of morality.

Our commitment to moral pathos is always in terms of rules and regulations, laws and commandments, that imply condemnation and involve punishment, and recipes that are to benefit the individual or the individual group. There is in essence no difference between the pathic state of one individual and that of a group of individuals, such as a group of citizens.

<u>So moral pathos</u> does not need our commitment, to its regulations or perpetuation, as a state, but it <u>is in itself our automatic reaction, our blind reaction, to a call to ethics, to personality and community</u>. We are not to get into a relationship with the messenger but we are to read the message and take it on board.

*

166

Any pathic state, whether established or not, testifies to the religious impulse rejected. Once established, however, such a state is sanctioned as the norm and one finds it difficult to see around it. All the same, what of those who reject all training or upbringing, or who have never been trained or brought up to come face to face with the evil in themselves? What of those who have never experienced the religious impulse and have therefore not even had the opportunity to accept or reject it? Needless to say, they will see no sense in the establishment of a public pathic state either, since they have no notion of any private pathos. For them the public political state is either something they need to challenge, criminally, or else they fall in with it unquestioningly, as though it were real. So from that point of view there is not much to choose between the criminal and the 'good citizen', if by good, here, we mean merely an abiding by the rules of citizenship. Mind you, one ought to know the difference between abiding by the rules and just plain not infringing against them. Those who have never been brought up and who have therefore not grown up either, may go through life like slaves of appearances and one is astonished by the vigour with which they defend laws for which they have no real respect against those who hate laws because they have no integrity.

Never having experienced the religious impulse because of a lack of upbringing is not the same as not yet having experienced it because of insufficient upbringing. Any attempt to educate someone when he has not yet experienced the religious impulse is foolish, to say the least. Once we have responded to the religious impulse and begun to acquire ethical habits, we have no use for education. Only our reasoned rejections of religion become hindrances to our true progress, and to liberate us from these we have educators, teachers who know from their own experience what it means to reject the religious impulse but who were then liberated by reason itself and enlightened.

Such enlightenment is rare and we do well to ask for more of it. We need many true teachers. They cannot be trained and they cannot be educated themselves by a teacher but they are enlightened by reason itself.

*

The religious impulse contains all we need for our wholeness. If we reject it, reason gives us a second chance. If we reject reason there is no hope for us and we turn into building blocks of the established pathic state. Here we live out our lives then, consistent with the standards and norms of Society. The eternal life has passed us by. What remains for us is that we play along until the death within coincides with the death from without. We are not necessarily unhappy or unfortunate. We help to make up the furniture for the room in which human beings abide. In truth we are things. We might have been, but we are not. To be a thing is self-defeating, is not to be. Those who live, know us for what we are, but we do not. Actually we know nothing. Neither love nor reason informs us. And yet, as we play along, we may make up our own world; no one and nothing may stop us. What we call nature is really an outline of nature. Our reality is really a reflection of reality. What we call life is a phenomenon. Those who mistake us and argue their case with us cannot for the life of them understand why their points of view never earn recognition or why their logic never takes hold. We exist virtually and our foremost interest is virtuality.

*

A political state is a pathic state. Like every pathic state, it exists more or less under the influence of reason. However, it is not only a pathic state but also an established pathic state. Individual pathic states can of course be established too, such as when a particular social stance is adopted. What matters in

168

each case is whether or not the rejection of the ethical order is methodically planned and organized.

Morality takes the individual out of himself, so that he shall no longer be content with himself in isolation, but it does not commit him or bind him to community. All the same, the call to community, the ethic voice, does not abandon us, however perverse our refusal to hear. While morality can take us half the distance, the urgency to go all the way always exists for us, however masked by our grievances against god.

So one great error is the attempt to make morality take us all the way. This cannot work. A law-abiding citizen is not yet necessarily an ethical human being, although an ethical human being may coincidentally also be a law-abiding citizen. He will certainly not be breaking any laws. His concern is with the truth, the good and the glorious and what he knows of these he communicates to others so that he too may possess them. As an ethical human being he is mindful of his mortality and therefore never disrespectful of laws and the law. He is ethical in that he acts from an inner ethical motivation and in the interest of the wellbeing of his community and the welfare of the members of his community. As he behaves more and more ethically, his community becomes more expansive, more defined and the members of it better known to him. His community has nothing to do with society and readily cuts across all social phenomena. Friends, acquaintances, companions, family relations make up a part of his community. So do the authors whose books he reads, the composers of the music he listens to, whoever stands next to him in the bus queue. Personal contact is what community is about, the maintaining and sustaining of that contact and of course the initial establishment of it. The children of Mammon are not capable of community because their primary considerations are material possessions and not the possession of their soul; the self and not the other; survival and not life. By comparison the children of the god who is merciful spirit do not neglect their survival but their chief aim is eternal life, here and now, on earth as in heaven.

Now the one we know as the Christ is communally power-ful. We are not to be ashamed of him if we want that commu-nal power for ourselves. It is the power that makes whole. There is really no difference between the Christ and this power. If we want this power we must accept this person into our minds and hearts. This is where the embarrassment comes in. We are willing enough to accept a thought into our mind and a feeling into our heart because we can appropriate these without challenge or risk to our established pathic state, private or pub-lic, biological or political. But the acceptance of a person im-plies an unpredictable change for us, while the acceptance of this particular person as Messiah or Christ or Lord involves an abandonment of our ego. As soon as we contemplate the possi-bility that Jesus of Nazareth is Lord we are forcefully made aware of our selfishness and egotism, and of this we are ashamed, so naturally we blame the one whose presence 'causes' us to feel this shame. We also feel guilty because of the actual harm we ourselves have done by harming others or neglecting others, so once again we accuse him who 'causes' us to experience this guilt, merely by dint of his presence in what might be our community.

Of course it is not necessary for the members of my commu-nity to belong to an organization that calls itself Christianity. What matters is that I know that all those with whom I make personal contact are creatures of god and therefore at least po-tentially members of my community.

Our spheres of personal effectiveness and influence overlap, of course. All the same I am responsible and accountable for my, not for your, community. Are there then as many commu-nities as there are human beings? Technically yes. And yet there is really only the one. All our ethical deeds touch on all human beings and the effect is eternal.

*

An experience of Jesus as friend is probably the most contemporary and relevant. The fact that we cannot rest after such an experience until we have made sense of it, is also the reason for our eventual ethical effectiveness. We call it an experience, and it is also an experience, but in reality there is more to it than that, especially if by experience we mean mainly physical sensation. The reality of Jesus as universal friend lies anchored in the eternal, and as the eternal comes to light for us, upon success of our search for it, so does the physically apprehendable person we call the universal Jesus. So we cannot enjoy his friendship separate from the eternal universe, and if this eternal universe interests us and we mean to find it out, then the temporal aspect of Jesus shows us the way and invites us.

How can anyone be eternally bound and also temporally effective? Such a condition presupposes an ethical good willingness. We cannot imagine how anything from the universal timeless realm could be effective in time unless it wanted, desired or wished to be so. Not a thing, of course, but a being, and then also a personal being would be required. And an experience of Jesus as universal friend does open out the timesphere of present, past and future to show and demonstrate, in other words to reveal, the eternally universal hinterland which extends into our immediate experience in timely fashion. One of the first impressions we have is that time and the realm of the temporal is not a hindrance or a barrier to our knowledge of eternal reality, which barrier presumably would then need to be deprecated and removed or overcome before we could have the fullness of life, but rather that time and the temporal is the precious gift of itself, by the eternal order, to created men, women and children. The temporal is bound to occur to us as an im-

171

poverishing hindrance to the extent that we become attached to it exclusively as to an order not growing out of the eternal order, and when we know nothing of the eternal, time must appear to us and occur to us as a slippery slope and a noose. We make a dreadful mistake then if we try to efface the temporal in order to enter upon the eternal. First we must step back from the temporal which we have forced to appear and occur as a lifeless, irresponsive thing to us, and this is a moral activity which must precede the ethical. The baptism by water and by fire is indispensible. We must be morally cleansed of all inappropriate attachment to our timely surroundings, which creates in us a passive appreciation, a wonderful appreciability of the world in its true sense, and then our interest must be drawn to the possibility of our involvement in that true world, so that we are stirred out of passive resignation and out of a merely refreshing appreciation of the marvellous into active participation in reality, as we become real examples and demonstrate what we have learned and now know.

*

The question is always: How can we sustain ourselves in the reality that is eternal and timely? There are those who become attached to the temporal order as though this could be separate from the eternal, but there are also those who flee into the eternal as though it might exist independently from the temporal order. Most of us have done both, have erred in both directions.

What makes Jesus today a friend for life, even potentially for those who are ashamed of him and find any mention of him embarrassing – and, let us quickly add, even for those who think nothing of expropriating his figure in a cult or using some idea of him to burden their fellow men – is his availability as an historic person. He lived once and he lives again.[i] This is extremely useful. If no one like this were available to us we would be in desperation either trying to find someone of that calibre or else trying to do what he did. The previous two millennia are littered with casualties attesting to attempts of both sorts and the failures can be enlightening. On one hand it is a kind of fatal pride that tempts us to undertake the messianic achievement of Jesus even though, or precisely because, we reject the real Jesus. A smart person makes use of what is available and makes the best of it. Jesus today is available and along with him the fully ordered ethical realm called reality, and the best we can make of this is ourselves as fully functional and wholly integrated members of an ethical community. While we are attached – even addicted – to society, even moral society, we can only have the foreshadowing of what is meant by fully functional, by wholly integrated, by ethical community.

On the other hand, it is a kind of fatal cowardice that would persuade us to harness an image of Jesus into service to mere survival, a feel-good factor as we go about our trivial business of making selfish ends meet. Not touched by the regenerating passion of Jesus we make a sophisticated game out of a christian religion and then those who would need the reality of god's mercy are put off it by this obscenity of a social accommodation.

Of course it always needs to be demonstrated that Jesus works. We can have the understanding of the Christ but at the time of crisis we do not put what we know into practice.

---

[i] Today I would say: He lived once and he still lives. The life he had, and to which he drew our attention so that we may have it, is never taken away. If we are killed, it is only the psychic life that stops, as it did with Jesus. His resurrection therefore came to its proper end when he was killed. It began when he became aware of who he was and of what was required of him. We today, (2017) if we have eternal life and an abundance of it, are also mortal.

Every time of crisis however happens to be a perfect point of practical application where we can once again put down ethical roots. Of course it has to be a genuine crisis. Either our customary existence is at risk or our creative work has got us into trouble. The fact that immediate comfort is available is not to be disparaged because it helps us to be able to think straight. But this immediate comfort is not meant to be the end of the story. There is nothing like the feeling of comfort to make us fall back into emptiness and uselessness.

Investments of good spirit in the natural world are all in a day's work. These are matters of personal instigation and support.

*

When we say that Jesus lived once and lives again, this tells us something about life. Not everyone thinks of life in a way that would allow such a statement to make sense. He lived and he lives again. How can anyone live again? He lived in the temporal order and now he lives in the eternal realm. His death describes the passage from the former to the latter. This passage, this death, had not until then been managed by anyone. It was the ethical act par excellence.[i] The main motivation for the achievement was compassion for those who died and got nowhere. It was a demonstration of what life in reality amounts to, and of the fact that real life does not come to an end, does not finish, but is eternal. It does take on individual characteristics for a time in the case of beings on earth, and a time is allotted to every being on earth, but even without such characteristics it is still life. And we human beings

---

[i] It is difficult for us to appreciate this supreme ethical act because we, thanks to this achievement, are able to have eternal life, whereas Jesus of Nazareth was, so to speak, on his own, because he was the first to be called upon to demonstrate the critical difference between eternal life and the life that comes to an end.

can understand this and live accordingly. We are fashioned in a way so that it suits us well to live in a reality that supports eternity on earth for a time.

How can we take advantage of this achievement of Jesus? What does it mean, to take advantage of this achievement? Do we indeed live as though one day our life would end or do we live in the knowledge that nothing can harm us ever because we have eternal life? And, knowing that nothing can harm us, do we stand by idly and watch those who live in fear of death or do we let them know what we know? Do we demonstrate for them what it means to live eternally? Do we set examples of life in reality? And is that then how we are fully at home in ourselves or do we forever knock ourselves out trying to make temporal phenomena do duty as eternal beings?

Let us by all means try to understand love as far as we can and then let us return it. It was merciful love that motivated Jesus to demonstrate conclusively what could be done in terms of god and human relationship. That same love motivates us today and we do well to concern ourselves with what the implications are of either ignoring that motivation or acknowledging it. Even with regard to our existence alone we are under pressure and in stress, and we can easily imagine what life would be like without those impediments – while it seems impossible simply to avoid or remove them. We can make sense of them. In the absence of this motivating love we would be free of anxiety – but we would also be dead. While we are troubled we have opportunities for more life and for a greater abundance of it. If we want someone to be more alive and to have more life we know to love them, which means that we give our life to them. Possibly they will at first be troubled by this and made anxious over it because no one likes to be reminded, even inadvertently, of a comparative shortcoming.

*

To give our life means to love. Those who give their life for their country love their country. That does not mean that they die for their country. To give one's life is not the same as to die. One may give one's life and one may be killed but those two are not the same. We need to be instructed. God cannot but love us and yet he is everywhere reviled.

There was a time when the spiritual realm and the temporal state were not connected. It made sense then to speak of the spiritual realm and of the temporal states, and of course on various parts of the earth characteristic and appropriate reference was made to both. Today the 'spiritual realm' and the 'temporal state' are one. It was on the cards that they should become one and then of course someone was needed to make the play, to instigate the process, to make the first move, so that the connection could succeed and so that others could then take advantage of what had been accomplished. Today when describing present reality one really has to begin with a term that accounts for the two being one. One has to acknowledge somehow that an eternal ordering goes on and exists of temporal matters. This is how it is in reality now. To the extent that we cannot see this and live accordingly we are entangled in spiritual realm and temporal state as separate, which places us in the past, though we may insist ever so firmly that we live here and now.

It stands to reason that this commonwealth of merciful spirit in action and passion cannot be countenanced or entered into unless we somehow take on board the role of its initiator and the work of its initiation. This commonwealth is not like a room we enter and then we are warm and cosy and laugh at those who freeze in the snow outside. It is like a room we enter and then we realize we have left a room and are free to disport ourselves. It is like a room we enter and there the host has our work ready for us and we learn to live for others. It is like a room we enter and below us the earth is a glorious globe so

176

that our hearts ache to inhabit the earth and be part of that living community of beings while we lovingly descend and when we arrive we yearn to have others by our side.

*

One wonders why anyone would choose to ignore or refuse this commonwealth of merciful spirit and insist on remaining in the past, clinging to a point of view from which the temporal state exists separately from the spiritual realm. Why is a temporal state attractive, or a spiritual realm desirable, while a commonwealth of merciful spirit in which these two no longer exist is experienced as a judgment from which one tries to flee at all costs? It is an ethical task of the first order to show, that this judgment does not originate with the commonwealth of merciful spirit or with its personal initiator and central governing being but with us who give more credence to symptoms of unruliness in ourselves which are brought to light by the reality of this commonwealth in actual influence upon us than we do to that commonwealth itself and its governing body. These symptoms of unruliness come to our attention to start with. They draw our attention to themselves even as pain does, and indeed they are in one way of another painful. For example, I feel weary at the moment and would rather lie down and sleep than continue with this writing. But I have had a good night's sleep, so what is the point of this painful weariness which makes me feel twice my weight and causes my brain to flow with the speed of molasses in mid winter? I am reminded of the time when I lived in Canada as a boy on a farm and was fascinated by the steaming breath of the cattle as they jostled for position at the trough into which the molasses had been poured; thick and creamy, purchased at the nearby Japanese sugar beat factory. A memorable image for me, and passing it on to you is an act of love already, an ethical decision which helps me come to terms with some of the negative attitudes I had begun to develop towards this weariness when I should have faced it as

177

one faces a simple fact. So I used art here to help me out of the first entanglement, and I assure you I feel at much greater liberty now to go on. Had I had no art at my disposal I might simply have repented of my sluggishness, in acknowledgment of the fact that it is I myself who place impediment in the path of life on its way to myself as its host.

So much for my obstructionist attitude. I would not have succeeded at this however if I had not had a fairly good notion of what lay behind this impediment, the revelation of which would be worth my while. If I had not had this greater goal in mind, I might well have imagined that the removal of the weariness was the main part of the exercise, so that I might be left feeling chipper and gay. Then the weariness would return and I would be in despair, having failed. Of course my idea of failure would be quite mistaken. I would have failed not because I did not permanently get rid of that feeling of weariness but because I did not really make contact with the reality I had obstructed. No work is complete until that contact is made. So I had to give of my life. I had to hand over willingly that feeling of energy which I would have liked instead of the weariness. It would also have been a pleasure to give in to that weariness and sleep, and I had to give that up, do without it, aim higher.

Now that I have succeeded in truth I can attest to the fact that what I have gained all in all is something appreciably greater than a lack of weariness or a pleasant feeling of energy. If I call it eternal life, surely that is my own business. What it amounts to, this eternal life, is obvious to me and perhaps evident to you too by now. The whole strength of it is beyond question.

The difference between the life we give and the life we get is crucially important from the point of view of an appropriate and sufficient understanding. The Christian tradition has often fudged this point, so that sacrifice took the place of mercy. Let me try to explain. I might have come up with the willpower to force the weariness out of my existence so that I might do my duty by the work load I had imposed upon myself in agreement with moral society. That would have been sacrificial in the sense that I would have cut myself off from the pleasure of giving in to the weariness, a kind of life, and my reward would have been a sense of proud achievement, another kind of life. The two kinds are not all that different, only that in the latter sort my ego has asserted itself over sense gratification in the interest of self- or ego-gratification. Am I really any better off? I call it a kind of life but really it is not life at all, only a temporary feeling of vitality or a forceful assertion of will, which amounts to the same. Really all of this needs to be simply laid down or aside as we work to make contact with reality, for the first time or again, and as we renew our real being in the commonwealth of merciful spirit, in which alone real life is the case.

We do not remove ourselves from this commonwealth until we give greater credence and acknowledgment to the presence or absence of that psychic life, to those feelings of negative or positive ego-gratification, than to the true reality, the commonwealth of merciful spirit governed by the established person called Jesus – the very mention of whose name causes my ego to bristle with indignation as it looks for insults to levy and stones to throw.

*

Why should the very mention of a person's name cause upset? This is a remarkable observation I have made, that when I mention the name Jesus in public someone usually is offended. Sometimes I refrain from mentioning it because I myself fear offence. It feels like a pang of conscience. Guilt seems to be involved.

The reason why I have anything at all to do with this person is that I promise myself certain advantages from it. I was not brought up to associate with people who spoke of him. Speaking of him now is a part of my task to come up with a workable ethic. Claims and counterclaims are made about him. When I see his name listed with that of the Buddha, Ghandi, Mohammed etc. I cannot help but find that inappropriate, and yet a great many traditional – I suppose I mean western Christian traditional – explanations for that finding fail to satisfy me.

I want to speak entirely from within my own personal thinking and experience here, and in addition to that, since my writing is itself after the nature of a venture and quest – I mean since it is also this – not only my thinking and experience but also my doing, here and now on the spot, is bound to play a role and make a creative difference. I fully expect that after every active step and after every period of passive endurance, something new is revealed to me, so that I can pass it on. Also, since I live in a human community, as I investigate myself I also learn about you, as you are and tend to be today, in general mostly.

Why is it then, first of all, that the name Jesus makes me cringe? Why do I use it as an expletive when I am upset or shocked or hurt? How curious, that even though I would very much hesitate to mention that name in ordinary conversation, it bursts out of me when I have just burnt my hand or barely avoided some mishap? "Jesus Christ!" is actually one of the favourite curse words among many people, along with "fuck!"

It must have to do with the social morality. The hypothesis is worth exploring. Society, the status quo, standard behaviour – all that and more: an unprejudicial analysis might yield results here. What does sexuality have in common with universal human nature in person that makes them both suspect in the eyes of society? Perhaps I should capitalize Society, in order to distinguish between the myth of a permanent order of companionship and fellowship based on similarity of appearances, such a appearances of behaviour, of action, even of being, and an incidental process of companionship. So we speak about English Society during the Victorian age and on the other hand of acquaintances who enjoy one another's society.

In Society, behaviour is fashionable. So to the extent that sexuality and Jesus are fashionable there is no problem. Where these two become substantial and meaningful however they cut right across the social sphere and they need to be marked out, denigrated and placed under suspicion. To the extent that we belong to Society – if the above meaning of the term can be allowed to stand for a moment – we are forced to trivialize or reject out of hand – what I would like to call the son of man. I would also like to call it the human natural power. This human natural power is common to both our sexuality and to the one we call Jesus. When we check in the Gospels how Jesus used the term 'son of man' we can make some interesting comparisons. The son of man comes from above and needs to be accepted if a human being is to have the benefit. At the same time he must be rejected and killed (presumably not by the one who accepts him) so that he may live again. This seems to be lawful. If we imagine this going on and being done in the case of a single individual human being, we may think of that human being at a certain point in life being visited by a human natural power, such as during puberty for example, when sex becomes an inward function. Now, we might say, this human being can either waste this power, ignorant of the lawful responsibility that is his or hers, and perhaps even take an addictive pleasure in such waste, or he can understand the nature of what it is that is happening to him and the responsibility that is his for the proper investment of that power.

As soon as he sets out to behave in terms of this power that is new to him, he is bound to be rejected by those around him

181

who have no understanding and who have themselves either wasted or made a habit of wasting that power and are therefore scandalized by anyone who displays this still raw power. It is not raw in itself but being presented in a raw form. If no one were around to reject these premature gestures of power, then the individual would be afflicted by whatever environment is his at the time. A more or less wise partner for example can make the transition easier for the youth who has this power visited upon him or her. There are degrees of it. He can explain how the strength which the youth demonstrates is in itself good but that it must be invested in a way no one else but that youth can discover for him- or herself. He can also set a continuous and repeated example of merciful power for the youth, and this alone can completely ease the transition, because due to that merciful human natural power wielded by the parental adult, the youth can cope much more readily, even thoroughly, with the transformational changes he is being asked, by his nature and spirit, to undergo.

Much depends upon the ethical readiness and preparedness of the youth when this human natural power comes upon him or her. Generally I differentiate in my works the five interrelated areas of flesh, spirit, mind, body and soul, and this can help us come to terms better with particular shortcomings and neglects that suddenly show up as afflictions when this power arrives in a human being.

We have to assume here too that the male and female distinction cuts across all five of the above mentioned areas of being and that it does not have to do merely with the carnal. Male and female sexuality play into the five areas of being. Female psyche is different from male psyche, female spirit from male spirit, etc. At the same time we have to keep in mind that areas of being are in themselves symptomatic. A whole human being, mature and active in community, is only liable to such areas of being but does not work in terms of them as separately accessible but in line with spirit, mind, body, soul and flesh as one.

Most important, we have to distinguish between vitality and life. On one hand we have energy, vitality and survival, while on the other we have life, by which we mean eternal life.

The vitality that comes along with the human-natural power, the feeling of energy and ambitiousness, is not real life, even as the romantic feelings that accompany our falling in love are not real love. There is truth, but not yet reality. Is it possible for anyone truly to fall in love and even upon the first signs of having fallen to ignore all those romantic feelings and aspirations in favour of active love learned? Is it even desirable? The point is that we cannot have the benefit of god's love in reality until we ourselves love in reality, so that the symptoms of true love are not for us to cling to, just as the symptoms of true life, as we find them too, are not for us to hold on to but we do well to <u>return</u> them.

It would seem that both life and love are first drawn to our attention in truth. We become alert and awake to them in truth. How do we become attentive to them? Sensationally. What matters next is that we do not mistake this sensation for reality. The purpose of the sensation is to let us know that there is now a certain something for us to be done. The reason for the existence of such sensations of energetic vitality and amorous attachment is not that we should indulge in them but that we should commence our search for real active and ethical life and love. As we begin that search, those sensations no longer excite or trouble us.

I say excite <u>or</u> trouble. We all know how the most glorious vitality suddenly switches over into the most depressive melancholy; how the most amorous romance suddenly becomes the most hateful affair. However, in the light of our knowledge of what these vital and romantic sensations mean and amount to, the change from happy to unhappy, from lucky to unlucky, only proves to us that the law of true reality not only is complete but cannot be broken. So in a sense we should be grateful that our mere romance has turned sour; but much better if we quickly realize, better late than never, that now it is high time to espouse the reality of life and love. There was no need to wait until our vitality turned sick and our amorousness turned sour. It was time then to return these sensations gratefully and to espouse reality. But now it is high time.

To return them – which does not mean to extirpate them, to feel guilty for having them, to repress them, but simply to say to them: "Yes, I know what you mean and what your purpose is, and I will go ahead and do that now."

And of course we realize how crucially important it is for our own acquisition of real life and love that we help those who are entangled in and enchanted by those sensations to appreciate that their attention is being drawn to life and love so that they might espouse it – and to help them espouse it.

*

So what or whom did Jesus mean by the son of man? Never, to my knowledge, did he say: "I am the son of man," any more than he said: "I am the Christ." Evidently he refers to someone or something for which he is willing to stand, with which he is willing to identify, which also exists in and for those around him, especially for those who declare and demonstrate solidarity with him inwardly, through believing and not being offended in him or his words. What he himself intends to demonstrate – at which he succeeds – is that the human-natural power of truth, as offered to human beings by their creator, can become for them active and ethical reality. His singular task is not simply to image forth some aspect of this truth, as many have before him, and in the end they died, as did Abraham and Moses, though they looked forward to one who would be in

184

person what they only partially realized, but to be that power in person. He taught them how to handle the various sensations, the experiences in his presence, warning against both high and low spirits, so as not to get carried away by them, but ever advising them not to fight those spirits either, since what was crucial was that the fate of the son of man should be seen through, so that the doors of reality should finally be open. Of course they had to be trained, as many as possible but especially those he chose, so that in the face of true reality on his return they would be able to accept him.

The same question exists for us today: Are we trained, and how well are we trained, brought up, educated, to accept and receive into us that one real universal personality so that we may really be who we are and be fully who we are meant to be.

That preparation is what we mean by ethics. And it all has to do with having life and having it in greater abundance, life being the gift of gifts. And the "kingdom of heaven", of the commonwealth of reality, could be described as our realm of ethical behaviour.

*

Now we understand perhaps a little better why we do not need to die, since Jesus allowed himself to be killed so that true reality, including him, might be open for us. Even as he became ethically one with that true human-natural power vouchsafed him by god, we today may become one with that now personified power in us and really live, not die. The earlier and the more thoroughly we understand our proximity to this personality called Jesus the easier it will be for us to continue to do so.

*

There are many reasons why we should be aware, and perhaps help others to be aware, of the time of the historic Jesus of

185

Nazareth as somehow separate and distinct from our own time. As I write, my intention and purpose is first and foremost ethical, consequently I cannot afford to ignore for one moment that my perception of eternal true reality, with which I am as much gifted as rewarded, cannot but occur as a closed book, as an impossible dream, to many who dip into these pages. One motivation remains in the strictest sense evangelical, in that I want to share good news. This is an aspect of how I have always been: even as a child, when something pleasant happened to me, I was nearly bereft if I could not tell someone about it. Indeed how few children are not like that. One of the first gestures of communication from the one year old and earlier is that he points something out for the appreciation of the mother. This urgency to communicate can be trivialized and even destroyed through indulgence in the mass media, but it can also be developed, articulated and brought to awareness, so that it accounts for a lifelong joy in the search, in discovery, learning and telling others about what we have learned – which, let's face it, no one else could have discovered and learned in just that way.

What I have called the evangelic motivation is, however, not the only one. I am really referring to my various reasons for writing this book, I suppose. In addition to the wish to let you know what has been revealed to me and what I have practiced, there is also my desire to grow. This desire for increase is strong in me, and if I had not cast my lot in with those who accumulate permanent quantities I would be trying to earn – no, to make – money hand over fist.

And an aspect of this desire to grow is the will to do. "We impress ourselves on the world," someone once observed during the course of a public speech – if I recall correctly he visited the school where I attended in Canada. Our will to do, to impress ourselves on the world, to make, to act – this streaming out of energy and how good it feels, especially if one can convince oneself somehow that one is being beneficial and admirable – this has given me the most trouble. And if this book is now turning once again towards autobiography, should I mind? Schopenhauer's 'World as Will and Representation' focussed my attention at school, but left me nervously dissatisfied. I suspected that what he described as world was indeed one way of looking at it as the foredoomed product of our both energetic and ignorant hands, but I carried within me even then the seed of a world that existed whether I reacted to it or not, and although in my teens I got into the habit of violent outbursts of energy that apparently needed to be structured, to be made socially acceptable – I climbed mountains, skied, read voraciously – I also had occasion to reflect on my childhood, a time of insecurity and intimidation during the war in the Germany of the early nineteen forties followed by a period of reflection and meditation in the countryside where my parents and close relatives managed to create a sanctuary of the self-sustaining sort. Uncles, aunts, parents and grandparents all pitched in together to grow our own garden produce, to raise rabbits, chickens, goats – they even grew their own tobacco, which always struck me as exceptionally enterprising. I shall never forget the mind-numbing scent of the large tobacco leaves drying in bundles suspended from the rafters in the attic.

In those days, after Germany had fortunately lost the war, I heard nothing of "repent and seek the kingdom of heaven." It was much more a case of: "You have tired yourselves out trying to impress on the world your notion of it as will and picture, now try to make the best of the spectacle as it all crumbles." It would have been an ideal time, come to think of it, for "repent and seek the kingdom of god", and no doubt here and there in the stunned would-be empire the opportunity was taken; not, of course, from an impulse of weariness and disgust with action but due to genuine insight into the heart of reality. For myself however, I must say, the time of reflection de-

187

pended on undisturbed fields and meadows and was nourished by fragrant umbellifers such as hogweed and hedge parsley, into which I buried my face. To this day I preserve under the skin of my memory the strongest possible impressions of clambering beetles and flies, and when they unfolded their wings to hum off into the distance I also spread mine. It was a sun-drenched pastime for me and I swear I never expected, when I set out on this section of the work in hand, that I would find myself once again transported into the gold of those moments. Perhaps they were in fact no more than moments, in comparison to long hours of drudgery in a state school which I cannot recall and which are best forgotten. I sometimes think of that drudgery, which still goes on today, perhaps with increased intensity, all over the globe except in the Australian bush and the Brazilian jungle, and I wonder is this an illustration of "the son of man must be handed over to the literate ... etc. and killed..."? one tries to make sense of one's grief. However, though they might have been intervals, these deep experiences of the child's joy in being alive, they were the seeds of my experience today. We know, alas, that for the grain to sprout the seed must die.

Ages have passed since then, as I reflect on my life in the light of those childhood memories resurrectable as enduring quantities of grateful appreciability. No, not ages, but an eternity – at least several eternities. As I lay my descriptive hand on those globes of potential vitality and life, they are not diminished and their surfaces are neither tainted nor strained. Neither rust nor the moth can harm them.

*

I was amazed, I freely confess it, by my sense of eternal history during that last section. It may be worth describing. Suddenly my life, as it lay so to speak behind me, seemed embedded within some endless matrix; what truly occurred to me

188

was: I have lived forever! Those experiences of my youth, even as I recalled them, no longer remained stacked end to end in linear time but they glowed from an inner source and their setting, or rather what they amounted to, was timeless. I am going to occupy myself with that theme for a while. I really believe I can hold on to what that is without diminishing it. I may be wrong. I have become forgetful these last two years. I may be my age, nearly sixty. My assumption is the following: If I bind myself round more securely with my eternal past, I will fare much better with the present. I have mentioned before that time past, present and future is precious to me but not essential. The eternal is essential. Time is existential. Good for you if you can sustain it, but don't worry if the eternal stream on which the temporal floats – whirling under the overhanging sweet chestnut branches – claims your undivided attention for a while. Dive. Which reminds me. I was able to swim under water before I had the courage to hold my head above water. I would squeeze my eyes shut, take a deep breath and push myself hard off the shore with a kick like a frog against the sandbank. Then I would swim in a large semi-circle until I arrived back at the shore perhaps a few feet along from where I had started. You see, I nurse the expectation that the very process of reading this book now will make you more ethical, more prepared for the merciful spirit and more capable of acting it out. So while I swam under water, until my breath gave out, at which time I always felt a delicious touch of panic like electricity coursing through my veins, I felt perfectly content. It was the breathing with my head above sea level that troubled me. Water in the lungs was like drowning. Eventually I learned to struggle along amphibiously. Only a year ago I floated ashore in Crete after a long swim at sea; I let the shallow waves carry me in through tangles of seaweed and over brilliant pebbles and I kept my eyes just at the surface of the water as steadily as I could, one moment in touch with the life below, dream like, weightless and carefree, and the next moment apprised of the boulders glittering in the hot sun, the driftwood fanned by the breezes and I realized I was at home in both worlds and might at any moment choose to continue my career on earth among the fishes. Gills would have been supplied. It was entirely out of a sense of loyalty to sheer habit that I agreed to the awkward, strenuous process of levering myself like a fresh-born colt into an upright position for the purpose of walking back to my wife and children who had no idea how close they had come to being husband- and fatherless.

On an airplane flight something similar happened to me, when it suddenly occurred to me that there might not be any real reason for me to continue to breathe. My attention became focussed, at some thirty-five thousand feet above mother earth, on the stimulus that evidently had until then caused my lungs to expand and contract – and it disappeared. I felt like the protagonist in the Tibetan Book of the Dead. Why breathe, if you see no need for it? Perhaps it was my privilege to turn into a mineral above the clouds over Algiers. My wife, who in cases such as this does by her mere presence cause me to espouse at least a fibre of common sense, noticed something and said: "What's wrong?" My garbled explanation alarmed her and she alerted a stewardess who administered oxygen. I resurfaced right away and decided that mineral being lay after all outside my province. Nevertheless I had nearly been willing to try the switch. I had toyed with it. So the suggestion of "repent and seek the kingdom of God" has often occurred to me as not only practical but also attractive. When I forget that the earth is my mother and the sea my father (I speak as a worker of art) I remind myself of that initial summation of the ethic relevant to those days as propagated by Jesus of Nazareth and his precursor. The ethic relevant to our day must of course have a much different slant to it, I say incautiously, hoping no one will right off the bat ask me to say what that is in so many words. Sometimes I tiptoe around the mystery of redeemed creation like a cat around hot milk. At other times I leap into the midst of it and splash it all about.

*

For me, the call to "repent and seek the kingdom of heaven" stands first and foremost as an ethical offering to the Jews prior to the Christian era, to help them through the coming and unavoidable crisis. Something had been preparing itself within the Jewish cultural consciousness, especially in terms of cultural self-consciousness, since "Father Abraham", and the culmination of it was about to be realized – let those who want to benefit take the following precautions and make the following preparations. The word went out to all Jews, but especially to those who were already biologically earmarked, so to speak, and had therefore come into an inner conflict with the standard Jewish society. This society, like all societies before and since, had sanctioned a status quo of existence in order to escape from the psychic challenges, threats and annoyances implied by real human life in progress towards ultimate cosmic perfection. That society too pre-empted historically while neglecting communally. Meanwhile the 'preordained remnant', which figures throughout the prophetic tradition of the Jews, was rejected by Society as obviously unsuitable and both figuratively and literally stood outside the gate. One gets the impression they secretly sensed that in spite of their status as outcasts they were also in the best possible position there to apprehend the newcomer who would 'set things straight'.

It would seem unavoidable that if something new is to be introduced, it has to start somewhere. The notion of simple faith in a single god had to put down roots somewhere. Since the subsequent incarnation of that god depended on that notion of faith in the singular god, that too had to materialize there. One might as well accept facts. But the incarnation of that god now

191

implied the unnecessity of state and nation and at the same time the necessity of ethical solidarity with 'the son of man', who was on the move, path-finding, transition-making, all-else-staking. Obviously those who were happy with the status quo did not take kindly to one who stood for change, and those who looked forward to political improvements had little use for someone who spoke in terms of blessedness. It has ever been thus.

*

Now we have it on record that some made it through the initial crisis and we can tell to some extent from their subsequent being and behaviour what that meant, both for them and for those around them whom they unavoidably influenced. When we ask: What was the attitude of these few guiding persons who had experienced in their own generation the coming of that new order of reality which included the 'son of man on clouds of glory and in strength', we receive a variety of answers. Some were momentarily overwhelmed and struck with a combination of unbelief and amazement. Thereafter they were fired by an ambition that surpassed all individual advantage. Some were stunned by the vista that opened out for them. Legend has it they travelled far afield to share their new-found knowledge and to help others prepare for the unavoidable change, so that it might succeed for them and not find them ignorant. An ethic of sorts existed everywhere, so that this new ethic was bound to meet with resistance, in the same way that the notion of faith in one god initially made it difficult for Jews not to see outsiders as at least potential enemies if they worshipped many gods. There was one important difference. The notion of might and anti-might, of political warfare and belligerent politics was part and parcel of a kingdom and state economy, as a people defined itself and grew to powerful self-awareness, through periods of correction – and eventually ended in destruction. With the advent of the new kingdom, the kingdom not of the world but of god, this notion of might and anti-might was seriously undermined by one of ethical strength which involved, among other precepts, the love and forgiveness of enemies and the ethical exploitation of persecution and seeming disadvantage. With the event of that order of reality then, these ethical precepts could be – and were – shown to bear fruit on an everyday basis, both in the lives of those who lived them and for those who accepted what they said.

It makes sense therefore to speak of an old ethic and of a new ethic. The difference between the two hinges on the attitude towards force and might; towards force and anti-force, might and anti-might. It makes no sense to attempt a line of development from the one attitude to the other. One either draws on might or one does not. One draws on it by supporting it or by opposing it. How can one not draw on it?

In order to be able to avoid supporting or opposing might, one actually has to draw on that new reality, and in order to be able to do this one must enter into personal relationship with the one who has realized it in himself.

But how does one enter into personal relationship with one who cannot even seem real until one espouses the reality he represents?

It should appear to be more straightforward for a Jew to accept the messiahship of Jesus of Nazareth – or shall we say: to accept the fact that the messiah or Christ foretold in their tradition is among us – because his culture should have schooled him to that end. However, the opposite seems to be the case. Perhaps it had to do with familiarity breeding contempt. Perhaps the very pride of his 'being one of us' gets in the way at the best of times of that receptive humility which alone can succeed. Let's face it, for all too many of us the very fact that a human being should be divine is itself unacceptable, for we dream of spectres and ghosts.

So what is required, really, is an ethic that a., helps us make contact with a reality that is available in its personal and universal fullness here and now; b., takes account of our status as Jews or non-Jews and recognizes peculiar hindrances in each case that need to be overcome; c., recognizes the capacity nowadays of all human beings, regardless of race, colour or creed, for a rational, universal ethic that is free of all external observancies or marks of membership and commits them entirely under their own independent and individual volition to nothing less than their own inborn humanity.

We cannot be truly 'reborn' once we have forfeited our inborn humanity. This discovery, or rediscovery, of our humanity must therefore be facilitated by the rational ethic we mean.

*

How does this ethic draw our attention to our inborn humanity, once we have so much ignored or wasted that humanity that it cannot but occur to us, upon reminder, except offensively, that is to say, involving incurment of shame or guilt? In other words, we have arrived at such a deplorable state of being that we resent being reminded of our human being, and now an ethical approach to us is deemed to be possible that will help us overcome, ignore or simply side-step that 'unavoidable' resentment and 'lay in' human being.

The definition of force and might has to be considered. For example, where ability and circumstances come together fortuitously, a woman will be a home-maker. She will take creative delight in the sort of atmosphere and environment for her family that brings with it a flourishing of the communal reality in which children thrive. If she chooses not to 'make a home', or if circumstances overly prevent her, a human-natural anxiety sets in and instead of being a home-maker she turns into an anxious house-keeper. It is like this with all of us. As soon as the creative realm closes for us, we find ourselves in the space of force and might. Possession is defined and experienced much differently. In the <u>realm</u> we experience possession incidentally and on account of use. In the <u>space</u> we need to be in possession under the law; hopefully under the law, because where the law breaks down, we insist then on our need to possess, in line with brute force and arbitrary might. The need, the fear, the possessiveness all figure large and, even more important, we slip into the habit of thinking and feeling in those terms. It does not occur to us that for one reason or another we have fallen out of favour or grace and must above all else try to get back into that creative realm. No, we are determined now to seek happiness in terms of satisfied possessiveness, allayed fear and a sufficient exercise of might. No longer is blessedness our happy experience but the hectic search for happiness has become our curse.

*

While we search anxiously for happiness, in ignorance of true blessedness and the means to it, we are on the wrong track, but at least we are on a track. While we deem ourselves in need of having our rights seen to, legally and mightily, we have the wrong source of satisfaction in mind but at least we deem ourselves in need. While we experience possessiveness, we want the wrong thing but at least we experience a want. While we take pleasure in exercising force and being predominant, we are being destructive but at least we are trying to be effective. While we are hoping to rid ourselves of fear, our hope is misguided but at least we still have some notion of peace.

And so on. Our humanity has not yet been forfeited in the case of all of these examples, only our human being is lost, and to that degree and extent we ourselves are lost. The implication here is that the man who is lost at least somehow senses it. If he doesn't, he must be insane or dead.

195

Our ethic, in other words, must allow us to distinguish between lost human being and forfeited humanity. The former is serious; the latter dead serious. Traditionally Christians have distinguished along similar lines between 'saving sinners' and 'raising the dead'.

*

Ethically however our business is not with the dead. It suffices that we know: there they are. It suffices that we know not to waste on the dead what pertains to the living, though they be lost.

Which draws to our attention the need for all ethical teaching to include him who teaches among those who would learn in a way that acknowledges their common mortality. We do not become immortal by denying or ignoring our mortality but our mortality is the soil in which our immortal being is rooted.

Ethically we must guard, and if necessary re-invent, a certain sense of our common mortality. As soon as we forget our liability to death we court destruction. Of course we may also go wrong in the opposite direction and suppose that we must die, and then there is presumably no end to our morbidity.

So a slight refinement of our ethic for the approach of death is in order. Not only shall it keep us mindful of our common mortality but at the same time it shall inform us in as great a variety of ways and means as is necessary of our mortality not as an unavoidable death but as a liability to death – to death and destruction.

Only in that way can the problem of pain be solved. In no other way can pain become meaningful and significant. Our mortality, our liability to death, reminds us of itself through pain. By way of all that is uncomfortable and inconvenient are we put in mind of adjustments to be made by ourselves, adjustments of a radical nature, which is to say of a nature primitive and instinctive.

But such adjustments are not generally written about in the newspapers, nor are they topics of casual chat in the sitting-room of the nation. Truth is not fashionable. It is we who must fashion in the name of it. So the question can arise with each individual pain, each grief or sorrow: What am I to learn here, to gain? Then we step back and ask a more timely question: How shall I adjust myself, so that I will not miss out? How shall I move or cease from motion? Shall I turn left or right or go straight? Or sit down?

And this prior question, prior to any knowledge we can have of a gain, points us in the direction of primitive instinct, of inborn humanity.

Not that we will necessarily find this well unmuddied. Let us first find it. And let us not wait until we are in pain, for then our senses are clouded and our task complicated, not least perhaps by a desire to be rid of pain.

*

Primitive instinct is easy enough to incorporate – easy enough to handle and make sense of, however we have to know well in advance what it is we hope to make and do here. A variety of unpredictable notions arise in the modern mind when primitive instinct is mentioned and we have to be ready for that. So we have to know for example what this primitive instinct is and amounts to in truth, before we mistake it for whatever we happen to find when we look for it. What it is in truth is inborn humanity. We want to get our hands on that, so that we can become ethically effective. If we look for it in ourselves now, under the heading (concept) of primitive instinct, and we come up instead with a garbled picture of self, then we know to discard this and to look again. Inborn humanity – or let us say simply: humanity – will immediately empower us with a perfect and genuine liveliness that is unmistakable. It is unmistakable because it carries within itself something no other experience carries. And that is eternal life, which is unquestionable, or rather undoubtable. It cannot be doubted but is certain.

So whatever else comes up or occurs to us when we search for the primitive instinct in ourselves, unless it is doubtless, undoubtable and certain, it merely amounts to something that covered or masked that instinct and we need to reject or disown it. It can however be turned into fuel for expression. We tend to do this as part of our creativity without thinking about it. The creative process incorporates the mud in the well.

*

But why do we want to be ethically effective? This in itself surely is a wish that has real life as its goal. The life that does not diminish or fade but it grows in variety and splendour for me in person has its roots of necessity in my ethical being and doing. It comes to me as a gift when- and however I am properly prepared for it. Now what I am saying is that there is available in me, to me, an inborn humanity that allows itself to be described as primitive instinct and, upon access, as powerful, perfect and genuine liveliness that is certain to my enquiring mind.

As a creative person I would not let it occur to me for one moment to think of myself as autonomous in thought and feeling and not open to the influence of merciful spirit. I know there are times when I must act or fall by the wayside and other times when I must intimately rely on the influence that is responsible for my own creation. These two go hand in hand and only an individualist or a despot would nowadays quarrel with such a point of view. Inspiration and authority do not contradict in a creative person, only in morbid reflection or heedless business. How do I know that the primitive instinct I have discovered in myself must be inborn humanity? I have had it revealed to me. But that revelation is of no use to me unless I exercise my creative faculty in one way of another, so as to come into ownership of that powerful ethical effectiveness that prepares me, in action and passion, for the gift of life.

I need to know how I can exercise my initiating authority in the case of this human-original instinct. The doing part of me needs guidance: how shall it present itself? As will or appetite? As intellectual application? As a suffering and bearing approach? What is the key to this sometimes apparently locked away source of power, and how can I get my hands on it? I am fully aware of my liability to death and therefore not very likely to behave unreasonably as I try to come to terms with an aspect of my human nature that testifies in itself to god's biological presence for me. This biological presence or readiness is equally of the order of merciful reality that I have described elsewhere as a commonwealth. The kingdom of heaven indwells me. I have no complaints about that, but I try to keep in mind that this works for me if I work for it but against me if I do not. Peculiar ailments and illnesses are visited upon me if I become neglectful in this department and for that I am grateful in the long run, though stupidly resentful at times.

How it comes to indwell me – this is of little or less interest to me now. I have stated the case and intend to explore the possibilities. Much better to demonstrate first the usefulness of some certainty and only then, if time allows, speculate on the origin of it, the faculty or cause.

I am not looking for the key to the underworld but to my inheritance. I do not want to possess what belongs to another or what another might possess but what only I can make use of, and if I do not, I miss out badly. My study of ethical motivation and effectiveness so far has brought me to the conclusion that such an inheritance must be available to me and that it is not merely an intellectual achievement that is required. This happens to be a very important point, namely that the nature of the key does not depend upon some ritual force of tradition sanctioned by society but rather on the panoply of my own abilities, capacities and skills. How shall I ask? With whatever words are available to me. I cannot rely on someone else to dictate the method or to lay down the technique. What counts for you are solely the results I come up with. Equally I await results from you. We are both individually and independently responsible for our ethical progress, and if I lean on you or you on me, then this may bolster our confidence but it cannot make up for what must in the end again stem from me alone and from you alone.

*

I cannot even begin this next section of my book without immediate reference to this source of meaning and value in myself. My inborn humanity exists for me always as ready potential, this has been revealed to me and I share the good news with you, make of it what you can or will. Ah, but now comes the next crux of the matter: What does the fellow mean by humanity?

Well, let me tell you what I mean by it. I mean the same as divinity. I might as readily speak of divinity. And if you ask me: How did you manage to get the two joined up? I retort: How did you ever get them divided? I am not being intentionally flippant. This notion of humanity and divinity as one is not so extraordinary as all that, but it does present a problem to us when we have made a virtue out of a shortcoming. You may picture as you like how it has all come about but god and man as one are historic fact and ongoing reality. If you still try to live as though this were not so, were not yet so, never could be so, then that is how it is for you and no one can help you. If I make up my mind that the air I breathe is poison I will suffocate and equally if I know that the poison I breathe cannot harm me I live. We can believe what we like and if we believe nonsense our existence soon follows suit.

I do not say that primitive instinct in me means pleasant survival. It might be much more pleasant for me for a while to steer clear of that inborn humanity/divinity, because I can be sure that once I make contact and allow myself to be quickened from there I will also have my eyes opened to one or two crimes I have committed against that very humanity/divinity and I confess that I hesitate on the threshold. The truth may wipe me out. That is a very realistic fear. What if I have succeeded for so long in my present life only because I have managed to pull the wool over my eyes? Will I be able to bear the disillusionment, the demystification, the sheer change of master that will be imposed on me? If my mind is wedded to the notion of money as substantial to life, will I be able to go through with the divorce? If people's opinion of me is a collective truth for me, how will I cope when my world falls apart? No, better continue the way I am, self-fooled but happy; impressed by the mighty forces that hold sway in the world and looking for guidance, protection, even self-definition, from there. I will make it through somehow.

And anyone who talks like this cannot be faulted. Better the devil you know than the devil you don't know. Obviously such a person has to feel somehow dissatisfied before he will look for a change, and that dissatisfaction must lie in the nature of his existence. If the authorities come along and say: He refuses to share our opinions, so we shall cause him pain until he does: this is not going to help our man search for his inborn humanity. Coercion creates slavery and rebellion, not voluntary humanity. If the so-called religious authorities cause him pain, then so much the worse.

*

201

The notion of humanity and divinity as one: Where does that come from? How can we rid ourselves of the false notion that they are not one and the same? And what difference does it make that they are? It is not even worth talking about unless it makes a difference to me, and there I can say that it does. Is pain not also from one way of looking at it a mercy and from another point of view a bloody nuisance?

So what am I leading you to expect if and when you fight your way through all those hindrances and you arrive where you hope to arrive? You will be quickened. You will be empowered. You will be valued. Those three probably sum up the lot of it. And what if it comes with such a relief that you shed bitter tears over your previous obtuseness or obduracy? Does that matter? But I tell you now, you have much better luck if your approach is self-denying from the start. You see, because of your faulty vision, your idea of who you are and what you amount to is cock-eyed. You cannot rely on it to fit into the order of power and meaning that is about to be revealed to you. Which also explains why so many of us are often so unhappy, and that is because we are suddenly influenced by this order while we are in an unprepared state, so that we mis-experience the good as bad. There are those whose experience of love in their life is at first noting but woe and thereafter disappointment.

Let's face it, it is really inhumanity, not humanity, that we refuse to countenance as one with god, and of course we are right in that. Is it impossible for men, women and children to be inhuman? I maintain that it is not. And as for our liability to dying, our mortality, that is our lot as human beings. Mortality does not adhere to humanity. If we die it is because in our being we have failed to satisfy certain prerequisites, not because we are human.

If this is difficult to grasp, then solely so because of our habitual preoccupation with popular things. Humanity today is whole. The essence of being is whole. Divinity is holy. There is the one who is both human and divine. We may have him along with his order of reality over which he holds sway. We also have his legacy, each one of us in his or her individual nature.

Not only may we have full participation in the eternal live community for which the world was created and in which the one who is human and divine plays the central role, but on account of his active passion we have in our human nature what it takes as individual human beings to prepare ourselves sufficiently for enrolment in eternal community and for the gift of real life.

How can something done and endured by someone else some time ago be biologically relevant to me today? I have difficulties with that entirely because of my wrongheaded notions concerning time and space. With a different upbringing and education I would know how to be in touch today with all who truly are and have been. Why do I suppose that a day takes me away from the previous day: how has time become adulterated by space for me? Why do I project my biological growth symptoms into what becomes for me then a kind of space-time continuum – and a wedge, a barrier, between myself and the preparation for life? Human nature is quite unique, we should not be embarrassed to admit it. Human nature is not like animal nature. It's the other way around. Our human nature transcends space, time and causality. But it must be approached individually. This is the lesson for <u>contemporary man</u>. There are men women and children, and human nature relates to each one individually, uniquely and in singular fashion. Mighty forces always exist as if to give the lie to that and as if to make it difficult if not impossible to act and undergo in any way other than collectively, but here again we have it backwards. These mighty forces, these 'powers and principalities', do not exist in any case so that our concept and experience of reality must encompass them but – it is our failure to act and undergo as individual human beings, as a man or a woman, in terms of our endowed human nature that allows such mighty forces to come into being and to seem real, when in fact and in truth they are mirror images of what we ourselves amount to, to the extent and degree that we neglect the quest for our individual human nature and venture forth into the world of things ill- or unprepared. Do we have a picture now of what goes on when, not satisfied with allowing these spectres and demons to come into existence, we even collaborate and cooperate with them? What does it mean, in the light of this, when we hanker for popularity and prestige, for renown and standing, for political power and for self-esteem? It means that we run away from our human nature and barricade ourselves within the confines of the unreal, the unnatural and the false. When those who busy themselves behind those barricades with the products of their technology and then wonder for a moment whether a trick here or a discovery there might be 'ethical' or not, we concede that the word must have another meaning.

*

Our own individual human nature – even this says a lot. Jesus refers to the pearl we may find here. He looks ahead to the time when we may actually find it and do ourselves some good but he does have in mind as he speaks that we are going to have to be shown. Today too, as always, when someone tells us about a great piece of good fortune if only we do such and such, we do well to say: Show me. If it's true what you say, that there is such a pearl of great price, give us some indication of the effect that has on our own life, and then I will judge for myself. So Jesus spoke about this pearl of great value which presumably he had discovered in himself and which, so he said, we would be able to discover in ourselves too. That was the implication, in any case. Meanwhile he would demonstrate what this pearl meant to him. I, who come from a different racial stock, look across to his Jewish culture and tradition and realize: Here was a human being like myself who – and then I translate into my own language, both what I owe him and what I come up with myself now, not just for your sake but for mine as well. What I have discovered is an inborn humanity/divinity in myself, a human-natural function, if you like, which allows me to make the sort of preparations that are required for my blessedness in life. I cannot in some way force the blessed life to come into me by activating this function. This has to be said, because we live in an age when people suppose they are forever only one small step away from forcing nature to afford them happiness on earth, by which they mean god knows what.

What sense would it make for me to go out into the real world and offer my services if as yet I had nothing of value to give? First I have to have life so that I can give it. When I have the gift of life, then I can be of benefit to others. First let me make the necessary preparations so that I will be judged worthy of this gift. Potentially I am worthy, that's true enough. But I have to realize that potential.

What shall be my approach to this inward deposit of inherited value? One is tempted to call it a deposit of glory. If I just let it lie there, it will do me no good. It will seem after a time like a trivial reminiscence. However I know it in truth to amount to a profound glory, to a weighty substance that sinks further down into me, after the nature of a tap root, I suppose, the more I pay attention to it and seek to profit from it.

So use is of the essence in my approach. The more I make use of it the more useful it becomes. The more I rely on it the more reliable it becomes.

Now even for every iota of preparation I make in application to this talent there is a corresponding donation of life to me, and I take that for granted in the best sense of the word. All the same, the life is after the nature of a gift and will not be coerced. As soon as I suppose that my talented preparation must result in eternal life, I make a hodgepodge of everything.

When I know a stone as a being and then take for granted that if I hit it hard enough it will split, I am still grateful to that being for behaving as it does, and at the heart of that stone the creative power chooses to respond to me. The law to which ethical being and doing resorts is gracious. Modern science is ungracious, forceful throughout and concerned with things inasmuch as they may be coerced. Beings approached ungraciously as things have no choice but to hide behind a plethora of appearances, all of which have one hand up in rejection while holding out another in acceptance. If we suppose that we are better able to survive because we have forced certain things to yield up to us certain appearances, our notion of certainty is worthless. This is not pessimism but insight.

*

The inherited deposit of human or divine nature within me is meaningless to me and useless for me unless I mean it or use it. Even whatever I say about it must somehow involve my meaning or using it. This meaning and use is truthful and practical.

It is interesting that although I cannot have a sensation of this source of true human nature within myself, I do experience a reluctance or hindrance each time I decide to apply myself, and every move I make towards my substantial individual being causes me to be confronted by an unwillingness which I have to overcome. It is as if again and again a skin or an ice crust grew over that area of my resourcefulness, so that every time I must in a sense begin from the beginning with an assertion of good faith. The more I think about it, the more am I convinced that this is quite a good arrangement, because it prevents me from indulging in foolishness. Nothing is allowed to enter but faith. The reluctance or hindrance is nothing but the measure of my other than faithful approach. If I were to try to force my way in, by will or intellect, I would come up with all sorts of things which would be neither useful nor true. Faith alone makes the true and useful connection, while will or intellect usurp and falsify. That those who have committed themselves to will and intellect find it difficult to come up with faith is no wonder. Faith has a bad press because it is forever being pressed into the service of one faith or another, and certainly we cannot find out via will or intellect what faith is. On the other hand, unless we come up with faith, our senses and thinking remain ill-founded, however impressive they appear.

So I would like to be able to say that an act of will is required of me, or an intellectual commitment, before I can have the benefit of the humanity inborn in me, but I cannot, because I know that an act of will may well leave me with a tremendous sense of progress and with much to show for my persistence, but it will be without foundation, while an intellectual commitment will supply me with masses of material, none of which will be ethically effective. That which is neither true nor useful cannot support life and will not be crowned with life, however great and demanding its claims are for itself or its renown in the world.

*

The curious thing about faith is that when we have lost it, we may have the most extraordinary notion of what it is we have lost. Rarely do we suppose that we have lost a faculty for the lack of use of it. If your hands were tied behind your back for ten years, you would have trouble using them if suddenly they were untied, but at least you would have been able to observe others using their hands during those ten years. With faith it is such that a few only know how to use that faculty, while for most of us it has atrophied. Blind faith and superstition play a much greater role in modern life than we readily suspect. Most of us use our ordinary senses in blind faith and we superstitiously rely on things to see us through crises.

Will without faith plays straight into the hands of the mighty spectral forces. Intellect without faith is a straightforward invitation to falsehood. It would be well worth our while to revive that faculty. Look at the table or the chair in front of you. Now believe that this table exists. Do not just look at it but believe that it exists, that it is really there. It may begin to look different to you after a while. Take your time. Make a repetitive exercise of not only seeing, hearing, tasting, etc. but of believing first and foremost. Remember that the wish, the simple wish to believe, leads straight into the deed, into the practice. Better still, believe in god that the air you breathe really exists. Real existence is quite a good ground for faith. If you have trouble with god, then think of the good. You must have some notion of what it means for something to be good. Begin then by imagining that god is all that is good and do your believing in that. If one believes whatever one believes in god rather than in anxiety or presumptuousness one has a very good chance, actually, of being able to make sense of god. If I believe in god that what I am writing is sensible, then god becomes more meaningful for me too and my faith has more context.

Ethics is pointless in the absence of faith. I cannot perceive the humanity/divinity in myself if I do not begin by believing that it exists. But now they will say there is something magical about faith because it can make that appear to exist which does not exist. Actually faith does away with magic. Magic is not believing but a belief, not faith but a faith. Just when we assume we are no longer subject to magic we are most constricted by it.

The son of man must be raised. Our natural male or female energy, our sexual energy, does not automatically come to terms with the world of beings. What does happen readily is mischief and chaos. Let us not reproach one another for how we cope with our sexuality, but let each one look to his own education in this respect, so that by example the rule may be followed. Even the teacher must set the example. Call it the rule of chastity, which allows me to reject all promiscuous expression of my sexual energy so that eventually it may culminate in generic strength. The rule of chastity channels sexual energy and does not repress it. Promiscuity wastes it. We can follow this rule easily once we have become proficient in our faithful approach to our inborn inheritance of perfect humanity. I may also believe that Jesus, who followed the rule of chastity to the end, exists in me. This will make it easiest of all for me to arrive at generic strength, and that is after all the object of the exercise, not that I make my own existence hard for myself. There are never any prizes for my causing myself pain. The generic strength is an aspect of the life that crowns my preparatory work in terms of this sexual energy now, and that strength will come in handy for ethical action in the world. It will allow me to face down the liar in you and to support you if you struggle under a falsehood.

*

It will also allow me to face down the liar in me at the same time, which amounts to the same. But what does it mean, that Jesus is in me? What sort of meaning does that have? I know that I am when I am, I have actual evidence of that at the time and the availability of that evidence depends on my actually wanting to be at the time when it matters to me whether I am or not. It's no good sitting back in speculative apathy waiting for evidence of one's being to be served upon a platter. I am that I am but I have evidence of it because I want to be. Really the evidence is a sign of an increase of being and let it be confessed that our being either increases or diminishes, it does not stand still like a philosophisticated concept in academic aspic.

Now if I love you and care about you, your being and mine unite. It takes time and practical application. It's as if I were inwardly holding and keeping you close to me, whereupon certain kinds of behaviour that are open to me and that would be of benefit for both of us come to mind. They come to my mind then, where as before they did not. As soon as I opt for this unity of our being it's as if I moved into another sphere of reference where advantages relevant to both of us come to my mind plus the urgency to attain them.

Unity or oneness of being is the burning factor here. It comes about due to my wanting it and due to love. It is more or less a description of <u>love</u>. Instead of loving you I can love my brother who is no longer around, or a certain writer who lived two hundred years ago. Regard, reverence, honour, even worship, all play into this which we call love. And even as it is a doing that brings my own being to the fore, as testimony, so it is also a doing when I love someone and our united being comes to the fore. And of course the better I know you the more I can love you. It's impossible to love a mere cipher. And how can I know you? By what you do, again. Even your wanting to be, evidentially, is a doing. Your loving is a doing. And all you have done can also be known by me and will add to the unity and combined substance of our being. I know you as much by what you have done as by what you do. All this opens out great possibilities for me. One can see how important ancestor worship can become and how good and bad examples in the past, more or less correctly evaluated or even fictitiously adumbrated, can lend ethical weight and purpose to our contemporary lives.

So who someone was and how we perceive him or her to have been and what that person has accomplished, all this makes him more of less useful to us today. It is something rather different from the gratitude we might come up with for someone because she has knitted us a jumper or secured for us the right to vote. There we would still have to ask: What was the ethical motivation, if there was any, and then it gets messy because judgment and possibly condemnation are involved, and all because we allow certain 'things' to matter to us when it should really be the personal being.

If I want to explain in any way sensibly why I consider such a union of being with Jesus of Nazareth to be of benefit and advantage to me, I have to relate who I perceive him to have been and what I consider him to have accomplished. Was what he accomplished of ethical value or merely a selfish indulgence dressed up for popular mass consumption? Would I be just as wise to unite my being in love with Adolf Hitler and Joseph Stalin and Genghis Khan?

*

I have not yet mentioned <u>memory</u> in this respect. In the case of Jesus one can get some notion of who he was, what he did and what he amounted to from the synoptic gospels. We must ask, as in all such cases, what did he do that was individual, singular and unique, which presumably no one else could have done? What use can we make of his accomplishments? What specific benefit can we expect and anticipate from uniting his being with ours? If we love an enemy, we rid ourselves of destructive motivations and morbid dispositions, and that is a specific benefit.

If we ask who Jesus was, we find out from the synoptic Gospels some slight information about his family, his racial and ethnic background. This is more or less incidental information. More interesting is who those around him thought he was or imagined him to be. This information is sometimes quite directly stated and dealt with in the forefront of the agenda of these three books. An ethical benefit we hope to gain from uniting our being with this human being will depend to some extent on what we can find out here, especially when we combine what we can know about who he was with what he did

211

and what he amounted to. It certainly was not clear to his contemporaries who he was. They looked for a title. They saw that he healed, they heard that he taught, but something about him caused them to feel dissatisfied with just calling him a healer and a teacher. There was a chance that he might fit in with the cultural tradition in terms of being "the one who is to come", i.e. Elijah. He was also hailed by the crowd as 'son of David'. After those close to him told him who some people thought he might be, he asked them, who they thought he was. So there is this certain amount of guesswork going on over who he is, and that being the case we should perhaps not be into much of a hurry ourselves to make up our minds, lest we fall in with theological jargon and miss the point of his personal being entirely. If we miss that, how can we unite our being with his? We would be trying to unite it with a myth perhaps, which can produce enthusiasm but nothing of lasting ethical value. He certainly seems very reluctant to discuss with anyone the possibility of his being 'the Messiah or Christ'. When Peter makes that suggestion he is told in so many words to keep it to himself, for the time being at least. He never says: 'I am the son of man' either, but usually after the Christ is mentioned he quickly steers the conversation around to the son of man, as if this were a universal term to which they might safely and profitably relate when they wonder who he is. One almost gets the impression he would prefer it if those around him focussed more on what he is saying and doing than on who he is. Did it not suffice that he was the person speaking to them? (An interesting expansion is possible: " I am the person speaking to you," also meaning: "Whenever a person speaks to you, it is I.")

When it comes to what he said and did, there is plenty of scope for manoeuvre. For me what has always counted for a great deal is that his speech was effective. Diseases cleared up, he mentions that those nearest to him were cleansed by his words, and he suggests that his words will have a permanent value, available to others and useful for them if they 'keep them', which to me means something like allowing them to matter to me, to influence my being, without necessarily becoming overly concerned with their logical meaning. In other words, first I had to want that they should affect me and only then would a meaning, the most suitable for that moment, become obvious to me. On another occasion the emphasis might lie elsewhere. Again, I have always been both very much concerned that his words should not become dead labels for me and have also been very much relieved when I found how readily they lent themselves to a fluid practical use. Especially in the fourth Gospel there is this emphasis on language which I find exciting. For example: It's not what goes into our mouth but what comes out of it that harms you.

Then of course there are all the so-called commandments, which for my money are all very practical pointers as to what to do and how to behave if we have particular achievements in mind and if we want to gain certain ends. There is certainly nothing about them of the threat, of the 'thou shalt not'. If you want to be able to come to terms successfully with this new reality that is about to come into being, then you would be smart to behave in this and in that way. Even right now, as I seem to be coming near the end of my days on earth, I say: Stick with me as long as you can. If in the end you fall away, don't worry, it can't be helped.

Then too he held out the promise that a lot of what they could not understand at the moment would come clear to them as soon as he would return to them after he had been killed – or rather after the son of man had been killed. The new reality would be upon them then, including a new sense of time. I find this extremely interesting. It tells me something directly about what is possible and available for me today here and now, if I want it and go after it in the right way.

Much of what he did seems to have been of the nature of a preparation. I know how much of my own time has to be spent on preparation, so I am always looking for helpful hints. The need for preparation, in my case as I see it, is tied up with the notion of a certain ongoing and repetitive eventuality, unpredictable to me as to the timing of it. This could be quite complicated, when I try to explain it; I am eager to avoid dead language. My personal experience is of something like an influence on me equally from within and from without and it seems to be very important for me that I acknowledge this influence and seek clarity as to what it amounts to, both from time to time and in the long run. What Jesus said and did has thrown the best light on this for me so far; which is not to say that the only help I have had in my life so far is from the Gospels. Also, I have come to this conclusion, to this notion of a universal influence, over a period of time and from the inside out, so to speak. I would call myself a man of desire rather than of will and intellect. So it might happen that at the end of my span I will be able to get on quite well with someone who began in his youth from a concept of god and a definition of faith. Meanwhile however I have to, so to speak, feel everything through from the start, test out all the practicalities and progress in my learning via the medium of communication.

To be perfectly honest, it all began with pain. It began with my trying to make sense of the wherefore and howwith of pain. Many experiences shocked me, took my breath away, left me reeling in perplexity and incomprehension. Was it something I had said or done? How did I bring down on me such punishment? Indeed was it incurred or simply the result of an accident? Or perhaps accidents are incurred? I am speaking about the time when I was eighteen to twenty years old. Pressure was being put on me, so I felt, by the parental adults around me, parents, relations and teachers, to behave in a certain way and at least to pay lip-service to a variety of values which to me were not values at all. I can describe it as a watershed when it occurred to me that I was becoming more and more miserable and that I was really not thinking for myself. As I then began to think for myself, I was not liked for it. On many an occasion, mind you, when I expressed, tentatively enough, my own thought, sometimes more or less by way of experiment, I was not very diplomatic. My questions were radical. When I inquired into the basis of, and the reason for, some of the time-honoured life-habits that were being pressed upon me, I discovered there was none; I also noticed that no one particularly thanked me for pointing that out, even indirectly. Later it occurred to me that this was quite as it had to be in my case, and I was able to make good sense of the statement reported of Jesus: "The son of man must be rejected." Mind you, the rejection of the son of man should not necessarily include the rejection of the person. I can recall three or four incidents when, after I had in some way laid myself open, so to speak, a mature adult person spoke to me in such a way that I was, as a result, both disciplined and accepted. I knew one person especially who was not very afraid of what was welling up in me and who, secondly, was not all that concerned about whether I liked him or not and, thirdly, who seemed to speak from some authority that I could not help but fall in with. Those were impressive and wholly memorable experiences. It was also done for me once by a young lady of admirable integrity who, in terms of my, at the time, rather arbitrary expression of sexual need, introduced me, by way of her own personal example, to the practice of chastity in a way that at one and the same time amounted to a rejection of my sexual advances and strengthened my personal integrity. It occurs to me more frequently than ever nowadays that the daughter of man must be rejected too. Judging by this young lady's maturity in relation to her sex, her female nature, I can only suppose that she had been brought up quite thoroughly in that department and that probably her parents had managed over a period of time to combine this 'rejection of the daughter of man' with an acceptance, an affectionate acceptance, of their own daughter in person.

Perhaps we should even speak of the 'daughter of woman' so as not to add to that political correctness-block that prevents so much understanding nowadays. In a culture where the expressions 'son' and 'father' are used readily to mean success and origin respectively, such a political correction must seem superfluous, however in our own political culture, possibly world-wide, sexuality for perfectly good reasons has become a critical issue, so a little extra effort with terminology pays dividends. So if instead of 'son of man' we were to say something like 'biological human succession' we ought to be on the same track at least, but we might do even better not to insist on any permanent translation of standardized terminology. Usually we can advance our cause better by thinking and feeling afresh on most occasions.

My own impression of the way Jesus behaved in relation to what we are just talking about is that he allowed the 'son of man' in himself to be rejected even though that rejection was usually not at all accompanied by any affectionate acceptance of himself in person, and therein lay the real strength of what he did, which was also the strength in which the son of man was then to arrive later. We will have to talk about that later when we touch on what Jesus amounted to. The strength he came up with so as not to 'call down fire' on those who <u>merely</u> rejected the son of man in him, actually mounted up. This expression 'mounted up' is a telling one. It rhymes with the prediction, by Jesus, of the son of man afterwards being visible in strength, or as strength or power, on <u>the clouds of heaven</u>. This process, or combination of process and result, of practice and pay-off, might be expressed in the terms of any one of all the various disciplines invented by modern man during the recent two millennia. The moral preparation terminates in ethical potential. Activity of the heart eventually bears fruit in various effects of the brain. Physiologically, a complete digestion makes available spiritual food. Unless you are merciful to the person next to you, your father in heaven cannot be merciful to you. Invest your talents and inspiration will find you. 'Every action resulting in an equal and opposite reaction' would have to be understood in a very specific fashion so as not to be wide of the mark. The automatic transfer of energy according to Mr. Newton, even as the automatic progress of spirit in the world according to Mr. Hegel, would seem, on the surface at least, to miss out on that precisely which is essential to the rejection of the son of man in combination with not being offended by the person of Jesus.

If we differentiate like this between the son of man and the person of Jesus, we have to admit that we can translate 'son of man' in a variety of more or less suitable ways, but the person of Jesus stands, historically memorable and thus contemporary for us. What he in person did and said had a great deal to do with the son of man, with this universal and human-natural energy that comes into our being, especially at puberty. What he said and what he did were of a piece, and this gives his message a physical reality in our time, as in every time. Even if they kill me, I will not betray my origin, my father, who is merciful spirit. Even if he should appear, to me, in the end, to have forsaken me – that cannot be helped. I will help myself out with a piece of art.[i]

*

What Jesus said and did was all geared towards an order of reality that, according to him, was on the way. Calling it the

---

[i] I intend this as a ference to Mark 15: 34, which itself is a reference to Psalm 22:1.

kingdom of heaven drew attention to the fact that this order was not created by people on earth according to the customary rules and regulations of a law-abiding state. If one asks people what they imagine he meant by that, their answers invariably refer somehow to earthly parameters. Those who say that this order after all did not arrive, point, for proof, to famine in the Sudan and war in Northern Ireland, less frequently to their own bad habits.

On the other hand, when we agree that this 'kingdom', this order, is within and among us, then we mean precisely the ethical foundation in our individuality expressed in, and as, community. We mean personal ethics based on individual morality. And above all we mean what is possible today and what we are capable of today.

This influence on me, from within and from without, of which I have become increasingly aware since I was a young man, is in itself good. There is the son of man, the natural male energy in my case, for which I am wise to be ready and which 'enters like a thief'. That is to be kept in mind. But there is also this steady influence which is good and which I want to acknowledge so that I will in fact experience it as good rather than as a terrible burden, of guilt or shame, of depression of heedlessness, of despair or cupidity or such like. It means staying tuned. The work I do is to a great extant such a tuning, such opening myself again and again to this good influence when time and again, on account of bad behaviour, I close up. The influence is whole. It is to make me whole, to heal me, to complete any unfinished development and to round out my experience. My chief method for dealing with self-imposed hindrances is to endure and suffer the pain or discomfort of them as gladly as possible. It helps me to do it gladly when I remind myself that such a pain or discomfort is after all a sign of good influence available, though blocked by something I am doing or have done. This is a totally practical consideration. If I drive

218

my car into the ditch I don't waste any time blaming it on the car or on the ditch and I don't sit down and lament my fate but I admit to myself that I didn't watch where I was driving and then take steps to get the ruddy thing back on the road. Why should I not behave just like that when I feel depressed or stressed? While I blame circumstances or my wife or get even more depressed because I am once again depressed, I only increase my burden. An order of reality is the medium in which I am suspended whether I know it or not and whether I like it or not, and while I comply, and every time I comply again, it goes well for me and I make progress – I become more real. Compliance means, in addition to a glad willingness or readiness to undergo and endure the inconvenience and misery at present, a whole series of clever moves which are mentioned and demonstrated or exemplified by Jesus as reported in the Gospels. All these recipes are mentioned that will help me comply easily and smoothly with this kingdom-of-heaven influence which is accompanied by a healing and whole-making agency to which I can subscribe if I wish.

The help I can have with the enduring and undergoing is appreciable. As I have said before, my ambition is not to make things hard for myself but to be ethically effective, and if I can do that with ease, then so much the better. When Jesus says: "My burden is light" I prick up my ears. It makes me think he might be suggesting that if I take advantage of what he has accomplished, I don't have to start every time with inventing the wheel. But what exactly did he accomplish, and how can I avail myself of the benefit?

If we unite our personal being to someone else's personal being, then our own personhood increases to that extent. It depends on how well we know that person and on who he or she is of course. Schoolboys will unite their young personal being with that of their favourite football player or their favourite film star and in this juvenile exercise of identification we have a picture of what I am talking about. There is an increase of albeit trivial self-esteem, energy, happiness and confidence. The football hero and the film star evidently possess and radiate these personality traits and they are neatly imported by our young hero worshipper.

The main personality trait Jesus demonstrates, so far as I am concerned at this point in time, is this creative passion. It allows him to achieve tremendous results. And what he radiates, in my view, is an incredible power. The passion is creative in that by giving into misfortune rather than opposing it he actually overcomes its bad effect in him so that it is transformed into a benefit. He is not the child of the spirit that fights fire with fire but of the spirit that practices hindsight and forgives. The fact that he could breathe fire if he chose[i] lets us know that his forgiveness is not automatic. I, by uniting my personal being with his to the extent I am presently able, can have some of that power and some of that creative passion. Should I reject it for some reason? Because I'm too proud? No, I want to be as ethically effective as I can and I am going to make use of all the help I can get my hands on.

*

It stands to reason that unless I want to be ethically effective I should have no power. Various thoughts have to be brought together here. It almost seems that they cannot even be properly understood separately. There is the new order of reality which is at hand and which we can embrace more and more. There is Jesus who can be a source of passionate creativity and creative passion for me and also of ethical power. There is the need to learn about this person Jesus, who he was, what he did and said and what he eventually amounted to. Then there is my act, ongoing and repeated, of unifying my personal being with

---

[i] I refer to Mk. 11:14 and 11:17.

220

his so that I can have a piece of this creative passion and this ethical power. Finally there is a spirit of healing and wholeness available along with all the interest I take and along with all I manage to do and undo in this respect. It sounds almost like a full-time occupation. Certainly it's not something that can be handed to me over a counter or magically instituted. I have to take a certain amount of trouble over it, and it seems that the more satisfied I am with myself, the less likely am I to take such trouble, and then I get unpleasant surprises. I can vouch for that. As a matter of fact this notion I have of a steady good influence on me both from within and without – I have arrived at it over a period of time, learning from mistakes, arduous bouts of trying to cope with set-backs I could not explain, seemingly unjust treatment at the hands of fate, an observable relation between attentiveness to matters ethical and the number of catastrophes in my life, the actual effect I can have on my environment and on the state of my being by means of ethical action, and so on. A long purification process partially resulted in my attitude towards this reality-influence – this affectiveness – as towards something that must be so and cannot be otherwise.

*

Of course this places the responsibility for my overall disposition in my own back yard. This is exciting because I much prefer it if I can manage my own affairs. <u>Disposition-management</u> is then par for the course. My existence is placed into my hands and this affords me that crucial sense of freedom that comes along with being able to call the shots.

Now if I try to sustain this ethical autonomy in my <u>self</u>, it soon breaks down and so do I. I have tried it often enough to know what I am talking about here. Out of my own self come only sporadic bursts of energy temporarily forceful. Whatever I achieve on the basis of these lasts for a while and then perishes, whether the achievement is inside or outside my self. And, by the way, in cases like this, I mean of the self, it is bound to be either inside or outside. Brilliant intellectual achievements turn out to be straw. Material progress turns out to be ill-timed, impractical and even harmful. I notice this even when I play the piano from my self. I cannot get my act together. Either I concentrate on technique and make amazing advances only to get so bored with music altogether that it nauseates me, or I revel in the sound and indulge in the sheer musicality only to notice to my chagrin that memory goes to pots and technique falls apart.

So what is the answer? Limited to self (not myself) I can do nothing. I feel momentarily all-powerful or full of life but it's fake. It makes a mockery of me in the end. When I stand back a bit, I can see that people around me, as in all ages, have broken their brains trying to perpetuate that which 'will not hold'. Usually they invent a spirituality that disguises for them the ultimate failure, so that they can lay the blame for it on agencies other than themselves.

It is after all I myself who make the decision to rely on my self and on the bad and false spirituality that allows me to fool myself. In such cases I do not unite my being with that of another being. The spirit of falsehood, of vain force and sensual indulgence, is not a being and has no being. The devil as such does not exist but we are never done trying to turn ourselves into devils; and strangest thing of all – when we fail we feel bad about it. So in that way, through these repeated and artificially sustained attempts to be selfishly effective, we remove ourselves miles from any ethical effectiveness. Our failure at being total failures drives us to despair and we accidentally become total failures.

The faculties of philosophy, of science, of religion and art, can all be pressed into the service of the self. My self is the self. Your self is the self. And this begins haphazardly. We slide into it unawares. It happens when we are not looking.

222

Then we automatically enforce and sustain the misdirection for the simple reason that we do not do the opposite. This is a kind of a catch. We suppose that we should be able to sit back and contemplate alternatives at our leisure as we weigh up the pros and cons of ethical and selfish effectiveness as though they share a common basis. The point that is so slow in penetrating our understanding is that ethical and selfish effectiveness exclude each other and that we are either involved in the one or else we do the other; there is no middle ground. A respite from selfishness is already ethically effective, but we must know what we are about. Not satisfied with mere respites from selfishness, we decide that our ethical effectiveness might be properly founded and successfully sustained. This is when we come to the conclusion that it might be possible for us to unite our being to that of an ethically effective being. It's entirely up to us. We are perfectly at liberty not to do so and to return to self-mockery and self-deception. Not only will no one stop us but many upon many in high and low places will smilingly extend the helping hand. When our turn comes to perish they don't know us.

*

We know that Jesus was ethically effective. Many of those who knew him began to worship in reality. Although they were puzzled about who he was, they recognized that what he said gave them a strong sense of humanity. Their attempt to place him within the pre-structured cultural tradition of the Hebrew tribal society and the Jewish State failed simply because he could not be thus placed. It can happen to us that we sit next to someone on a flight to Nairobi and have the best conversation imaginable without ever finding out anything about him or her, not where he lives, what he does for a living, if anything, nor even what his name is. We part at the end of the journey, aware of having spent our time constructively.

223

Who was that man? Who was that woman? It was the one we spoke to. That is what counts.

Who was this Messiah, this Christ the Jews expected? How did the prophets describe him? Clearly, towards the end, he was not to be confused with some political personality. One gets the impression that his being was anticipated in the realm of the supernatural. How that realm was imagined is anybody's guess. The more profound anticipants described a being who would somehow offer the possibility of a just existence in freedom from insecurity. One gets the impression of something like finally being at home in the universe. His day would coincide with a time of arrival at the long sought after destination. Biological changes were not envisaged. Not being an individual with political power, he would have to be someone who ruled over his own inward disposition and that would make him inwardly invincible, though outwardly vulnerable. This inward invincibility interested and excited the prophets in any case because they realized that the destiny of the Jews as chosen by their god could not possibly be played out in military conquests of the surrounding nations. The final direction of the path for the developing human being must therefore lie inward, towards self-conquest. The god of Abraham had responded to faith. The one who would lead the Jews out of their outward perplexity inward would be an expert and specialist in faith. However no one knew what he would look like. Hardly surprising therefore that eventually only a few trusted this itinerant preacher and healer. People then as now wanted their selves to be boosted and their egos to be bolstered, so they were glad to unite their being with someone who performed spectacular healings, but when it turned out that this person rejected his ego and denied his self, they went home to their wives and children. All the same, many recognized his powerful personhood and expected a great deal from their acquaintanceship and even friendship with him. A remarkable episode is the one

224

where he tells his audience that if they would have any part in him, they must eat his flesh and drink his blood. Is it any wonder that this made a certain kind of solidarity with him impossible for them?

Others wondered what he meant by that, as do many of us today. A man is a being of flesh and blood. When a man lays down his life for another, he renounces his claim on his own flesh and blood. If someone lays down his life for us and renounces his claim on his flesh and blood, it has to be up to us to take advantage of that act and to accept that gift of life, and we can do that by way of our own flesh and blood, incorporating what is being presented to us. My spirit is able to ingest and to digest. All the same, in reality I long to have within me, akin to the food in my stomach, this being's flesh and blood existence. Jesus called this 'food indeed' and 'everlasting food' and 'food onto eternal life' and we find it so difficult to imagine what goes on here because we have become accustomed to opposing flesh and spirit, which is not wise. Rather flesh and spirit are two sides of the same reality. Also we think of human beings as animals, which is most unfortunate, because as a consequence the spiritual side is lost and the flesh and blood side becomes dead matter. Human being as flesh and blood and human being as spirit are not opposed. The spirit that is god may motivate our every move, while the flesh and blood of Jesus ensures us his being in ours. Our being is informed by the being of Jesus in terms of flesh and blood.

It helps if we thoroughly first come to terms with what it means to us that we are beings of flesh and blood, not merely of spirit. Human being implies both. It can in fact be shown to have been one of the chief correctives Jesus brought to bear on our attitude towards human – shall we say: towards the human mystery – that in human beings spirit and flesh and blood are to be unified. In the so-called Gospel of Thomas we have this re-

225

markable encouragement to "make the two one", which carries implications far and wide into the evolution of all life-forms.

Our flesh and blood being as divorced or separate from any spirit at all is inconceivable because we would no longer be. We can view being in terms of form and content, substance and matter, spirit and flesh, burden and carrier, but finally we must keep in mind that these are useful conceptual devices we have invented as we try to achieve or recapture the inherent meaningfulness and significance of our being. The argument that invention itself can be creative or destructive, holds of course. More than ever today do we need to ask why we came up with certain tools, for our hands or for our will and intellect, but if we forget that they are devices, and that their purpose does not rest in themselves, we cannot examine our motivations for producing them.

Spirit form one point of view, flesh and blood from the other – this is how we human beings can approach human beings. When we look at animals, plants, minerals and elements we are still in the presence of beings, like ourselves, and therefore this two-handed approach is still the most useful, but flesh and blood refers more appropriately to human beings, perhaps, than to other beings. Of course we could make a case for stones bleeding, if we imagined it would be useful to do so. Crucial is the epistemological insight, therefore, that we either get to know beings, we ourselves being such and therefore also being mercifully incapable of stepping outside our skins – or we try to get to know things, badly inspired, priding ourselves on some falsehood of a notion of utter objectivity (or mere subjectivity) which amounts to the sort of dehumanization which we need to overcome.

*

"Eat my flesh and drink my blood," – it is the tangible side of that activity which we have called 'unifying our being with that of another.' It is also the side that needs to be especially emphasized when we begin to spiritualize one another, turning beings into myths, drained of flesh and blood. I am not entirely happy speaking of two sides here, because people will always try to find a name then for that which has those two sides, as when we speak of the two sides of a penny. When it comes to spirit and flesh, then each one of these in reality implies and presupposes the other. Which is not to say that one cannot indulge in spiritualism, shunning the flesh, or that one cannot 'lust after the flesh' in the absence of spirit. And one will in fact do one or the other to the extent that one ignores the achievement of the one who has married spirit and flesh, good spirit and chaste flesh, in person. By way of that achievement we have become capable of contemporary existence, but always and again in person, such as in your or my person.

The trials we sustain in our lives, sustaining them rather than running away from them, prepare us from both the side of spirit and from the side of flesh and blood. Normal behaviour is no protection against the temptations of mere flesh or of exclusive spirit, against spiritualism or concupiscence. Extraordinary measures are required. To that end Jesus suggested various disciplines, commandments, words. Much of what he purportedly said amounts to helpful hints on how to deal with the terrors and horrors, the shame and guilt, the hatred and infatuation, that set in due, on one hand, to the approach of the new reality and on the other hand to our unpreparedness. The initial advice to repent and look for this order of being is after all extraordinary, but then admittedly also given to those who are in dire straits, since those who are happy with themselves as they normally are cannot be expected to undertake emergency measures.

So the sum total of what Jesus says and does effectively deals with this emergence of the new order of being in himself, for example, and in others, for the love of them. We need to keep hold of his advice, otherwise, when the emergency is upon us, we have no mind of it. Mind you, we can apply some of his suggestions at any time, and should perhaps do so especially at times when we seem to ourselves perfectly alright. I myself at this moment am in no pain whatsoever but as I reflect on that fact – and such reflection on one's present state of being is healthy – it occurs to me that at any moment a depression may set in, a misfortune may arise, I may behave badly, someone may insult or praise me, and in such a case I want to be able to respond ethically rather than making matters worse. So I open myself, in the present case by way of my writing, to the good influence, even though I have no sign or evidence of it. In that way I make it less likely that some barrier will inadvertently be created by me, which will show up as a depression, misfortune etc., and I also become more alert and awake, which will stand me in good stead if I do suddenly commit some stupidity or find myself in some painful experience. As soon as such a painful experience is upon me, I am at liberty to take moral pains in the interest of my growth, my improvement or rehabilitation. I call them moral rather than ethical pains because I take them primarily so that I may find repair, though I fully realize that the fruits of such activity are secondarily of use also to others. As soon as I come to the end of such a moral bout, I look about me for an ethical task, primarily ethical, so that my new growth will be invested. This is better than collapsing or running away until the next pain visits me.

I describe this because some may suppose I advocate hedonism in relation to available goods.

The son of man comes like a thief in the night. To the degree that we are not ready we make accusations of injustice and evil, perpetrated by our fellow man, by circumstances, by god or fate, when we should quickly strive for intimate contact with that creative energy that is male or female so that we will not continue to mistake its effect and to shrug off our responsibility and to fly in the face of god.

What Jesus teaches in terms of the <u>son of man</u> we usually try to learn in terms of nature. But with our 'Natural Sciences' and our appetite for legitimate objectivity we spoil our chances, so that with all our knowledge of nature we know nothing of human nature and as we ourselves as a consequence decline, what we seem to learn of ourselves is bound to decline too. Jesus in his ethic begins with human nature, with the son of man, and it seems that even the elements fell in with that, which should not surprise us. Once we know a little better what to expect and what not to expect from human nature, our ethical activity is to that extent firmly based and we ourselves, with a view to reality, are in with a chance.

*

Once we begin to understand the son of man as initially distinct from personality, we become freer as persons to do the one necessary thing. Or let's put it this way: I myself as a person am not really free to act until I give my true human nature its due. By my true human nature I mean a variety of processes and events that are to some extent predictable but that cannot be manipulated. An attempt to coerce or trick true human nature backfires. We find ourselves in the presence of that which must be respected, honoured and obeyed. Here is productive cause for wakefulness and attentiveness. To be alert of the existence of the son of man is the first duty we have as maturing and mature human beings. I hope no one objects too much to the way I almost equate Jesus' use of the expression 'son of man' with true human nature. I certainly do not apologize for coming around, at this stage of this rational ethic, when the beings we take an interest in are explicitly human beings, to the ethic of Jesus as I see it, for I too, in the interest of my ethical being and behaving, if I want to mature and be fruitful and not get stuck in states of being, have to unite my being with one who is greater than I am and I find there that Jesus rather splendidly fills the bill and fits the description.

My human nature at the moment is such that I am impressed by its gravity. I want to work an example through. This gravity is what I differentiate from onsets of lethargy, heaviness, tiredness and laziness because I look with respect on what I know to be true human nature. I think of gravity as an essential attribute of human nature. Gravity to me means principally earth-bound. Earth, terrestrial existence, familiarity with earth-environments, gratitude for limitations due to birth on earth with inherited equipment suitable to the task of living on earth – all this is what gravity amounts to. It can amount to that, and if I make it my business to respect human nature, then it does so for me in reality.

Remember that everything I say about human nature has to be true for me first of all, otherwise I spin a lot of straw. True human nature is not accessible as something upon which you can make pronouncements while it has nothing to do with you as a living human being.

So simple respect of human nature yields me a recognition of it as gravity and this is added to my knowledge of it. Let's say that for us now our knowledge of human nature starts as gravity, and it works for me if I respect this. Try it yourself. It is bound to work also for you, but it is up to you to try it. One has to start somewhere.

I can report that the lethargy, the heaviness, laziness and tiredness have receded, like a bank of dark cloud before the sun. I have done the work on the preceding page and find myself in a kind of limbo, as if I had got rid of obstructive rubbish and had to think carefully now about what to do next. If I don't think carefully, I am liable to fritter away what I have gained and then I would be worse off in terms of that lethargy, so that it would probably turn into melancholy, the prospect of which I do not relish. So I return my attention to the son of man, to my present experience of my human nature as a matter of fact, al-

230

ways aware of the tentative 'my' as I make my approach. As I honour true human nature now I become aware of my liberty, of my potential freedom. Where previously a receding bank of cloud outside my window towards the east impressed me as a suitable symbol, now it was a seagull hovering in mid-air, as if deciding which way to turn or swoop next. Again, as in the case of gravity, where respect was required so that I did not get entangled in lethargy etc., so now too am I tempted – to take liberties, to make arbitrary and heedless decisions, to feel comfortable with a lack of an immediate sense of duty and responsibility, to stop and be content with what I have half achieved as I look ahead to a veritable mountain to climb. All these temptations fade as I continue, in spite of my disinclination, to honour human nature which is undoubtedly active in me and therefore passive too. The lethargy threatens to return and I respond respectfully. The work is more difficult now. I ask for help and I get it. I unite my being more thoroughly with the being of the one who saw true human nature through to the finish during his own existence on earth – that is what I mean by asking for help. Compare it to a trustful leaning in a certain direction, inwardly of course, as on the shoulder of a strong friend. My task may now be easier but it is still a task, still a burden. I am at liberty to toss it off or carry it. The plough share is in the ground but I can "look back" if I like. However the warning of Jesus is fresh in my mind and I carry on. I am moving very gradually into the realm of obedience now. Since I am at liberty to go on or quit, the obedience is perfectly free. The temptation to down tools and walk away is overcome now as I obey human nature. I cooperate with necessity, with a certain forward thrust which I experience in myself. Temptations are laboriousness, cheerlessly grim determination, an unaffectionate resignation to the unavoidable chore, and half-heartedness, a going through the motions and notions and maybe getting away with it. I also get a cramp in my chest and an onset of timidity. Special efforts of obedience to true human nature definitely make a good difference. I get the impression that I am near the end. It still feels like a weight that lies on me and now I am reminded to suffer. This had not occurred to me until now. Human nature has to undergo, to bear up under, to endure and to withstand. To the degree that I cooperate with human nature in myself I too endure, obediently. A symbol presents itself to me in the woman I observe in the backyard of the house I can look at as I lift my gaze. She hangs up washing, empties garbage, sweeps and wipes windows, hangs up more washing, busily and patiently at once, as she walks in and out through the door numerous times, neither fast nor slow, just efficiently, so there I again have something outside myself to be going on with and I never reject that sort of comfort. I straighten my stooping shoulders and remind myself to be "exceedingly glad" as all these potential problems and threats to my peace of mind pile in on me.

Then suddenly I'm done. The pressure is off. I have no sense of immediate reward but I am in no doubt as to the value of what I have accomplished. It amounts to something, what I have done in your presence. Also I have learned something. My knowledge has increased and I have honed a few skills and maybe acquired a good habit, of persistence perhaps, and of endurance. My attitude of respect, honour and obedience to true human nature as it exists on my behalf or for my good, has been affirmed and confirmed. What I look forward to now is an infusion of strength, after a time. Then I will be able to speak, to that extent, of <u>my</u> human nature. I will own what I have inherited and worked for. As I down tools now I am cautioned to guard against self-indulgence for the time being.

*

Our true human nature, or just plain human nature – let's get back to its beginning in our gender, as our sexuality. Do we still have what it takes to come to some understanding here?

Sex and gender – sex and the erotic: destruction or creation? In spite of what some say, I remain convinced that we are all born male or female, and I would not insist on going exclusively by appearance. How we capitalize on this, well, it depends, I dare say, to some extent on genes and circumstances. But let's not forget the autonomous individual person. The person I am is not in the same category with my genes and my environment. The person I am takes a stance vis-à-vis his world and his inheritance. The person I am, that is I. I am not an ego, or my ego, not as a rule, in any case. When I am my ego, or an ego, I am in trouble, and I would have made a deal with the powers that be, that they should remind me, painfully if necessary, of the fact that I as an ego am a predicament and a snare for my fellow human beings, if I did not know that such a mechanism is in any case firmly in place. When egoism besets me, I am no longer in touch with my human nature, and when egotism has me trapped, I have begun to take pleasure in a resistance to my human nature. Now mind you, the test of egoism and egotism depends on my human natural instincts being intact, and while this only luckily is the case, I am an accident waiting to happen. What I mean is, that my human natural instincts have to be intentionally in place. I must actually desire to be human naturally intact, otherwise how can I use that condition as a parameter – I mean inasmuch as I hope that its absence will tell me something?

*

What I am suggesting is that I can be perfectly sound in terms of my gender (male in my case) and that in addition to this highly satisfactory state of affairs for which I may be duly grateful, I may also persist in it and do my bit in order to continue to persist in it; which is good news, surely. Doing my bit, as I call it, involves on the one hand (the two-handed hands-on approach is usually the best) a discriminatory attitude towards son of man and person, or true human nature and individual

233

person, and on the other hand an attentive alertness to such violations of the frontier, such unethical trespasses, as are indisputably implied by sexuality.

No use speaking of trespasses unless borders exist. The border between nature and personality needs to be sensed, sounded, confessed, recognized, acknowledged, understood and whatever else just happens to be on the cards during creative living. That's it, let's refer to creative living. The word 'life' by itself has become meaningless through the widest possible spread of abuse during the modern centuries. Speak of creative living, of the two-handed approach, of an awareness of what true human nature amounts to as distinct from individual personality.

Because what we have in mind is, once again, ethically to make the two one; and before we correctly know them as two we cannot possibly unite them, in ourselves or on the moon for that matter.

I feel urged once again to look closely at the use of the term 'son of man' by Jesus in the various Gospels, because here we have the clearest example I have come across of person and nature both sustained in distinction until in the end this 'amounts to' something.

*

The term 'son of man' is used by Jesus in the synoptic Gospels almost in the sense of a law. One gets the impression that this son of man moves with a necessity of his own. One has the choice of cooperation, which betokens success and benefit, or of ignorance, followed by degeneration and disaster. Those of us who are not of the Hebrew tradition may justifiably feel alienated by an attitude to human reality and by a terminology for the depiction of it which is peculiar to a race other than our own. And yet the entire Christian tradition to date has accommodated,

234

in its own peculiar fashion, the teaching and personality of Jesus, so that nowadays we really have two quite disparate traditions against which we may hold our contemporary experience and understanding of this singular human being in whose shadow we may wish to exist though his life as light is available to all.

I myself am certainly reminded strongly of my own experience and understanding of it when I read such statements as: "The Son of Man has power on earth to forgive sins." Within us exists a power by which we may put at ease someone who is torn between despair and a desire for joy, and yet how often do we really put that power to good use? This disturbs me. Someone near me is troubled by anxiety and by the physical symptoms of prolonged anxiety and instead of coming powerfully to his or her aid, I become anxious myself and withdraw from that person. The power of the Son of man within me does not come to the fore. I should be able to say to that person: 'Relax, you have nothing to worry about, you can trust the world around you,' and then that person will taste relief and his or her physical symptoms will disappear. I ask myself, is my overall attitude correct? Am I really sorry when someone is in pain and do I wish he were not in pain? Perhaps I am ashamed of this Jesus and of what he stands for when I am confronted by callous behaviour and by indifference that is being acted out. What, after all, does this Jesus stand for if not for partial concern and tender affection?

*

So we have Jesus quoted as having said: "Whosoever shall be ashamed of me and my words, in this adulterous and sinful generation, of him also shall the Son of Man be ashamed, when he comes in the glory of his father with the holy angels."

The annoyance we feel with ourselves, for example, when once again we have emptied ourselves of all truthful perceptiveness due to some mindless activity, is just such an experi-

235

ence of shame in the face of the one who purportedly spoke those words.

The historic narrative and record of Jesus as a person in history is available to us in the three synoptic Gospels. We have precious little to go on and not all of what we do have is recorded in the same way in all three books. What seems to matter much more, at least to me, is the most singular resonance this record produces in myself as soon as I concentrate on what was said by him. Often he refers to the Son of Man but on some occasions he refers to himself, so we do not feel right about simply equating the historic Jesus with the Son of man. Nor does it make sense simply to say that he presently identified with the Son of Man.

If now for Son of man we substitute 'true human-natural being' we are perhaps more readily brought to the appreciation of that generic being which seems almost able to lead a life of his or her own in us at times, so that we 'do not know what came over us' or we are 'beside ourselves' or 'not entirely ourselves' – in addition to being men and women of integrity and truthfulness. What does seem to me to be the case is that Jesus, while aware of this truthful and natural human being, (which has relevance to us in whatever time), saw himself as potentially identical with the Son of Man and as destined to demonstrate, in the particular of his own personal action and behaviour, the universal relevance of this 'Son of Man; of this general human being which generates a life with which we are not necessarily all that familiar. A generation of a unique life is involved and Jesus, by acting this out, makes it possible for us to understand, for one example, why we are beset by various difficulties and problems and how we might turn them to our benefit.

So one way of looking at what we might call the ethical achievement of Jesus is by recognizing his willingness, on one hand, to demonstrate and make plain for once in the flesh, how

236

this generative human being operates and under what sort of circumstances it can and needs to grow, to flourish and bear – from seed to fruit, as it were – and on the other hand to make available for others, for a few, for several and for many, the complete and powerful personal substance of an accomplished existence which allows them then to steer or travel a similar course, within the liberated confines, of course, of their own unique individuality.

The power to regenerate, to restore and heal on all fronts, by empowering faith, is amply demonstrated by Jesus in person, if we are to credit the Gospel documentation. Hearing about this, however, only allows us to admire, it does not put the power to do the same, to be regenerated and to regenerate, to be healed and to heal, into our own hands.

What does put this power in our hands, if we but knew it, is that he, in the end then, handed it over – which act also conformed to and coincided with that truthful human nature to which he so often is quoted as having referred.

The point here is that the Son of man "must suffer many things and be set at nought," (Mk. 9:12); that he "is delivered into the hands of men and they shall kill him," (Mk. 9:31); that he is "as a man taking a far journey, who left his house and gave authority to his servants," (Mk.10:34); but also that "he came to save that which was lost" (Mt. 18:11) and that "he is not come to destroy men's lives but to save them", (L. 9:56) and even "to seek and to save that which was lost." (L. 19:10).

We should take care not to fall into an unethical, pseudo-scientific objectivity here by assuming that since this is as it must be, what is that to us beyond the fascinating historicity of it, for "truly the Son of man goeth as it was determined, but woe unto that man by whom he is betrayed," (L.22:22). Mark adds: " – it had been good for that man if he had not been born." (MK. 26:24)

237

The importance of our attitude towards this truthful human nature in ourselves, this accomplished Son of Man, is therefore not to be underestimated. If we are not careful we will be among those who do the killing rather than one of those who realize that while this human nature "must be killed", we ourselves may know that this is as the seed which is *killed by circumstances* so that it may sprout, flourish and bear fruit. The ethical notion of suffering and enduring intelligently and meaningfully comes into its own on those terms. We are not to try to escape from conditions and circumstances that kill our truthful human nature but we are to bear with this for the purpose of the restoring and healing that comes as a consequence and so that we may have this substantial power that results for us and for the good of others. This otherwise impossible task becomes possible and even easy for us ("my burden is light") to the extent that we lean on the personality of Jesus insofar as we have made ourselves aware of it, and this 'leaning on' we have earlier described as our uniting our being with his, person to person.

*

What is the reward? What does it all amount to in the end?

There was a time when a man's time on earth was idealistically viewed as the suffering preparation, in terms of a Christianity, for a reward not this side of the grave and in hope of an eventual – who knows when – return of the Christ who would finally bring justice into the world. Something was definitely to come right on the other side of the grave and something else was to be righted in the future. Meanwhile nothing much was working out. The kingdoms of the earth still failed as they always did while personal liberty and good fortune ebbed and flowed as usual in accordance with some arbitrary moon. Very rarely does one hear of anyone who realized the kingdom of god and gave cheerful evidence of this to the world, irrespective of its contempt or admiration.

238

And yet it sat deep in the message of Jesus that "after me the kingdom". Many times does he prophesy the coming of "the Son of man in the glory of his father with the holy angels". In Mark 9:1 and in Mathew 16:28 he states that "there be some of them that stand here which will not taste of death till they have seen the kingdom of god come with power". The Son of man will "rise from the dead", (Mk. 9:9) he shall "rise the third day" (Mk. 9:31), they "shall see the Son of man coming in the clouds with great power and glory" (Mk. 13:27) and "see the Son of man sitting on the right hand of power and coming in the clouds of heaven." (Mk 14:61,62). Also "the Son of man shall come in the glory of his Father with his angels and then he shall reward every man according to his works," (Mt. 16:27). The coming of the Son of man shall be "as the lightning (that) comes out of the East and shines in the West" (Mt. 24:27) and "as the days of Noah were …" (L. 24:37).

But "the kingdom of god does not come with observation" for it is "within you", (L. 17:21). It is within and among us.

Gradually, during the days and years of early Christendom the disappointed search for the kingdom of god without, or even outside, results in a compensatory doctrine of 'soon'. Very rarely is the individual or collective misfortune correctly understood as the present kingdom of god unprepared for, and the coming Son of man unwelcome. And this has not changed. The world as such is no closer to the kingdom of god than it ever was, neither is the individual human being as such. But let us take one thing to heart: Our inhabitation of the kingdom of god does not get us into the newspapers or into the history books, for these inadvertently record the failures to prepare and comply and never in terms of possible preparation or compliance.

All this aside though, what we need to take on board is that the kingdom of god is in fact upon us and that the Son of man reigns in that kingdom. Now all depends on how we see ourselves in relation and comparison to this. If we are to become aware of the *material earth*, of the *cloudy sky* and of the *starry universe*, it will not do for us to sit in a close-walled chamber entranced by the vicissitudes of our psyche. We must step outside and come to our senses. The same goes for our awareness of the Son of man and the kingdom of god. This commonwealth of reality in which our truthful human natural being is at home will make us or break us, roughly speaking, depending on which way we lean. Not that we should come any the less to our senses, but faith, the parent of our senses, is essential. What sort of faith? Simply faith, in god. What is god? God is merciful spirit. This means that he does not hold our past nonsense against us. If we wish we had done otherwise and were otherwise, this spirit cannot but flow into us, for our contrition and repentance involves the being of the one who was utterly contrite.

As we turn ethically towards the world, our actions and what we gain by them coincide. This may not be the simplest thing in the world to explain while our language is geared to accommodate itself to halfway measures, however it is nonetheless a fact.

We cannot make sense of modern-day experience until we credit the contemporary availability of all that is eschatologically foretold by Jesus. Of course we may have to create a language for ourselves that is neither crippled by a hedonistic materialism of the mere senses nor impoverished by an addiction to superstition or to outworn dogma. As we lean towards reality, we must be willing to participate with it in the creation of the language required for a personal presentation of that reality. Also we must get away from trying to lay down for all time a pattern of static law. As we work on our contemporary ethicality, we gradually leave behind such presumption. The words of Jesus will always be powerful but his language is not for us to imitate. If we must paraphrase, let us at least steer clear of the temptation to paraphrase the words of Jesus. We have our own contemporary reality to express as we communicate what we learn by reflection and experience.

What is eschatologically foretold by Jesus and what is available today is a link with reality. No longer do we have to fight for an approximation to reality and tire ourselves out to be rid of evil energy before we can succumb to an aesthetic appreciation of phenomena – which is still no true rest. No longer do we have to limit our horizon to good ideas, perfect laws and solicitous angels in order to avoid the presumptions of rampant individualism and still we can only imagine the true life from an impenetrable distance.

Of course our watchwords shall be such common denominators as chastity, humility and patience. But let each one find within himself and herself the desire for a significance of those words that is more and more appropriate to his or her own contemporary needs. Do not ask: What means chastity? But rather: What does it mean to me? Then see how far you get with that meaning. And when you have finally discovered solid ground in yourself, tell the rest of us. Leave the guru to stew in his brew. Why should he feed off your deplorable imagination? Deplore it yourself and look how quickly you make headway. By all means search the scriptures, holy or wise or simply innocent, but observe, while you listen to them, that you do so. Then their language will always and again be fresh. These words on the page in front of you here and now make no claim to a mighty publicity or to an endowment of magical thrills. Their task is to fortify, to edify, and finally simply to praise. However as you turn the page, that purpose may have changed, so that you find yourself confronted by a challenge to your understanding and by a seeming threat to your spiritual conveniences. What you do then is again entirely up to you. He who offers me a potential skill must leave me at liberty to rise to the occasion. Even the aroma of an incursion on my individuality, be it by force of trickery, inten-

tional or accidental, destroys my sympathy and subverts communality for a while.

*

There is Jesus the historic person with whom we may unite
our personal being, in terms of one another. There is the Son of
man who shows the way into the kingdom of god here and
now, especially to those who make it their main business in life
that he should do so. Meanwhile there is the Christ, the Messiah, the returning or coming Son of man, who appropriates for
us the future just as the historic Jesus appropriates for us the
past, while the Son of man, in transit as it were, appropriates
for us the present.

Not to worry that here we are confronted by fragments. Even
when I speak to you I am aware of your present impression on
me, and I am aware of your past as you reveal it to me even as I
find out eventually who you would like to be in the future, what
your aims and ambitions are and also what you look forward to
and what you fear. In your case too, as in mine, there is a past, a
present and a future entity, which are not fragments but facets of
the whole. I do not push your future self, your hoped-for blessedness, for example, beyond the grave by telling you to put up
with the turmoil of your existence as best you can until the day
of your death, when everything will come right, but I say to you:
Let us together endure your despair with an eye to one who
showed what it means to endure to the end and then watch how
your blessedness takes place. Meanwhile I try as best I can to
make up with my own patience for the lack of patience I may
notice in you and I try not to hold your incessant complaining
against you. For I know that this is merely a symptom of the despair in which you appear to me to have taken refuge. In line
with the present Son of man, any mercy I show you makes it
possible for mercy to be shown to me, whereas my recrimination

against you would imply unavoidable recrimination eventually-visited upon me.

*

If we view Christianity as a religion, then we must also admit that Jesus of Nazareth was not the founder of that religion. He was not the founder of a religion, but Christianity as a religion was based on him by others. How this happened is not the easiest thing in the world to describe. Whichever of the four Gospels we look at, there is never the slightest suggestion that a movement of cultural proportions is intended or that an external body of dogma is envisioned to which 'the faithful' or 'believers' are to adhere so that they might be safe in the world and secure in the 'hereafter'. This is not to pass judgment on Christianity as a religion but simply to suggest that Jesus was not the founder of a religion. This distinction is important because when we wonder whether or not we should link our ethical progress to Jesus, that does not yet imply that we should become adherents of the Christian religion. Our adherence to a religion is something specific in its own right and not necessarily based on true ethical principles. The endless, pointless quarrel about the difference between a good and not so good Christian stems from just such a misconception of Christianity as a religion founded by Jesus. A Christian is *obliged* to believe this and that, so as to have membership in a church community. That is something quite different from discovering in oneself the perfect law of the Son of man or from assisting in oneself in the growth of one's universal human nature. The two concepts of community do not match and behaviour is guided from quite a different point of view.

If our chief concern is to get through life as painlessly and pleasurably as possible, we may well be good Christians but if we experience in ourselves a hunger and thirst for eternal life here and now, none of the religions in the world can help us, not even Christianity, because then our inner being must be at native liberty for us to arrive at contemporary solutions to modern, individual problems. Guilt and shame, misery and grief will all have to be looked at in a positive light, not as something to be rid of so that we can get on with our customary existence. 'To be condemned' then means not to have reached out sufficiently yet to that greater being which looks to us for companionship. It does not mean that God has rejected us.

As soon as we become members of a church community (a pleonasm, really) we cannot really afford any longer to be welcoming to all other human beings because we will always be measuring them according to the cultural yardstick we have adopted. The fact that Jesus of Nazareth was Jewish does not prevent us from recognizing in him a human being, but as soon as we know someone as a Christian or as a Hindu we can no longer take communication with him on a non-prescriptive human-natural level for granted. One gets the impression, when perusing the Gospels, that Jesus was very much aware of the cultural differences between Samaritans and Jews for example but that he had little trouble in distinguishing and working with the human-natural predispositions in each. He does not seem to feel obliged to look down with pity on the goyim or even on the mixed race Samaritans. More often than not it is the 'outsiders' who show the true faith. In other words his sense of community was human-natural and simply personal.

*

We adhere to our customs with a tenacity born of lazy spirit. No sooner do we overcome this than our spirit takes flight. It lodges in novelties as readily as in ancient peculiarities and we cannot say why or wherefore. Only it does matter to us in the end, if not sooner, that our spirit moves. Indeed when we speak of our spirit we may mean much the same as some mean by their will, except that successful motion and not merely a flippant or cranky stirring is meant. A *moving* spirit then is like good will,

244

for good will too must participate, and we must know that it does. Remote on a hillside overlooking all it purports to control, neither spirit nor will makes sense – nor does it make ends meet.

What we know of the Son of Man through Gospel text leans heavily on this notion of moving spirit and good will. "The Son of man has nowhere to lay his head," (Mt. 8:20) (L. 9:20) for example. This is no image of restlessness, by the way, but of transition. All we associate with passage, from one to another – transformation, transubstantiation, transcendence etc. – projects this Son of Man quality, this energy knowingly on the move. What our own Western culture has learned to assimilate on that score it has wantonly projected. We today must learn to make it entirely our own, for we have begun to believe in these projections and they have turned into virtual world, as substitute for real world. Only a few will escape the seductive drag out there or the allure of the drug in here, and since they cannot know ahead of time who they are we must speak to all.

*

The way energy ebbs and flows in us is itself a sign of the times. By this I do not mean that it is an indication of how far we are along the way – towards arrival at some utopia – but of what the special requirements are today if we want to take best advantage of what is available to us. Indeed it is up to those who know that they are responsible for their community, to interpret these signs, not so as to get others to do what is necessary but so as to be able to do it themselves.

This ebb and flow of energy, for example, which coincides with political turmoil and social apathy, not to say 'with war and peace', and which shows up in our private lives as periods of anxiousness and panic alternating with times of indifference and carelessness, with loose energy and adrenalin addiction, is not in itself a 'true state of affairs', even though we might like to imagine that it is. The ethical approach to these and related phenomena reveals rather the human spirit in search of freedom. Neither does a 'true state of affairs' lie just below the surface, waiting to be intellectually perceived.

It is our ability to suffer that comes into its own here. Beginning with our private lives, here we experience the misery of being intellectually out in the cold. There is physical illness, which makes no sense to us because we have lost the rational point of reference. Unhappiness besets us like a punishment from God and we feel singled out due to cruel injustice while experiencing the temptation to call ourselves fools for our pursuit of the truth. Bad habits of thought, indulged in for the momentary relief, turn into death threats and it occurs to us that we have nothing to live for.

Suddenly the compulsion to take out our frustration on our environment exerts itself. We are going to change the world even if that means merely to change appearances – and even if that implies nothing but destruction. We feel we have just cause to inflict pain. We create disorder and call it a new order. We are evidently not loved, so why should we love? We are not even liked, so we have reason to hate. – This profile of non-suffering shows how the unethical approach takes its toll. Masses become apathetic whereupon masses engineer a revolution.

*

When faced with death, we can either run away from it and die or suffer and live. In fact we can suffer and have more life. An intellectual understanding of this is possible but what we need is a passionate concern. We are born with that passionate concern and no one can take it from us.

When we read in the Gospel according to Mark, for example, that the Son of Man "must suffer many things and be despised" (Mk. 9:12) we prick up our ears. Why 'must' this be? It sounds almost as if something like a natural law is involved here. Is it possible that here we have a clue towards the understanding of our misery? Might it make sense? In Luke we read: "The Son of Man must suffer many things and be rejected by the elders and chief priests and scribes and be slain and be raised the third day," (L. 9:22). That is a case of despising and 'setting at nought' with a vengeance. Right away we ask: Does this apply to the Son of Man in ourselves? Must our own true human nature become contemptible in the eyes of certain outside agencies and be destroyed? Is this unavoidable if we are to really and truly live? If so, then we would be wise to cease from labours of clinging to our reputation, to our standing in Society and to our justification and assertion of our self, because we are fighting a losing battle. It would mean that all those psychic labours amount to our running away from death and therefore to dying, against our will and in utter frustration, increasingly miserable as we try to repress the truth about it.

*

When I equate the expression 'Son of Man' with 'our true human nature' I am not suggesting that the latter could be used for the former within the context of the former. What matters for me is that within the context of our Western culture we find an expression that will do duty for us similar to that done by 'Son of Man' in the context that was envisioned by Jesus. When I speak of my true human nature I am, by the fact of saying it is mine, indicating that I have accepted, as working within myself, this agency of which I always wish to take account. When we speak of 'true human nature' we mean it insofar as it may be accepted or appropriated, in other words in its potency. Not power, but potency. We have the power as soon as we agree to cooperate with this agency, in other words as soon as we make its business our own, which includes our patient and knowing acceptance of any dire pressures from 'outside', which we do well to choose to suffer intelligently. It would never do for us to pretend that we still live in a time when the Son of Man is not yet return-

247

ing or coming, as modern man pretends. <u>One of our tasks is to rise from the moderns.</u> It happens to be a complicated issue. True human nature is not ours until we acknowledge it as both creatively fertile within us and at the same time affective from without.

In this apparent duality, of course, lies the difficulty. It brings us back to what we mean by suffering rather than 'flying in the face of god' or 'being in pain'. Death reaches both outward and inward, and for that very reason, if truth be known, so that the Son of Man as the 'being one' and as 'the coming one' should both be acknowledged and made one by us. Running away from death therefore means a denial of true human nature, whereas through suffering in a certain way we are able to employ death and the signs of death as invitation to life.

We do well to think of suffering as work. Ethical suffering, as we might also call it, to get away from the notion of it being the same as being in pain, is of benefit both to me and to others. A work stems from it. In the case of Jesus, his work was his exemplary behaviour which could not but shine evidential light and fire the imagination of man. From our contemporary, privileged point of view beyond all times and ages, we can fully appreciate the ethical prestige of Jesus in terms of both its productivity and counter-productivity in the world, having "come not to bring peace but a sword, etc.", on the one hand, and on the other hand making available the peace beyond understanding to those who espouse his cause.

So if we can view our present misery, whenever it happens to be upon us, as practicably indicative of available true human nature then we not only accept the word of Jesus: "blessed are those who sorrow" (Mt. 5:4) but we also have our work cut out for us, because we know that even though we have no individual evidence of this true human nature at that present moment, we nevertheless allow it to place our misery in perspective so that we may get our hands on it and shape it, and by so doing we testify then, do we not, to that true human nature, which then does give evidence of itself as 'ideal inspiration' if you like, or as creative energy, or as fortuitous events in our life, but in its own good time and not at a time we choose. We work with the 'being one' so as to be ready for the 'coming one'. Insofar as the two dovetail we have true human natural being.

The view of our misery against the backdrop of true human nature allows us to suffer creatively.

However, we must get away from imagining true human nature as a static matter of opinion or as an extinct-scientifically objective force-field patient of application to natural laws. It only seems like that, and only at such times as when we have started to disown our misery, by saying: This has nothing to do with me, I need to be rid of it <u>before</u> I can even begin to be active and effective. Also there is more to suffering than quietly putting up with our misery and enduring in the sense of gritting our teeth and hoping it will soon be over. Such mock-heroic holding out, in the absence of any evidence of our knowing what we are doing in terms of true human nature that would be ours, still has nothing about it that can be called ethical.

*

We have to admit, I'm afraid, that it does not lie in our power to 'suffer creatively' – that is to say: to suffer – unless we understand our own physical and spiritual limitations in the light of the god who would do us good. As soon as we suppose that we might usefully alter our state by imposing our unregenerate will on conditions, circumstances, surroundings and environment, we actually and virtually shut ourselves off from that major source of good which cannot in any other way be accessed by us except outwardly by way of ethical attitude and approach to circumstances. How do I speak to the next person I meet? How do I behave when I feel too hot or too cold? Do I acknowledge at all the existence of my community? The fact that I live on the earth rather than on Mars of Venus, what difference does that make to me? When I get a headache, how do I cope with that? If someone insults me, belittles me or shames me and I have unavoidably reacted, what is my next move? Do I recognize the rights of other beings on the earth and am I willing to acknowledge my human responsibility towards them? When things are not going my way, do I try to change them, into other things, or do I search for the beings I have misunderstood?

Questions such as these pertain to my ethical outward behaviour. I am in a position to address these and related issues once I have taken into account, with sufficient good habit, my true human nature, having made it mine, owned it in other words, otherwise I have no power to overcome any egotistic dependence on things or even to recognize that they are not beings. In order to be able to cope ethically with the outward world, more specifically with outward world, or simply world, I must be inwardly intact. At least the tap root must be in place. Then, as I interact with world-being, and as I notice that here and there I am on shaky ground, I may take pains to put down subsidiary roots, but this cannot make sense to me until that initial good habit of creative suffering has been established so that I can even recognize world as being.

*

Why must the Son of man be "set to nought", despised and killed? Why must this be? What sort of a law is at work here? Why do I write this down and not talk about it to someone? Because the letter kills?

The illusion of human nature is rich and strange. We like to elaborate upon it artfully. We like to imitate and to explicate and we do it with a passion. We do not like it that our human natural passions, emotions, feelings and senses should be de-

250

pressed and repressed, as they are automatically by circumstances beyond our control. So we let them play. Out in the open we trust them no longer, they have too often betrayed us. We provide an interior time-space for them, to allow them breathing space. However there is more to this than 'Ersatz'. It is not simply a case of letting our pony trot within the fenced confines of a pasture so that it will not run off and tread the neighbour's crops. The worker in art makes concessions to mortal sin but he aims at blessedness. I do not mean the <u>artist</u> but the <u>art-worker</u>. He imagines the life of pleasure but limns and trims it to the life of truth. With every fantastic move he makes, he annexes yet another patch of down-to-earth reality. Here in the person of the art-worker then we have the one who shows us the natural man under duress and in stress, set upon by circumstances outside his ken and given to ambitions and foibles that reveal to us the full extent of his mortality. The art-worker is the one among us who says with every one of his works: Let the natural man find his way. Make room for him and observe his passage. Let him come to no harm but neither isolate him from the elements, against the truth – against death.

The natural man is incomparable first and then irrepressible. Let us above all be aware of his inner own sanctity. Those who know art for what it is and for what it amounts to, have the natural man always within range of their experience. They do not insist on a picture of him that is ideal or in any way predetermined for that matter but they honour his transience, even if they do it in pictures. Communication with him in images suits him admirably. Let us suffer him to come onto us.

In terms of the natural man we may suffer and know what we are about, for the natural man finds his way among the ruins of antiquity as readily as in the traffic of the big cities and he travels in each of us, whether we know it or not.

*

251

Let us suffer the natural man to come onto us. What we do without thinking is reject him. And he must be rejected in the sense that any experience we have of him – or of her, since we may equally speak of the natural woman – has to succeed, even in awareness, as an initial reaction in unawareness. Most of us are not born with a serious talent for creative art-work, though we may all readily acquire the skill that then allows us to overcome the disadvantageous effects of our initial and automatic rejection of the natural man or woman. Would it be better if we spoke of the natural human being?

In any case, we cannot help it; to begin with, we reject this inscrutable being that stirs in us and we cannot have it otherwise. What counts is that we get to know more and better the effects of our rejection, so that we are not ruled by them, making our decisions according to them and supposing that we live and die when in truth we are only stimulated by the evil of our resistance to natural being and experiencing the effects of it.

When those effects are upon us, it is time to suffer the natural human being to come onto us. When we do this, others have the benefit of it too. True art has this as its chief goal, that the true human-natural being should be revealed where reaction to it and rejection of it has set in and accumulated.

*

It begins with puberty and adolescence. Think back to the time when you began to dream those dreams that frightened you. Notice in your breast right now how the image of a certain person makes your blood boil. It starts with unknown, unfamiliar disturbances of our organs. They are bound to seem unpleasant, inconvenient, terrible, devastating. What we generally, today, refer to as our sexuality is on the move during those early years when we are sons and daughters and not yet husbands and wives. The teenager is strapped into a system of preplanned achievements because his elders are frightened of how he is developing. Something happens to the young when they begin to look in on themselves and the terrain is both singular and unique. They panic. I know that I panicked. I also hid that panic quite successfully from those around me. They too managed to hide it. I hardly ever hid it from myself. In that I was blessed; I cannot take the credit for it.

I would like to believe that the individuation of my male sexuality caused me the greatest difficulties. I suppose it makes sense. The change from boy to man, as from girl to woman, is central to our development. No one explained to me that 'the Son of man must be raised.' No one discussed with me the issue of emerging human-natural being. That was not part of the culture of my teens. Granted, I was unique. But so are you. If you were not, if you were one of the popular masses who pride themselves on their identity, you would not be reading this book.

I write now from the reason of my heart and I work out this reason artfully. The central theme of the book is by no means lost. It runs underground. This reason of the heart was frightened out of me, I guess after the age of eight. It was not frightened out of me suddenly, although there was no shortage of sudden frights, but over the period of the next at least fourteen years. I have always been a late developer. Better late than never. But beings develop at their own rates. Those who standardize life are the frighteners. In spite of my own development, successful in the sense that 'I made it through' I myself have at times been a frightener. My heart contracts with regret. When I notice that in myself, I know there is hope for me.

"The Son of man must be betrayed into the hands of ..." but woe to those who do the betraying. I know both the betrayal and the woe. I am an ordinary human being trying to find my way, certain there is one.

In those very early days, prior to the prolonged fright, even the second world war could not touch me except of course very

253

indirectly through the mortal pain of my mother who fought to keep me and my sister alive, while my father fought too in a sense, in Russia, mostly to keep himself alive.

I would like to make clear that what began to perplex me from the age of eight onwards has never been explained to me. It was belittled, repressed, knocked out of me by well-meaning parental adults at home and at school, but it was never explained. I hope I exaggerate. I feel today that the betrayal was thorough. Not I was betrayed but that energy pulsing within me and longing for acknowledgment. It found no raw outlet as such, and that was just fine, because that would have meant real trouble, but neither did it come up against any genuine, transforming strength. I grew up outwardly but not inwardly. School twisted me every year and dropped me gasping into incredible summer holidays when life went into reverse.

I try today to set my own three children an example of human strength and weakness, and of informed faith in life. Can anyone do more? I could teach them French and promise them careers but where would be the point? It frightens me when they begin to challenge my authority but I have experienced a worse fear and I hope they learn even from my stupidities.

During puberty boys and girls become aware of each other as male and female. This is a drastic discovery, depending in character and intensity much on how they were brought to that point. Ethical art is also a case of a 'proper' upbringing. That word 'proper' would annoy me if I did not know that I meant by it that which pertains uniquely to a singular human being.

There is really no need to refer directly, in abstract terms, to the regenerative instinct in a child's presence. What brings a child much more successfully round is forbearance and frequent clearance of the communication channels. We know, we wise grown-ups, that the raw energies of the heart must be channelled to the head before strength can come about and we know to expect their premature, precocious, presumptuous attempts to avoid that destiny, so the onus is on us, surely, to prepare ourselves and to be prepared, for "as the days of Noah were, so also shall the coming of the Son of man be," (Mt. 24:37) and "...in such an hour as ye think not, the Son of man cometh" (Mt. 24:44), so "watch therefore, for ye know neither the day nor the hour when the Son of man cometh," (Mt. 25:13) and equally: "The kingdom of God comes not with observation ... for the kingdom of God is within you. (L17:21)

*

Of what nature then is our parental preparation, so that we can do children some good, rather than hindering their passage from youth to maturity. In our community many children look to us for guidance. What I intend to say here applies not only to the children of my own family. It makes a great difference how I speak to the boy or girl at the corner of the street or in the queue at the butcher's. Our general attitude to the young is under discussion here.

At the same time I intend this to be an example of ethical action specifically in terms of the 'Son of Man' approach to reality, where the true human nature that stirs in a young person may be countenanced and at the same time honoured. Or is it the young person him- or herself we must honour while we countenance that true human nature? [i]

Our perplexity here points to the duality that appears to be setting in with puberty. It makes no sense to speak of a union of individual nature and universal personality in the case of a

---

[i] Compare Lk. 12:8-9 – Whosoever shall confess me before men, him shall the Son of man also confess before the angels of God, but he that denieth me before men shall be denied before the angels of God. Also: Lk. 9:26 – For whosoever shall be ashamed of me and of my words, of him shall the Son of man be ashamed, when he shall come in his own glory, etc.

child, only in the case of a mature adult. As adults we recognize that we as children had, and children we know now have, a oneness to which we ourselves have for some time aspired and with maturity we achieved it, but we went through an often painful period when our childhood seemed lost, and as we tried to make sense of this and to fight our way through the threat of meaninglessness, unworthiness and incompetence, it may have helped us to learn in one way of another that: "… the Son of man is come to save that which was lost," (Mt. 18:12) and that: "…the Son of man is not come to destroy men's lives, but to save them." (Lk. 9:56). Also – "…the Son of man is come to seek and to save that which was lost." (Lk. 19:10) Certainly I myself had no explicit help from that direction at all, I mean in terms of organized religion. Once in a while however some adult in my vicinity would make a remark that opened a window for me or that eased my existential pain. My gratitude today stands. What they pointed out to me was sometimes quite simply that a human being has to go through some quite crucial developments at that stage of his life and that the difficulties I was experiencing did incidentally signify that I was a human being. A part of my motivation here is that I would like to pass on the favour. Had it not been for the odd encouraging remark, who knows where I might have ended up.

So we can easily imagine 'the child' as all of a piece and not divided in 'itself', in him- or herself, even during periods of grief or high playfulness, when it seems to become even more obvious that the child is 'all grief', or playful to the point of self-forgetfulness, if indeed there is a self to forget. I also find it tricky to refer to 'the child' as himself or herself, surely because gender is not yet established, while it seems wrong to say 'itself'. In German we have the neuter article, 'das' Kind, but the possessive pronoun limits us again to male and female.

It becomes rather difficult, by comparison, to imagine 'the adolescent' as 'all of a piece' and undivided. Individuality can become a problem and personality an issue. One feels almost inclined to say that they are bound to become problematic and an issue. They draw attention to themselves. Indeed they come into being. Where there was the one, namely childhood, there are now more and more the two: individuality and personality, during development towards adulthood and maturity; towards manhood and womanhood, more specifically. This development, this passage from the one to the other, is not automatic by any means. Very few actually get through. Most get stuck or over-shoot the mark. This sounds like a terrible thing to say but we do well to face it. The immature adult is neither a child nor a man or a women. Development is either arrested or distorted or over-stretched. A child, by the way, is not immature; is not childish either, unless spoiled by immature adults.

*

One thing we can do now is come up with a nice theoretic pic-ture of how individuality broadens, personality depends and a man or a woman, singular, unique and whole, is the result. An ideal that would be, and we could hold it up in front of one an-other and urge one another to realize it. We could, in other words, make life downright uncomfortable for one another and get nowhere much ourselves.

Something much more useful would be working examples of broadening individuality and deepening personality, so that we might develop a taste for this, a desire for doing it ourselves be-cause we can tell what can be gained.

These examples need to point human beings to their own in-dividuality and to their own personality and they need to be offered by someone who has indeed worked out how these two can be made one.

My own individuality is unique, like no one else's under the sun or ground. Indeed my individuality is my reason for being on the earth, so naturally it would make good sense for me to find out as soon as possible what it amounts to. At the time of puberty I began to get opportunities to do this, and those few adults in my vicinity who had a notion of what it means to grow up and to be raised helped me with it. When I speak of individuality characteristically broadening, I insist that this can only brought about, as an ongoing process of insight, reflection and experimentation. It certainly does not just *happen*.

The period of growing up and being raised implied a time when I as an up and coming person, along with caring persons around me, took an interest in my individuality as a source of knowledge as to who I was, what I should be doing and what I might eventually amount to. Of course I hourly and daily acted out this individuality, sometimes absurdly, sometimes rudely or deceptively, often haphazardly, but then those were the raw-materials I had to work with. What I wish to emphasize is that individuality is not a state or a quality but a spring of action and passion that demonstrates the aforementioned knowledge for the one who is involved in it and involved with it, and preferably knowledgably and carefully involved. Also others, who can be indirectly involved, can bring care and insight to the process and do everyone including themselves some good.

*

This spring of action and passion, this source of energy, of generative capacity, needs of course first of all to be noticed, to be identified, otherwise it takes the person over. This does not mean that this creative energy is dangerous or bad, but rather

258

that on that particular occasion when it took that person over there was not enough personality. We could talk about it in terms of face and race. Human race looks for its face, which the human being must supply, otherwise the human racial impulse is experienced as a negative or destructive force. The face is supplied in terms of reflection, which is a thought process.

When we reflect on the human individuality in terms of depression and aggression, we make still more headway. In the case of the aggression, when we find ourselves wanting to be aggressive and to attack, we need to know that the creative impulse is upon us but that the aggression must be repressed. That we can differentiate between the two, between the impulse and our experience of it, this is important. We must learn to take the responsibility for our experience of the creative impulse and we must be careful not to confuse or conflate the two. Awareness comes into its own here. An attentiveness to our state of being is of the essence. To note that we feel or even are aggressive is not enough, because we need to know that we are misconstruing the essence of life. There is the essence of life, at that moment available to us, and there is our misconstruction of that tremendous event, by which we cause the aggressiveness. What is of the essence, literally, is that we repress this aggressiveness and so make good the misconstruction. This takes presence of mind, lots of preparation in terms of a good grasp of this teaching, and eventually a good habit of behaving like this in the emergency.

In the case of depression we should have an easier time of it, but it depends on our temperament. Again we are being creatively motivated, but this time our potential aggressiveness is being repressed for us, by no matter what, and all we have to do is agree with that and be glad of it. Again the understanding is of the essence. Of course if we resist the depression, misunderstanding the reason and purpose of it, we fall foul of it and are personally dragged down – just as in the case of aggression, unless we repress, we are personally carried away.

*

The greatest difficulty usually seems to be our reluctance to accept that a creative motivation underlies the aggression and the depression. Let's stick with those two for the moment because between them they sum up an almost tragic modern predicament. It's as if a special dispensation were required before reality can be understood not to be based on appearances. In the presence of those who know, however, we are much more likely to catch on, because our depression and aggression rubs off on them and infects them, whereupon they deal with it rationally, in themselves, and with us mercifully. As a consequence we become curious. Their ethical behaviour by example and through immediate influence instils in us a desire for moral integrity and possibly for ethic power. We get a sense of, a taste for, the satisfaction from doing good. We become capable then of sustaining that extra dimension to our being which could be called the foundation of reality.

Our individuality then broadens in the sense that we are able to allow for the individuality of others. An exciting development takes place. Not only I am unique but you are unique too. To some that comes as a marvellous revelation because right away they get wind of the potential. How can both of us be unique and yet at the same time more communicative than ever! They experience the communicativeness as soon as they allow for the other one's individuality. So now they wonder what it is they share with the other one that makes both of them unique. On the surface it sounds as if one were saying that one and the same thing makes both of us totally different. The apparent contradiction and absurdity is caused by our bad habit of thinking and imagining in terms of things, not beings. The paradox which is frequently switched on in such cases sheds a poor light. Thing-bound logic has to be got rid of altogether, deeply ingrained though it is in our modern strategies of spirit and flesh.

The energy in me is not different from the energy in you. It is one and the same creative motivation. It urges us to get up and do. However it contains in itself nothing moral or ethical. Neither can it be experienced as such. The only evidence we have of its existence is negatively, that we become aggressive or depressed, or positively, that we do good, that we do ethical work. The aggressive ego is always an emergency, while the depressed self is a distinct advantage; if we have that in mind we can respond ethically in both cases.

In view of all this now, our individual uniqueness becomes apparent as soon as our personality draws attention to itself. Remember, we spoke of puberty in terms of a beginning of this polarity, where we become aware of a two-ness in ourselves, of individuality and personality.[i] Concentration on individuality at the exclusion of personality would falsify our insight and make us narrow, just as personality at the exclusion of individuality makes us shallow.

So at the same time, off and on, as we distinguish in ourselves this motivating creative energy, allowing for it in one another, we also become capable of attitude, of disposition, one might almost say: of appropriate language. We have been talking for a while, but now we learn to speak. There is quite a difference.

---

[i] The often quoted passage from Goethe's Faust I comes to mind: (Faust I, Verse 1112-1117) *Zwei Seelen wohnen, ach! in meiner Brust, Die eine will sich von der andern trennen; Die eine hält, in derber Liebeslust, Sich an die Welt mit klammernden Organen; Die andere hebt gewaltsam sich vom Dust, Zu den Gefilden hoher Ahnen.* (Two souls live in my breast. The one wants to separate from the other. The one clings to the world, in lust for life, with clinging organs. The other forces itself out of the dust, into the domain of noble ancestors.)

We present ourselves in a certain way and we do so for a reason. What I mean to imply is that we are well advised to do so and to overcome any hindrances to it.

Personality is our contact, first of all, with other beings and the world at large, but it is not an accidental contact. Personality is originally my wish to be myself. This wish to be myself meets with satisfaction as I undertake to come to terms with you – and with other beings, (not things). To come to terms with – to discover or invent a common language – this is what lies at the root of personality. We can tell how this wish is, of course, energetically and individually informed; just as in the case of all creative energy and information, if we know what we are about, there is noticeable a personal trait; and this is reassuring, in that it lets us know that we are on the right track, while in no way should we tire of working on: now our personality and now our individuality.

*

It begins with puberty and the essence of it is the process of maturation. But we are not talking about a plant here. For all this to work out, rational intelligence and good will must be part of the process. This is always a risk, that one speaks of ethical progress as though it might happen anyway. And of course it makes good sense that a human being should become ethically aware and capable somewhere between the age of twelve and twenty but equally we know fine well how many influences work in the opposite direction or in no direction at all, so that more often than not what someone has managed by the age of thirty, say, is a type of social morality, but of true ethics nothing is known. The desire for it has been buried under concerns for survival. If the urge for genuine morality is awakened now, the task of distinguishing profound personality from a liberal individuality is much more complicated, mostly because of all the bad habits that have been formed. 'Bad' here is whatever stands in the way of real ethical development, and a social morality may in itself present just such a hindrance. Of course there is no need to break down such hindrances prior to any real advance, and in fact such a kicking over of moral traces is in itself no guarantee of anything worthwhile at all, but it can be understood as a beginning of the search for the good. My main point here is that the best time for ethical growth is while youth is ready to mature.

*

Personality and communication go so much hand in hand that we could nearly say they are one and the same. An ethical personality says everything. It is also a very rare achievement. It must be informed and resourced by our individual human nature if it is not to become false, but at the same time I myself must be the one who does the personal communicating and who is aware of his individual resources.

Now here we have arrived at a point of no return again where we have to be careful that it does not happen to us as it does to so many. We agree that there is this opening discrepancy or growing distinction between personality and individuality. We feel alright about that because it agrees with our own experience, both of ourselves and of others. We are also able to some extent now to identify personality in ourselves, informed by individuality, and we are able to take account of individuality in ourselves, personally communicated. We may be happy enough with this teaching because we can readily enough apply it to ourselves, to our experience, and we can, so to speak, own it.

What happens now, usually, is that someone comes along, or a small voice in ourselves comes along, and asks: Ah, but how are these two, this individuality and this personality, now that you have begun to identify them, to be unified? There must be an agency in the name of which, or by means of which, or on account of which, this can succeed. – So the ego, the I, steps forward and says: Let me be the one. I will invent and reinvent myself suitably for every single given occasion that comes up. Leave it to me. I will let you know how I get on. I will harness your intellect and make all the necessary connections. I will count on your willpower to supply the justifiable motivation for doing and reason for being. Sacrifice your body to me, your senses, your feeling, emotion and passion, and I will present you, in exchange, with an ever growing body of testable and provable knowledge. It will excite you at first and you can take all the credit for accumulating all this knowledge; towards the end this knowledge will even seem to you, for some time, nearly complete – most significantly so when you begin to tire of it and to lose interest in it. However not to worry. If there is any life left in you, I will start you on something else, to keep you occupied and out of harm's way, while gaining recognition for my efforts, which is alright by me because I gain something much more important meanwhile. What that is you might have known at one time and you might even have regretted losing it but soon you will be so insensible to it and so addicted to this so-called objective or subjective knowledge that you will thank me for helping you out. It's all quite simple. Instead of referring to yourself, refer to your ego or self. That's me. Instead of espousing your responsibility, espouse me. Turn me into your messiah, if you like. You will never know the difference, I guarantee it.

So speaks the ego, the self, the I, or whatever else we want to call it – notice, not him or her. The ego or self is genderless. Whatever it manages for us becomes equally genderless. We can sign away our entire manhood or womanhood if we like. We are no longer male then, and certainly not masculine or men, but sexed males. We are no longer female, as at the beginning, and certainly not feminine or women, but sexed females. A certain

264

undeniable prestige readily attaches to sexed males and females; they are admired and imitated. They bestow their autographs.

Once I have begun to become aware of a distinct individuality and unique personality in myself, and also in others, and I understand that these two must first be identified before – and so that – they may be unified, then I myself am the only one who can bring this about. It is not up to my energy, my intelligence, my awareness, my sense of conscience or duty, and certainly not up to my self or ego, but simply up to me. This is the beginning of <u>true ethical maturity</u>, when I can refer to myself and not mean my self. It is also always and again the end of our immaturity, however often it should set in.

*

This difference between a person and his or her ego is of such importance that I never miss an opportunity to comment on it. There comes a time during any discourse on any topic that impinges upon reality or truth when one cannot avoid speaking in the first person singular. So for example when personality and individuality are properly identified, it can only be I myself in whom they can be made one. This 'making one' is the ethical act per se and it cannot be delegated. We can neither teach with integrity nor preach with propriety unless we make our unified and whole being individual and personal.

However it must be emphasized that once we have managed to sustain the duality of person and nature for any period of time at all, we are no longer merely human, that is to say human in the sense of the humanist or the anthropologist, but we have become capable of being – shall we call it: fully human?

This difference between merely human and fully human has to be understood if we are to avoid the ego-trap. Those who are merely human readily class themselves with the 'other animals' and see in that no slight. Being above the animals in any sense of the word 'above' causes them unease because they can only imagine this in terms of abusive control. However we are lower and less than that which we abuse and once we are above it we bear an ethical responsibility for it.

So to be fully human means to be in creative cooperation with good spirit. Who am I, while I am in creative cooperation with good spirit? I am fully human and myself. Whatever I do while I am fully myself, whether I build a house or reflect, pray of take a bath, write a word or help a child cross the street, is done cooperatively with good spirit. When I refer to myself therefore, in contrast to my ego, I mean myself inasmuch as I cooperate with good spirit. My relationship with the being who embraces all beings is such that I cannot conceive of myself as outside that relationship. Certainly my personality does not take me outside it, so I know that this being was personal before I am.[i] As for my individual human nature, I can only conceive of that as created.

From such a point of view now I am able to claim honourably that I am both naturally individual and ethically personal. It does however take some small effort for me to sustain such a point of view. My ethical awareness allows me to refer to myself as fully human, but as soon as I lose that awareness, I become merely human and stand in need of correction.

Now that small effort, small though it is, seems to be all too often too much for us and we would rather expend great individual energy or make laborious personal efforts – when it comes to what we call doing something, or working, or being diligent and industrious, little realizing that outside the cooperative relation-

---

[i] Compare: Gospel of John 8:58

ship with good spirit we cannot do anything of real value or true worth, however much we are admired for it and emulated by those around us.

*

No man or woman is good. That would be like saying we are good spirit, which would be absurd. On the other hand what exactly are we, if we have nothing of good spirit in ourselves? Can we call ourselves human beings? Beset as we are on all sides in any case by spirits that militate against our human being, we have no choice except to be ethical or perish. All non-human beings depend on us to make the right choice. Look how we dig and delve, how we poke our scientific noses into everything in any case, not a thing in the world is safe from our critical spirit, it seems we cannot help ourselves, we must be connected by a cord to all that is – so why not make it ethic relationship; why not introduce into every meeting with beings around us our concern for their welfare, since we alone can assure them that, even as, by doing so, we ourselves become fulfilled.

We can invite good spirit into ourselves. We can receive it; it presses in upon us in any case. Do we not know our misery?

Once we have good spirit in ourselves and not just in one or more of our parts or members, we are in the enviable position of being able to conduct ourselves with perfect autonomy. You might say that our name finally stands for something.

*

The interest we take in beings around us must however be free of <u>critical spirit</u> if those beings are not to don their thing-masks in our presence. Watch what happens to the person next to you when you criticize him or her. Immediately a defensive mask goes up and you can no longer know him, though what you do come up with at the time will probably satisfy you because those appearances of fearful defensiveness will seem to justify your thirst for evidence. So it is with things. Through them and by means of them beings give us enough rope to hang ourselves.

The critical spirit is the main offender of the modern age and those who participate in it really produce the modern age. Two thousand years ago, when Jesus of Nazareth was asked by the authorities "are you the Messiah?" his response created such a crisis that those who had stage-managed the affair ushered in the critical spirit which has plagued mankind ever since. The need for evidence, for a sign, was finally satisfied, as it were in cosmic proportions. Thereafter it became clear very quickly that the critical spirit produced quite readily the evidence it needed to justify its existence. If the thirst for evidence, for justification, is upon you, do not search in your breast for faith in personal good spirit, which would dissipate that craving, but league yourself with the critical spirit and soon that craving will be satisfied – of course for a short time only.

What exactly is that craving for evidence and justification that causes us to behave so stupidly? Is it not just simply an unavoidable reaction to a challenge by our capacity for faith? The modern age is singularly faithless and yet one can see everywhere evidence of a cry for faith, of a deep-seated need for that true foundation of all our senses if knowledge is to be down to earth and practical for human beings, not for demons or angels. Dozens, hundreds of different faiths make not a jot of difference to our modern predicament because they are not faith and in them faith is not elemental but dogmatic.

*

The "abomination of desolation"[i] is what the critical spirit produces, in fact what it is, when left to its own devices, so we have to be careful. A calculated offensive against this spirit is inconsequential. Really what we have to do is quietly get out of the way, step back and offer our condolences. The message must be clear: you are not wanted.

At the same time let us countenance our soul's cry for faith. That we have a capacity for faith is as human natural as that we have eyes, ears and a nose, but we limit ourselves strangely to the use of the latter. What have we to fear from faith? Only the loss of our ego. But that is always a great loss, so it seems, in proportion to our personal identification with it. It begins, perhaps, with a desire to be more interesting or significant in the eyes of those around us. It is 'their eyes' that matters to us, not our own. Right away to that extent we have lost faith.

Or we arrange our life in such a way that the modern prejudices prevail. We would like to appeal to the norm, to the prevailing standards of morality and we cannot help ourselves but we must take pride in how close we come, as we call the total agreement perfection while we 'humbly' consent it may not be achieved, however … etc. etc.

What my words amount to at the moment is not criticism but a critique. The difference is vital. During a critique we limit ourselves faithfully to a response to that which is faithless, and our response may be personal and instructive. But criticism is a faithless reaction to faithlessness. When we are critical, we have not overcome the effect on us of some faithlessness but we merely cast it back with renewed force.

---

[i] Compare Mk. 13:14.

The hallmark of faith itself is always that we need no evidence or justification to come up with the truth. This is frightening, of course, for those who insist that – and whose existence is based on the supposition that – nothing can come up except as evidential or justifiable.

So the first degree is simple faithlessness, which stems from neglect. The second degree actually incorporates an insistence on the impossibility of faith.

The terrible truth is that faithless sensation invents for itself an external (extinct) body of proof, thus ensconcing itself in a kind of witlessness. One's purpose is then to preserve that witlessness, perhaps to call it objective-scientific fact. What it really amounts to is a crying shame.

And why should we all be so eager to demonstrate our bondage to the critical spirit? Because it instils in us the delusion of self-importance. We do understandably become attached to that. Year after year it becomes harder to give it up. Why should we not be as we seem? We may well be as we seem, who can say. Our self is the one thing that needs no proof, being self-evident – strange as that may sound. The self-evidence of our self can be injected 'worthily' into our perception of 'reality out there' too. Let no one underestimate the consolation of an 'a priori' aspect to reality. Its effect is that of an article of faith. We have an article of faith here that firmly nails down the lid on the coffin of dead faith. The self-evident self is projected into the world of objectively scientific things; beings haven't a chance with us now. It only remains for us to be led by the hand by some 'historic process' now, towards some unavoidable nirvana/catastrophe.

*

No ethics can thrive within range of the critical spirit. Ethical thought is distorted and falsified by it. Ethical feeling is simply killed off.

We should not suppose that the senses can, in the absence of faith, be 'channels of perception'. The critical spirit automatically moves in and takes over. It becomes at once 'modus vivendi' of and 'raison d'être' for the modern man and woman. Should we fight it? Are we not perfectly content in our belligerent, indifferent shell? Are we not always so close to perfect success that the remainder may be ignored?

The only way to rid ourselves of the critical spirit and of our dependence on it is via a thoroughgoing critique. This means that we voluntarily and intentionally, and if necessary quite contrary to appearances, distinguish between our individuality, our unique and singular nature, and our personality, our power of communication.[i] The critical spirit knows only the assertive or deserving self. That view of the self we must shun utterly and not attempt to engage with it in any manner of form.

*

A critique of the self is not possible, but a critique of my self, by me, is. The outcome of such a critique, and the achievement of it, must be, incidentally, the destruction of my self, but more importantly the resurrection of myself. Such an ethical transformation is much to be desired. It brings us back into contact and community with reality and the world. Precisely at times when we feel we have nothing to learn any longer we should take ourselves in hand and question every

---

[i] You might say that the critical spirit moves in where the 'sword brought by Christ' has separated personality from individuality. It enters where it 'ought not to be'; (Mk. 13:14 again.) What ought to be is personality and individuality as one during ehical work.

move we make and every word we speak, because at such a time we may take it for granted that we are carrying an egotistical burden.

I refer especially to myself at the moment. I am more than content with myself. I have no worries. I am liked and esteemed by those around me. From painful experience I know that now is the time for me to search in myself for that pattern of life which is being obscured by my ego as it gradually accumulates in painless reaction to things around me. Immediately I sense also in myself the power to reach out and to meet reality halfway. That power presents itself to me so that I may take it up and wield it. I do so in the interest of a work, this present work in particular.

This power I have now is neither individual-natural nor personal-communal but purely and simply ethical. It is the <u>ethical power</u> that allows me to marry all opposites and contraries, given that those are in fact properly differentiated. It is also the power with which I may look through things into the heart of beings. Neither the magic nor the fascination of things can withstand this power, and a similar power meets it from within the beings with which I engage. I stand now in a working relation with those beings, where power engaging with power is productive of celebration, a work not to be underestimated because it brings into focus for others, you at the moment for example, the life relation, or live relation, of all beings, regardless of their stature. It also then brings the experience of this live relation to bear on some of those who have as yet no inkling of the inherent breakdown that slumbers in things or simply awaits its turn.

*

Ethical power can actually be felt, but only during the exercise of it and never at any other time, such as during periods of

272

idleness or when we are plagued by vain ambition. Were we to describe this feeling, it would again have to be done ethically; in other words the description of it, to be accurate and true, would have to amount to an ethical work.

There is to this power both a developmental aspect, best described perhaps as my support of its being and my inward recognition and celebration of the fact that it is, and that it is an environmental deployment, where we act this power out. The feeling of the power, and even the intention to feel it and to embody it, is developmental and it is one with the intention to act it out when the time is ripe. With reference to this ethical power then, premature activity is as wrong as indifferent development.

We should perhaps mention that it is impossible to have a feeling of this power, an emotion or a passion for it. Ethical power does not lend itself to a one-sided development, neither merely of the heart nor only of the head. Feeling is not the same as feelings or a feeling, nor is emotion and passion the same as an emotion or a passion. Neither is vision and sense the same as a vision or a sensation. This has to do with the truthful doctrine of our human body. We are certainly not capable of sustaining or supporting ethical power while we still confuse body and flesh. Visions, sensations, feelings, emotions and passions are carnal and therefore neither patient nor capable of powerful investment. Whatever is based on sexuality, for example, can neither stand nor hold. Indulgence in carnality destroys us. The very notion of a genuine human body, compared to flesh, depends on a soul, and those who have lost their soul can only come up with carnal power, which can make a big noise in the newspapers but does not change hearts and minds to the good.

So when albeit at an advanced stage of our own development, we set out to develop this ethical power, we do not do so in order to feel powerful and to entertain emotions and passions, or to have visions and sensations, but so that we may eventually make a good difference to our community and environment, to our neighbourhood, family and acquaintances. It's no good getting all fired up to change the world when within ourselves we have nothing to support good change. Being full of ourselves is no substitute for ethical power and no basis for ethical action.

So even for the purpose of ethical power and action we have to distinguish between our body and our flesh, between feeling and feelings, between real power and sensations of mere power.

Neither is the desire, the wish or the will, to feel this power any use to us because once again we are more than likely to get sidetracked by carnal ends. I am glad once again to go into this in detail because after all how often do we come across anyone who has all those fundamental issues decided for himself once and for all time. No, we all falter and mend, we improvise and experiment; we need to renew our commitment, examine our motivations and confirm our strategies, from day to day, if indeed we hope to do good rather than merely fooling ourselves and others.

So when we feel this ethical power, in the interest of development towards performance, we do not get a feeling of it. If we ever do get a 'feel' of it, or for it, then this is after the manner of an invitation, so that we may come up with the goods ourselves, just as our falling in love is so that we may get up and love. If we fly into a passion because our love is not returned or because our good deed is not recognized, then we have obviously rejected the invitation.

*

Ethical power is faith-based and the more of it we have, the better off we are. It does not depend on will, wish or desire but simply on our intention to have and use it. Once again we cannot have it without using it. I sit here now, for example, and I know I have this power even though I have no sensation of it. How do I know I have it? What kind of knowledge is that, if it does not begin with sensation? Elsewhere I have called it faith-knowledge, while hoping no one will suppose I have in mind a creed.

I find it interesting and ultimately quite exciting that this power allows me to use it in a variety of ways. As I mentioned a moment ago, I can feel it, so that I feel powerfully, but can also think it, so that I think ethically and powerfully. Now since I have learned that my soul can be mental or bodily and that feeling and thought are like its two hands, I do not make the mistake of supposing that real thought excludes feeling or that true feeling can be separate from thought. We know by now that our soul is available to us as our mind, as our body, or even in itself. When my mind and my body are both con-sciously involved by me in some process or activity, then this I call physical action. All this cannot come true for us except ethically. My mind is the visible aspect of my soul. This sounds contradictory, but only because we confuse flesh with body and spirit with mind. You should not imagine that you have access to someone's mind except in the visible world, where that someone as a whole person is available to you. Even as you read these words here now, my mind is not there for you, and there is no reason why it should be. What is there for you is your body and your soul, at least in the making. What you feel as you read this, the sense it makes to you, any pas-sionate commitment that results from it, that is what you have and that is your immediate business, all else has to do with critical spirit and at best it is pointless. Let your invisible body be affected by these words and then through it your soul will become more functional for you. Your soul is neither visible nor invisible. Do you suppose it has to be one or the other? Not so. You might as readily suppose that reason should rule all. As soon as we come to terms with our ethical power, we have less and less difficulty with such dualistic concepts that depend on things and on the critical spirit.

So we can simply cooperate with our soul and do this ethically and powerfully. Ethically powerful feeling and thinking are possible for us too, with the emphasis on the one or on the other. Then we can do physical work, where our mind and our body function in unison. Of course in all these cases we must know what we are doing. Mythically these are the four compass directions of our work as it streams out from us.

*

If you would like to know my mind, specifically (even as I might wish to know yours, though that is impossible for me at the moment since I do not know who you are) then you have before you these words and sentences, the manner of their choice and the style of their presentation. You may notice the kind of language I use, how I couple my phrases and how long I go on before I come to a full stop, that sort of thing. This is my mind and you may see it there visible in front of you. How can I know my mind unless and until I reveal it to you? My own mind is there for me once I have entered upon communication. My mind exists in the light of day once I have placed it there and nowhere else. What business have I turning my thoughts and opinions this way and that, juggling concepts until they abide by some alien imposition? What business have I with opinions and thoughts? What I write down for your sake and for the sake of others here and now, or how I behave and speak to you if ever we should meet in person, that reveals my mind to you – and to me too of course. As soon as I come upon a thought, quickly let me transform it, for every moment is precious in its newness and we never exist the same way in the same place twice.

When it comes to my invisible body, I have to tell you about that before you have any notion of it. My body is not readily manifest like my mind. So for example I tell you of my sense perceptions: the brass lamp, with the green glass shade standing on the table in front of me fits into the general visual environment of the room in which I am warm and alone, aware of my wife and child who will soon get up on this Tuesday, March the tenth, and have breakfast, if all goes as usual. I am glad to be able to communicate this to you, happy to be of service. At the same time I feel I should remain keenly aware of my level of performance, of the need for truthfulness. All this, the sense perception, the gladness and happiness, the awareness and sense of duty, amount to my body, and I could tell you much more. There is my sense of contentment at the moment; a sudden feeling of apprehensiveness on the other hand coincident with a change of circumstances which I need not describe, is more a case of my body being threatened, so that I need to do a repair there, as it were, and this has to do with the evil which threatens us all from time to time. This might be a good time to reflect on several possible attitudes to evil when we are threatened in body, mind or soul, or perhaps in flesh or spirit. Being ethically powerful now we are able to face the truth in relation to some of these issues; we should not hesitate to wield this power as much as we can and of course wherever some ethic conquest can be made.

*

If we think of evil as an attack on us, which is not the only way to look at it, then we can observe, almost, how the first thing to go is our ethical power. Part of the attack is that we suppose it to have been a thing, and when we cannot recapture it as a thing we feel downtrodden and contemplate despair.

This despair is an evil aimed at our soul. But remember now that your soul is capable of manifestation as our mind and of production as your body, and it is this capacity, really, of which you despair. You fear you will no longer be able to feel or to think, and this fear does in fact paralyze those two faculties. Physical activity seems to be out of the question.

A quick rearguard action therefore can be imagined as a kind of falling back on our soul and holding out there, in the knowledge that in cooperation with our soul we cannot be vanquished because here our ethical power originates. We can, so to speak, trust our operational soul to see us through the despair.

This is an imaginative approach to the notion of evil. It helps us to think it through a few times so that next time when we are in despair we can right away, as soon as we notice it, own our soul and leave the rest, otherwise we will surely resist the evil and add melancholy to the despair, which is dangerous. The further we get away from our ethical power, as we suppose, the more do we become a prey to destructive thoughts and negative feelings.

*

"Whatever you do in my name ..." was how Jesus of Nazareth put it, and this is the same as the ethical power we mean. Once we know that evil commences with us by rendering us heedless of this, we actually shun this evil. Again, imagination plays an important role. As we shun the evil that would displace it, our ethical power gains strength. Any exercise of our power is better than any attempt to merely cling to it, which always fails in the end. On the other side of the coin there is the danger that imagination turns into pictures. It is enough for us simply to reject this, so that we do not become tied up in our mind or trapped in our body. Ethical power must be exercised in the light of day. We do this even as we reject the critical spirit, for example, for it too would darken our soul and deposit us in a world of things.

*

This is the way evil commences with any human being, you and I included, that things seem more attractive, more meaningful and important, than beings.

Imagine for example how in the realm of appearances we make no distinction, for years perhaps, especially as children, between what we look at and what we see, between what we listen to and what we hear, between what we touch and what we feel. It would not occur to us to speak or think of a realm of appearances, because what we see, hear and touch exists for us automatically in itself and in relation to all else. On closer inspection a fruit tree or a fruit bat reveals to us more of its individual properties, but even these then right away deliver to us more of the relation of that being with others; with a few others, with several others and with many. (As soon as we say: "with all others" we risk picturing a finite universe and the betrayal of a being has started). Now technically we should not even speak of a relation here, because prior to any separation there cannot be a relation, so we would describe that childlike, initially quite innocent state of affairs more accurately if we just limited ourselves to observing what there is not, namely, a discrepancy which is then later, once evil has entered the world, so to speak, recognized in such terms as appearance versus substance, superficiality versus profundity; the very duality of heaven and earth as two different realms or kingdoms stems from our impaired vision, which is an evil impairment, because we can no longer see creation and creatures wholly and completely. We can go so far as to say that the fact of these two words existing testifies to the double vision under which we labour, but language is also a blessing that allows us, if we so desire, to aim and work for a relation of the two from a position of 'relative' comfort.

So the trouble has started when we notice that we can either look up or down, left or right, for or near, but not both at once, and also that we often feel inclined to look only up or down and insist that the whole of reality should reveal itself to us there, and that is really the start of the world of things, sometimes pointedly referred to as 'this world' in classical Christianity and confused even then with the world in any sense.

Duality, double vision, doubt – "offence must come into the world but …" – then the relationship of beings, the completion of experience, the wholeness of reality and the holiness, even, of nature, if you like: this encompasses the sum-total of our human existence, experience and work. From an ethical point of view, it all makes sense again, even the pain, because we are involved in being and doing and no longer much afraid of things or addicted to them.

*

The one-sided, or single-eyed (as it is sometimes called) approach to reality can become fascinating because it offers us the delusion of progress out of pain. Always and again when we cannot make sense of pain because that would involve pointing the finger at ourselves, we point the finger instead at reality and indulge ourselves in vicarious suffering. We feel disadvantaged and unfortunate and then take it out on beings around us – not just on human beings, but on animal, plant, mineral and element beings too. They withdraw from us and we are left with things. We continue to take out our aggravation on them now, which is like beating a dead horse, and we have proof that the horse is guilty because is it not blatantly refusing to pull our cart? No wonder that finally a shout goes up that even God is dead, when here we had produced the thingness of all things, in our misguided enthusiasm, while we lost the ability to love god.

*

The fascination of things and the critical spirit go hand in hand. We are ethically empowered, as human beings, to turn away from both by turning towards god, towards merciful spirit, with persistence if necessary. This turning towards god is a physical move. Our body and our mind are involved. Both our thinking and our feeling play a role. Indeed what part of us can we afford to leave behind when we turn to god, since god is equally within us!

In that sense we can even describe ethics as the power with which we turn to god in the face of whatever would dissuade us from doing so. But such a description is not worth much nowadays because the word god has become almost meaningless. Some of those who are closest to god call themselves atheists because they reject Churches and Religions, while some of those who give themselves out as devout merely cling to an idol. Probably in that respect not much has, after all, changed during the past two millennia, except appearances. The appearance of the idol changes as does the appearance of true religion, while the sum-total of truth and falsehood, of evil and good in the world, very likely remains the same. Let those who want to change the world beware that this urge is not a substitute for a change of heart. A change of heart brings along with it a changed world for us, as anyone will testify who has made the change, but changing the world in itself, what can that mean? It must be a delusion. Can I be changed by you? Can you change me? Can a husband change a wife or a wife a husband – to suit themselves? Those who have proselytized, reasoned and evangelized in the interest of uniformity have brought misery and calamity on the heads of many, including their own.

Any ethic worth it salt must place into the hands of individual human beings the ability to become members of community if they should choose to do so. A member of community has not forfeited his individuality but he has learned to invest it. He does not let his ego run away with him but he represses it in the interest of more ethical power. He does not value any part of any human being above any other but strives to bring them all under the mastery of the personal truth.

*

Now that we have this ethical power identified and in our grasp, we may know it as the <u>rational affection that binds being to being.</u>

Even at this moment we may exercise this power to demonstrate how it operates on this level. We assent to it as much as we initiate it. This is not a paradox. We know that as soon as we turn towards other beings we find that they are turned towards us. We ourselves, alone among all beings, are at liberty to turn away from creation and to distance ourselves from our own inner source of life. We turn into things and all beings around us appear to us to be things. Our ethical power can turn this around for us so that we can bear to face our error and see through the masks donned by beings to protect themselves against our deadliness.

While we exercise our ethical power, we come across no things. The beings we countenance right away persuade us of their genuine existence in the same world along with ourselves. But we have to be on our guard against people who deny their humanity. It is enough that they do not espouse their humanity to make them snares and traps for those who do. But again, our exercise of our ethical power lifts us beyond any risk. We know how vulnerable we ourselves are and we can recall how often in our life we have allowed ourselves to become just such liabilities to others around us, and no doubt we will do it again. But we have a skill of exceeding usefulness now and it is entirely up to us how often and how much we make use of it. Indeed every human being who has ever lived has dreamt of such a singular capacity for moral truth and wholeness because it alone renders life eternal.

We know it as power and thereafter it comes out as a skill, a capacity, a function or faculty and so on. Analysis of it leads nowhere. Always does it integrate distinct individualities into whole realities. This is not easy to describe because along with the description must always come the demonstration and we would all much rather step into ourselves and cease from participation in natural reality before we presume then indifferently as we suppose to observe and represent. Take for example, however, that dichotomy so beloved of the age between nature and art. Separate idols are invariably created because surely one tires of the running imperfection in both camps as one attempts to reside entirely in the one or in the other. Let all be art, we say, and we curse nature so that it shall not interrupt us, and for a while our science, our theology, our very society turns into a veritable conundrum until it takes something like the Lisbon earthquake or a demonic attack of the heart to make us realize we have gone out on a limb. Then we return to nature and hug to ourselves, hopefully for all time from now on finally, the concepts of liberty, equality, brotherhood, so that nature shall no longer be falsified – only to discover in our very hearts the original horrors of vanity, jealousy and greed against which no natural goodness can hold out. The modern approach has ever been to vacillate, so that memory must be short and energy intensified or we might have to face the insufficiency of our egos.

Now look instead how we can lay aside gradually our modern prejudice and presumptuousness by developing, on one hand, an art that inclines both ingeniously and graciously towards our human nature and on the other hand learning to conceive of our human nature as gratefully and responsibly inclusive and representative of all nature, both in general and in the particular. How long do you suppose it will be before the power to behave with ethical effectiveness will settle within your flesh and accommodate your spirit? No one can say but you may be assured that not a second will pass between your readiness and our endowment. Then art becomes natural and nature artful so that the two go hand in hand, as it were one in marriage, although of course, all along, the nature we mean is human in the sense in which humanity is the essence of all being. Nature and art are now the two-handed approach to reality, in reality, because each hand is informed, motivated and guided by the ethical power at our disposal. Of course this power is demeaned and vilified by us while we try to impress ourselves upon the world or while we try to change the world to suit us, especially while we still derive some small pleasure of satisfaction from willing or moaning. Circumstances affect us in manifold fashion, events cut across our expectations and plans, let us not be lulled by periods of relative peace and quiet. "The best peace is relative," you argue, when you should say, quietly to yourself: "I have not yet found the peace that is good."

*

In praise of modesty: Let him praise modesty who is troubled by unnatural pride. For here we have an outward exchange

284

between beings of all types and kinds that takes failure into account and thrives on it as the lowly cucumber on the compost. I would make myself modest if I could but I cannot, being born within range of a physical perfection to which I must needs aspire unless I pay heed to the facts, circumstances and events of the world as they impinge upon me, to render me miserable in my immodesty or to enrich me if I modestly approach.

Let me say from the outset that this modesty is ethically powerful. I shall for a time extol the so-called virtues, though I insist on their rootedness in ethical power.

*

How difficult to extol modesty modestly! And yet it must be done. How much less likely I am suddenly to fill my mouth with words. A modest connection with other beings – a modest rationality – it would see us through the past when we reflect on what has been gathered and considered worth keeping.

Why should the modesty of a man link him to his memory? Perhaps if that man has pitched himself too far ahead of his role in contemporary society, he cannot help himself but he must, if he would save his skin, espouse modesty. By his skin I mean his temporal being as viewed in the light of day. One may walk through the world anonymous and yet have one's finger on the pulse of the times, though mere observation here means nothing. One observes what is old. The past has happened, though memory relives it. And the past is attached to us, whether we know it or not. We remain at liberty to own or disown it. Modestly we may revalue what has, so to speak, passed through us without leaving a trace. We may shelter in the past. It brings us no crown of glory but it leaves us alone where we may heal.

Being an auathor by choice (not my own), I heal in the past tense. It has never particularly weakened me to be left alone by circumstances. I can speak from past experience and record my voice, literally. I make use of my gift then. I am able to become my own circumstance and reflect on my role in the past. I freely admit the past is a stage. It would not occur to me to live in the past, though that happens readily as soon as we make no time for being who we are and what we amount to. We live in the past and wonder why nothing succeeds – whereupon immodesty sets in, for we must somehow prove to ourselves that we live in reality, even though in truth we do not. This immodesty takes a variety of shapes and sizes but we may always know it by the way it causes us to insist on ourselves. All depends then on the number of immodest ones around us. They will sustain us while we lean on them and force their recognition. How can they help it? Our immodesty is in their best interest, and theirs in ours.

How different is the will to power (might) from ethical power! How immodest is this will!

*

How does our modesty support our relationship with other beings?

Here we have to reach deeply within ourselves to discover the root of our connectedness with all creatures. In our modesty we realize we are creatures. How we picture or imagine this is up to us; the fact remains that like the air we breathe and the plants and animals we eat we are creatures. I once observed an immense modesty in the eyes of an animal as it died – when I had killed it. The shame I experienced helped me to discover modesty for myself. I learned about the infinite variety and irreplaceable worth of all that which appears for a time.

Modesty keeps us in touch with the moment. The here and now can be appreciated modestly. Is it not the appearance of a thing that leads us into all sorts of metaphysical confusion, while the appearance of a being is measure in the particular, with which we cannot go wrong? As soon as we transgress particular appearances – or fail to forgive those who transgress them – we lose our sense of measure and are no longer able to relate as a being to other beings. Then we struggle to achieve ends and to uphold standards that have no real existence and are therefore alien to life.

So we need to call to mind, frequently, that things appear the way they do because we have transgressed against beings, and that beings appear the way they do because that is how they are created – and the appearance of a creature is a blessed event. We as human beings have a singular function here, which could be called the <u>benediction of all creatures</u>, namely the saying of: Thus it is good. In that way we do what we are uniquely created to do. Thus it is good, as the appearance of created beings would have it. Accustomed as we are however to fighting our corner as things among things, such a notion must seem to us irresponsible and trite.

*

At any moment of the day we can switch from the will to power, which is egotistic, to ethical power, which involves good will. If we are not yet able to exercise ethical power as such, then let us practise modesty, let us be modest. It is a way to be and assures us being. It is inadvertently ethical and takes us away from our preoccupation with things; with viewing, or rather mis-viewing, beings as things.

Modesty is therefore rational. Being rational it embraces the irrational, in this case immodesty. It is in the case of modesty

287

that we discover successfully the difference between true rationality and the supposed rationality of things.

This supposed rationality is not easy to pinpoint because we indulge ourselves in it and also it comes over us. So usually it has happened to us before we can come to terms with it. The missing ingredient, in comparison to <u>true rationality</u>, is care for being and for other beings, even for one. A healthy anxiety may accompany this care, as may the stress and strain of genuine application. As soon as this care goes missing or is left out, the anxiety, the stress and the strain, remain destructively. It is the care for another being and for other beings that makes our anxiety productive.

*

The test of our rationality is how we deal with the irrational. We come to the conclusion that we have only a short while to live and therefore we must rush. This would be a blatantly irrational move. Or we take ourselves in hand and we say: Now we are going to plan every move we make and then act accordingly. This would be equally irrational. In both cases we leave out of account the pain and misery of our existence as it comes and goes and we can neither control nor predict it. A human-natural modesty helps us preserve a sense of proportion. Because it is human-natural, this modesty, we can be modest. We can choose to be modest, right now. Not that our irrationality disappears from view now as though it had never been, but it appears and occurs to us safely in proportion. This means that the energy we had invested in it is not lost to us. It was misinvested energy and now we have it again but in order. We have it in order to do, to act, to behave, to conduct ourselves, to work and create.

This highlights the basic difference between the rational approach and the non-rational or irreverent one. Rationally we are always creatively in touch with our surroundings, our circumstances and environment. A reverence for other beings informs and involves us. The irrational approach is not irreverent in the strict sense but the individuality of other beings is overlooked. Irrationally we treat others as though they were inordinate extensions of ourselves. This borders on irreverence, because it is precisely the individuality of beings that is honoured by us when we practice reverence, but neglect is not the same as destruction. Irreverence is destructive. Irreverence and dishonour go hand in hand, though neither knows the presence of the other.

Modesty is a state of being and a way of being. By way of modesty we can become rational when we notice ourselves being irrational. No one can be irrational on purpose, by the way. We can however be intentionally irreverent, which is terrible and terrifying.

So we do well to counter our own irrationality by way of modesty. I feel I should tell you how you make yourself ill by leading a life of dissipation. You turn on me suddenly because you want to be left to your kind of behaviour and of course you have a right to insist on doing as you please. I notice your approach is irrational and at the same time I feel tempted to return that irrationality. You reject my wisdom and I resent you for it. As soon as I notice it, I do well to be modest. This is modesty as a state of being. Your irrationality has a chance of dissolving into rationality against my modesty.

If it should occur to you actually to attack me, irreverently, because you feel I have infringed against your right of self, then my modesty can only protect me but it cannot help you. You have become, in the most profound sense, careless and you need to be cared for. If I can come up with this care, for you, you are in luck, but if I insist on my modesty, then I will be safe from your irreverence but you will have only the woe of your misdemeanour.

*

A <u>critique of false rationality</u> is of the essence. What needs to be brought into perspective is what we mean by <u>reason</u>. Usually we suppose that reason, reasonable behaviour and rationality go together. You could not imagine an unreasonable person being rational or an irrational point of view being sustained by a reasonable person. If we are to relate, as beings, to other beings rather than dying as things among things we must trace our ancestry, so to speak. Not always are we able to come up, it seems, with the good willingness to alleviate one another's need for an origin. We do ask one another, in a variety of ways: How did I begin? Where do I come from? and we do well to ask one another rather than expecting an answer from within our individual self because the true origin of human being, and therefore also of any particular human being, must be communally perceived.

And this too is where reason, true reason, puts in its first appearance.

So not the individual ego sustains reason, its application and performance, its exercise and presentation, but our communal interdependence. I depend on you and you on me for the discovery of our reasonable human origin and ancestry. Prior to the modern age, all the various world-wide cults of ancestry testified to this common human need and capacity for reason. The search was tied to pictures and recall, to images and memory, to iconography and dream, and we know of the many puppet masters who comforted their society by way of the preservation of corpses and the production of statuary. We today know, or at least we should know, that our reasonable human origin has no social source whatsoever and that the question: What is my beginning and where do I come from? can only be answered by way of a gradual and sustained cooperation in community. In a very important sense we have to prove, by our words and actions to one another and for one another, whose children we are and what nature of offspring.

We fancy ourselves as biologically in a category of our own and this is how it should be. But our reason for doing so may be sound or unsound. While we formulate the <u>origin of life</u> in some chemical compound, so that it may then culminate in us who do the formulating, we are more to be pitied than to be admired, though once again we demonstrate to all and sundry where the shoe pinches, and that it does. The ego-centric drive will never permanently tire of attempting to duplicate itself and in the name of this demonic urge the "eternally ruminating monster"[i] digests those who will not perceive.

Life has no origin. Or what exactly do people mean by that? Do they wonder how one moment there was life where previously there was none? Of course we might quite sensibly and helpfully suggest that life originates in our relationships with one another and with god, spiritually determined. However outside there, among the things that stimulate our fancy, there is no life, neither original nor permanent. We do well to sort out our thoughts on that point.

*

---

[i] From 'Die Leiden des Jungen Werthers', J. W. Goethe. A reference to what the young protagonist sees when the curtain of mere appearances is drawn aside.

The truth that reason is not individual but communal in origin must seem at first, like all truth, indigestible. We tell one another to be reasonable, accuse one another of being unreasonable and irrational, pretend, even, to come up with reason and rationality out of our egotistic self so that we can flaunt it, as incontrovertible, without realizing that reason does not enter into any of this. What we do is base our life and existence on a false premise.

Perhaps we need to ask: Is it possible to base life and existence on reason? Is reason not much more at home in the company of such concepts as angels and grace, love and beauty? Can it be a reasonable argument, for instance, if it leaves out of consideration how the other person at that moment feels and thinks, indeed how he or she is?

Instead of using the word reason, perhaps we should resurrect 'demon' as a more suitable expression for what comes over us when we want to settle matters once and for all at the expense of anyone who cares and largely indifferent to all other points of view.

The demon asserts itself, is asexual and always right because it cannot be proven to be wrong. The demon comes over us as from a bygone age and makes use of us for its own ends and purposes.

What are those ends and purposes? Simply the destruction of all matter.

We find this difficult to believe, because often it seems quite the opposite, namely that matter should be structured and constructed.

But matter as conceived by the individual ego is always blamed in the end for not rising to that ego's expectations. Our individuality becomes egotistic as we reject the communal, so as soon as we touch matter, it so to speak shrinks into itself and appears as a thing, which only proves to the ego what it has always expected: that matter is useless and worthless.

We can observe therefore how human individuality, if we do not give it its due while reaching out for reason, becomes egotistic, insisting on itself and on its rights at the expense of the communal, and then, as the material world shrinks away in horror, our egotism becomes demonic and we take revenge on that which we ourselves have deformed. We ourselves are responsible for the deformation and it is no use pretending otherwise. False reason, or the demonic, is symptomatic of our ego, even as our ego is itself a betrayal of our individuality inasmuch as we become social rather than communal.

*

Here we have to make a few peripheral observations. The difference that is conventionally made between society and community is not all that obvious, and from the point of view of 'social beings', that is to say: of people in society, the difference, if it exists at all, is one of size and somehow related to the difference between the affluent and the poor. We speak for example of 19th century society, of Roman society at the time of the Caesars, of being social or anti-social, right to the point where we choose or refuse someone's society or – companionship. Substitute *community* for *society* in these cases and you get at least some of the flavour of the difference. Those who live in community (not in a community) talk and confess their sins to one another, they rely on one another, share advantages and griefs. The blood tie of family represents yet another dimension and we may note that it plays more readily into the context of soci-

293

ety than community, where entire families would see themselves as socially defined but the various members of the family might at the same time demonstrate widely differing communal preferences and habits. Compare also how we use the terms 'a community' and 'a society'. The NSPCA is not a community, while the group of like-minded individuals who try to live self-sustainably in the backwoods of beyond, with right call themselves a community and describe themselves as having opted out of society.

One cannot 'opt out' of community. This points to a fundamental definition of society that can be called the contractual relationship. One can opt in or out of that contract. One can play by the rules or break the rules without altogether opting out, although one may have to *pay one's debt to society.* Equally one can opt out without necessarily opting into another relationship, in which case one more or less 'drops out'.

It is really not until we begin to think and feel for ourselves that the question of our society and community can be answered by us. We may be *born into* upper middle-class English society or into the society of Chinese peasants, but any communal definition is subsequently *acquired* by us, or not, in line with our attitude towards those around us and due to the way we behave and conduct ourselves. We can choose to limit our contact with others to the realm of the social. In that case we observe rules and standards, abide by them or go against them. The most unconventional individualist, indeed the criminal in or out of goal, may still be exclusively a 'social being', in that he or she knows nothing of the human contact that comes with community.

So here, finally, we have to take a stance. If we know something of human contact, we soon realize that it lends itself to true community and trust and that the contractual association must seem alien to it.

What I am coming around to here, of course, is the observation that society is intrinsically demonic and based on *false reason*, while any undertaking to be *truly reasonable and rational* demonstrates the characteristics of community.

*

We can do without society but we cannot do without community. Community allows reason to be born and to flourish while society demeans and undermines it – we follow suit either socially or communally. We become 'social beings' or communal beings. Right away we notice that a social being is a contradiction, since society, far from allowing us to be or encouraging us to be, teaches us to short-circuit being, to leap over it metaphysically and *go straight into business*, which is mistaken for doing and action. The energy released during business is then mistaken for life. The control of this energy is called reason and its fulsome application is called rationality. In society we have no need to be, because the magic of association supplies us with an external (extinct) substitute, the likes of which proliferate all around us. A *social being* is therefore no being at all but a mental construct which needs to be forever justified, excused and underpinned by expensive sacrifice during wars, epidemics and catastrophes.

In society the onus is on each individual to be perfect and finished so as to be able to reflect to every other member of society the conquest of external or internal energy. The energy must first be produced, otherwise it cannot be encapsulates, railed, formulated, categorized etc.

The social contract – and every social contract – stems from the fear that comes over us when we have denied being and we discover how things begin to gang up on us, to overwhelm and ultimately destroy us. As beings under our irreverent touch contráct, we agree on social contracts, to assure us that this is not our fault and that we cannot help it; also that this is unfair. Take for example the social contract due to which we feel justified and even obliged to punish evil-doers. Whence do we derive the right to cast stones? But of course the evil we mean is defined in line with our contract. Certainly a madman should be constrained for his own good and for ours, but should a murderer be murdered? Should a thief be incarcerated? Should those who hate us be hated back? Of course from within the logic of society only one response is possible, is reasonable and rational, but the reason first had to be defined as ego-control over energy intentionally released. If that is the reason, then all is well with the world and God is in his heaven, nicely out of our way.

The communal being, by comparison, feels exposed and vulnerable in the presence of others and finds this useful because it allows communication. As one being relates to another or to several, there is no need for a disguise of responsibility because guilt is not incurred. Above all else, no agreement is sought on the topic of defence against the fear of the irrational. By comparison, most communal agreements are tacit, not in need of being forever refashioned to keep conscience off the scent.

And the mirror image in which the spirit of community delights to view itself is every individual person. Our sense of community is sharpened as soon as we meet someone. In the eyes of that other person we detect the possibility of reason and right away we take rational steps to make room for it in ourselves and to testify to it for others.

*

"I am a busy man." This statement would do nicely as the initial confession, once we have decided to ignore social contracts and to espouse communal being. A busy woman too is a 'social being' who knows nothing of community until she regrets this.

Business is that release of energy during which we become unaware. Thereafter we need to keep busy, to remain unaware. Strapped into a system of obligations and duties we reap the satisfaction of the moment and fool ourselves as to our long-range effectiveness. Conscience is not necessarily eliminated but in the absence of awareness it has no choice but to accuse or indulge.

*

Business is the modern equivalent of action, just as action was, and still is, in many ways, the ancient substitute for being. Ancient man knew nothing of being, but desired it or imagined it. Contemporary men, women and children know being as the one prerequisite for life. This does not mean that they all have the same notion of what it means to be. They reject business out of hand because the intentional production and subsequent structuring of energy is alien to them. By action they mean doing based on ethical relationship, inclusive of passion.

But nothing so much defines contemporary being as the role of imagination. When modern man imagines, he does it only halfway. When we moderns give reign to our imagination and end up with a lot of mental pictures, which is to say internal sensations that are like external sensations, and then we try to reproduce those internal sensations almost as if to get rid of them, (to express them) but also to boast about how well we can do this, then we are modern. We are neither reasonable nor rational then, neither communal nor ethical, but at best social individuals who adhere to a moral contract while we busily

297

produce energy so as to turn it into products, into structures of one sort or another, and all for the sake of a simulation of life.

It becomes almost impossible for moderns to imagine what it means to imagine. Contemporary, communal imagination is, for example, unproblematic. Within a context of communal, reasonable and rational being, the effect of the world, of beings, on ourselves, is not separate from our own effect on the world and on other beings like ourselves. We are in no doubt about other beings being like ourselves. A thunderstorm or a sunrise, a rocky promontory, a violet under a hawthorn hedge, a ewe with its twin lambs, these are all creatures like ourselves, and when we contemplate their similarity to ourselves we realize that a natural bridge exists between them and us that serves communication by a variety of means. Imagination is the oil that lubricates the transmission of substantial content, of good spirit. By way of imagination we place ourselves more readily at the disposal of other beings, human or otherwise. No trace is left in the mind of the stuff that dreams are made of. Not that we should be ashamed of our dreams or that we want to demean them but they do not pertain to the light of day. One is well enough aware of that adulterous culture that worships the half-light out of fear of both light and darkness, but once we fully espouse the light we are no longer afraid of the dark and the half-light becomes superfluous. Magic loses its fatal attraction. The wise man is no longer the one who interprets dreams but the one who frees us from our attachment to them. Modern interpretation seeks to make the supposed content of dreams meaningful and useful for our existence and in this it is mischievous.

At an advanced state in our ethical development it occurs to us that other beings are really likenesses of ourselves, of us as human beings I mean; no, even you, as a human being, are a likeness of me, as I am of you. It is the work of poets to highlight this likeness, so that love may prosper. If we make it our priority to know what we like, this shows a total lack of imagination and gets us nowhere except into trouble. There is a vast difference between liking, as that word is commonly used, and being able to appreciate another being as a likeness of ourselves. As soon as I perceive that human-natural connection between , say, a certain garden and myself, my human natural affection begins to flow much more easily. The likeness exists, as a fact, and our imagination can help us take advantage of it. Nothing is pictured because our imagination is distinct. It reveals water as wine but it does not mix the two.

*

Imagination, therefore, as a distinct human faculty, has nothing to do with mental pictures or dream images.

These mental pictures have to do with our five senses and they are incurred via sensation, accidentally. Mental pictures are not images. A certain smell calls up in me past experience, when I crossed the Atlantic as a child in a converted freighter, four decks below sea level. The smell is a combination of rancid fat, paint, machine oil and vomit with something like Jeyes Fluid mixed in for good measure. A sniff of any one of these ingredients places me, accidentally, among those bedraggled passengers again and I can picture how it looked, recall the sensation of sickness, of wretchedness. I 'see', more or less correctly, the bunks, the oil-painted floor, the iron latches on the bulkheads, the endless metal stairs clanging underfoot. Recalling how is was – for this I need no imagination. As soon as I bring my distinct imagination to bear on this recalled experience, I am returned to the light of day and I realize that for a time the past had a power over me. I did not know this at the time. It pleased me. What my distinct imagination helpd me do is recreate the rational perspective that allows me to see and feel actual beings and not just their shadows.

Imagination therefore is to accompany sensation and not be a substitute for it. When I see the cloudy sky – if I do not at the same time imagine it, the process of seeing eventually grinds to a halt. Imaginatively seeing it is not even a process but a lively exchange of affection. Sensation as unimaginative process has been studied and analyzed to extinction by modern philosophers, and what this never yields is satisfactory understanding. The epistemological pursuit of <u>bare sensation</u> is a dead end.

Imaginative sensation is even to some extent redemptive. The mess we have made of our sense organs, due to lack of imagination during processes of sensation, can be cleared up if we consciously involve imagination in all that of which we try to make sense.

*

All the same, we need to ask again: What is imagination? How do we fare better for it? How do we miss out or go wrong if this faculty is unused or misused? We should never forget that all our human-natural faculties are there to be used properly by each one of us or else they will seem like snares to us and we spend half our time or more looking outside and beyond ourselves for causes of structural complexities and for mechanisms when we are really looking at symptoms of our own half-heartedness and of the resulting shift in responsibility, the distortion of morality and deformation of personality – of <u>modernity</u>.

Now we speak of <u>human nature</u> and of <u>human spirit</u>, and rightly so, and we have become quite accustomed, culturally, colloquially and within our various thought disciplines, to apply these terms in a great variety of ways, even to the point where at times we seem to be speaking the same language but when we probe we discover disconcerting chasms of misunderstanding.

We do well, for example, to stay away entirely from speaking of 'the human spirit' as though we could take a definite one for granted. Let us instead say: human spirit. It makes sense to speak of human spirit; it does not make sense to speak of the human spirit. At the moment we are concerned with making sense, not with the creation of mythic comfort, such as becomes a priority in the case of some poetry.

So human nature and human spirit are usually mentioned separately, almost as if they referred to separate entities. We have to dig down deep here to be able to make sense of imagination itself, which will in turn lead to immeasurable enrichment of our ethical disposition.

We know that in some cultures, and more or less during various periods of culture, nature and spirit are presented as for all intents and purposes mutually exclusive and even at war. One is nearly being asked to take sides, either against those who argue for nature or against those who marshal their forces on the side of spirit. This struggle between nature and spirit could go on forever while a certain pre-modern historic event is left out of countenance. I feel inclined here for good and useful reason not only to introduce this term pre-modern but even to juxtapose it to that recently fashionable term: post-modern. Also let's keep in mind that historic is what happens in time, not what we make of the past or what we have made of the past.

Pre-modern eventually therefore is explicitly what we would have to take into account if we wanted to avoid modernity and be contemporary. 'Pre-modern' is therefore a corrective term and we use it admittedly from within our regrettable modern habituations. It is a term that allows us to apply the modesty we have taken such pains to gain.

We call that pre-modern which lives and influences us whether we are modern or not, but needless to say the term is only useful to us in inverse proportion to the extent to which we have left our modernity behind.

Now if we think and behave as though our human nature and our human spirit were indistinguishable, each adulterated by the other, and if we say we are happy with this business of tossing one moment on the waves of nature and flying the next moment in the face of spirit, there is nothing much that can be done for us because we are like the fool who says in his heart there is no god. This ignorant confusion of spirit and nature is massive and the word massive refers specifically to it.

Massive existence is existence on the thinnest of ice. The natural catastrophe or the spiritual nemesis is just around the corner. This is not on account of perversity or because of overweening or morbid spirituality; these are modern. It is simply on account of indifference to, and estrangement from, the truth. Imagine that the truth has stretched a reliable bridge across a chasm in which boils an uncontrollable torrent, but we insist on preparing to get to the other side by leaping across or by wading across. Eventually we are bound to try it and perish. History urges us across and will not forever be refused but we refuse to take cognizance of the bridge.

So the first step out of this foolishness is possible because nature and spirit are in truth discrete and as we take that step we testify to that truth. It means that we make room in ourselves for a fundamental doubt, which is however a doubt only in comparison to our previous false certainty. It is a real doubt instead of a false certainty and therefore such a step implies ethical progress.

It is also a step that requires for once a modicum of distinct imagination. By describing it as distinct we imply a freedom from both nature and spirit, a lack of mindless attachment. Such mindless attachment may be evidenced when our dreams spill into our wakeful day and we become entangled in superstition and magic even though we pride ourselves on our rational stance and reasoned progress. So it is due to our distinct imagination, to our cleansed eye, so to speak, that we are able to perceive <u>nature and spirit as discrete in truth</u>. That is real progress.

This also lets us know that an effective beginning to our escape from massive entrapment can be undertaken by us in terms of this clarification of vision and distinction of imagination. I am implying here that the two amount to the same.

*

In modern terms, from the point of view of modernity, we cannot make sense of human nature and human spirit as discrete. What we can do is clear our vision, or render our imagination distinct. As soon as mental pictures enter our field of vision we may decide to imagine instead. We then lose our previous sense of progress but it was a false sense. After a time of distinct imagination we will make real progress. If any of our senses at all are compromised, this will show up as mental pictures and can be dealt with in one and the same place, which is most convenient. It is true that if we clear our eye, our whole body is full of light. Clear vision, uninhibited by pictures, is required to be able to sense that nature and spirit are discrete.

If we take the pains and make the effort to find this out for ourselves, we are much better off than if we wait until that fact is forced upon us, because then we are in trouble. It is no use going any further with our enquiries here until that point is well and thoroughly taken. In a sense, your nature is everything you are while your spirit is everything you do, which leaves everything that happens to you, inwardly and outwardly. Now even though same thing happens to two of us: one of us takes it in stride, the other is bowled over by it. So it all depends on where and how we are situated, with regard to who we are and what we do. While our being and doing are in a massive muddle, we cannot really be said to exist responsibly, so we cannot respond to whatever happens to us. We are at the mercy of events. Good luck and bad luck are all we know, as happiness and unhappiness. Being able to respond to happenings prerequires one foot in nature and one in spirit. It means knowing that on one hand whatever we do must be underpinned by who and what we are, just as who and what we are is determined and shaped by what we do. This type of knowledge is responsible. If we cannot fall back – indeed if we do not fall back – on that sort of knowledge in the event of an event, we are overwhelmed, undermined or bypassed.

Now if, under the duress of events, we behave in a modern fashion, then this could be described as doubt and indecision as to nature or spirit; not nature _and_ spirit, but nature _or_ spirit. Our doing might be specifically affected, in which case we will try to manipulate the event and our reaction to it. We will not be happy until we have somehow convinced ourselves that we have done all in our power to right a wrong or make good something bad. This would be fine in itself, except that any wrong or bad we identify appears to us that way because of our one-sidedness, so that any manipulation at all is ill advised. What we really should do is allow ourselves to be reversed into our being by circumstances until we have a better foundation under our feet. _Suffering_ would get us out of the misconception that the world is wrong just because due to some event we cannot do as we are accustomed.

Instead of our doing, our being might be affected. As modern beings we stand in doing <u>or</u> in being, and we switch from one to the other half-consciously and half-accidentally. The world continually affects us but as modern beings we are affected not on the whole but either in our being alone or in our doing only. Now if we are affected in our being alone, by some event, we right away feel threatened in our identity and begin to justify ourselves. We feel uncertain and panic because just as we needed to rescue our functioning when we were affected in our doing, so now we need to rescue our identity, our sense of self-worth. In our modernity we produce and try to support a self as long as possible, because a self, so we hope, will be there both in the case of threatened nature and on the occasion of threatened spirit. When we begin to suspect this self, we turn into nihilists, manufacturing yet another identity that is half established, either on being alone or only on doing. Or we adopt a religion so that our self will attain to some mythic structure.

A clear eye, distinct imagination, allows us to discern between ourselves as being and ourselves as doing, between ourselves as natural and ourselves as spiritual – at the same time. It means we are persons. Right away we are also of course aware of being affected and willing to respond. Our own natural and spiritual affection is born out of this personal awareness.

We understand now that while we attend to our nature, our spirit is not idle, and while we exercise our spirit, our nature is not absent but involved. It takes time now to discover who and what we are, and it takes more time to learn how to be spiritually active. Continually the world and the beings in our vicinity affect us; we do not have to wait for events, to be persuaded

305

that by dint of our very existence we are loved. We should not hesitate to call this love, this affection that streams out from beings around us towards us. Our own <u>affectionate perception</u> is therefore of the essence. We might as readily call it perceptive affection.

Natural development and spiritual progress go hand in hand now because we know what we are doing. We return to our pre-modern state in which spirit and nature are discrete; events no longer need to remind us that they are, but if they do, we know soon enough what is going on and which way the wind blows.

*

It is in our works that nature and spirit are to become one. Our imagination serves to keep us mindful of their discreteness. Obviously if we do not know them as two, we cannot make them one.

Human spirit and human nature become one in our ethical works. As I sit here this moment I am aware of my human nature as a peaceful coexistence with my immediate surroundings. I can describe my human nature in detail. What is most interesting about it right now is its static appearance. This is reflected outside my window. Not a breeze stirs the branches of the trees and shrubs. A single robin on a wire cleans its beak, then perches motionless. A neighbour walks out into his yard, deposits a shovel into a coalbunker and re-enters his house. Shirts, towels, socks and blouses hang limp on a wash line. I let you know about my human nature right now by choosing to notice what I tell you about. I use my imagination, so that my nature does not get confused with my spirit. Of course my spirit is involved, for have I not decided to describe to you my nature. As a consequence, even this description, within the context of this book, is an ethical work, an example of spirit and nature married. I am tempted to analyze that last statement but that is due to a residue it has left in my mind, of a pictorial nature. An extra effort of imagination deals with that. I can, if I like, continue now to describe for you my human nature which has become less static and more fluent in the meanwhile. I sense a degree of agitation, of excitement. I feel like rushing off to do something else. This feeling clouds my mind and spoils my field of vision. Once again it is time for extra imagination. Rest sets in. Along with the rest comes an irritation of my trachea and a flow of mucus in my sinuses. This has to do with my human nature and it lets me know that I have something to suffer, so as to enrich my human nature. I do not fight the natural inconvenience but I make room for a change or adjustment of nature that is signalled by the inconvenience. My throat feels almost normal again now and my nose has stopped running. Next my back begins to hurt, between the shoulder blades. I think of this as a natural tension. An effort of imagination translates it into a work-related strength. Now my back no long hurts. Bear with me, I know what I am doing. My stomach is next. It feels bloated. A variety of nonsense floods my mind, disturbs my eye. If I were to mention the details of this nonsense I would get involved in it, so I simply strengthen my imagination. I do not engage with the nonsense, neither negatively nor positively. The heaviness in my stomach is still a signpost. Some imaginative suffering is of the essence. These are tiny details, meticulously ordered, because I want to give an indication of what it means to know one's nature as discrete. Not that I have to limit this knowledge to mental disturbances which I translate imaginatively. My human nature, like yours, is also in itself wholesome, let us not overlook that. It is healed. I am able to rely on that, to take stock of it, to draw on it for sustenance. After all I am not my human nature. I know much of it that I do not sense at the moment but memory serves. So my human nature as wholesome nurture is a part of the equation. The modern mind forever contrasts nurture with nature and this is unfortunate; it also leads to misfortune. I can tell now, by the way, that the pressure in my stomach is being digested. Interesting, in a way, how the suffering of that inconvenience, or of that unpleasantness, brought me round nicely to that other half of my nature which is inherently wholesome and innately whole. What I notice now – let me tell you about it – is almost a burden of well-being. This is a pleasant, a reassuring burden and I completely submit to it. The rest I mentioned earlier becomes plastic. I am able to mould it as I wish. This is not easy to describe. It allows itself to be compared to the putting on of a comfortable cloak. The security of it, as I assent to it, is tangible. Now I feel sleepy, and as I attend to that, knowing and acknowledging it, a refreshing cold sensation comes over me. I stretch. A new strength has come into me. Keep in mind that I work as I describe my nature. It is not a lazy description, as by someone who has no real interest in, or involvement with, what he describes. Neither is it an unimaginative description, where mischief gains the upper hand, in the name of cleverness, brilliance, etc.

*

I can as readily turn to my human spirit now and let you know how things stand.

I look away from my nature and take care to observe, with distinct imagination, the discreteness of my spirit and nature. I also keep in mind that my human spirit dispenses readily with all mental pictures, thereby becoming one with the spirit that is god. In the past, the difficulty with talking about human spirit has sometimes been that one has pictured it, perhaps unaware that one does so, and one ended up more or less sounding as if one were discussing smoke, fog or spectres. Upon closer inspection those foggy spirits (ghosts?) are dissipated.

My spirit at the moment delights in its companionship with the one who is its source. It refuses to be dogmatically incarcerated, so it can behave spontaneously and joyously. I who am aware of it notice every moment the motion which means my spirit. This is somewhat awkwardly put but what I wish to say is that my spirit, when I look directly at it, is pleased to appear to me in some guise, such as for example as motion. The fact that presently it appears to me as motion, does not mean anything else to me. I simply accept that and, my work being what it is, I move on. I make this observation for you, the reader, and am aware of myself as a worker, a writer in the name of good spirit. As soon as my spirit appears to me as somehow self-centred, or self-interested, or self-sufficient, it also takes on at least a hue of the spectral, and that lets me know that I am not any longer looking at my spirit but at some falsification imposed upon it by my self; right away I clean up my act by an effort of imagination. Speculation about spirit, about pure spirit or spirit in itself, is alien to me too. I know that it is quite possible for me to interfere, if I am not careful, with my human spirit's unpredictable love of my nature. I experience this love, even at this moment, as longing and desire. In this longing and desire I recognize an opportunity to facilitate my spirit's relation with my nature through work and to consummate that relationship in another work. All my works, even such as this one in hand, are such consummations of the relationship of my spirit with my nature.

For the moment, of course, I am interested chiefly in my spirit (not as such or in itself, mind you) and there I have to mention, in addition to motion, also the longing.

Next I notice something to which I can only refer as pressure, and I believe I mean specifically cerebral pressure. I assume that what is required from me here is attentiveness. It is the pressure of invitation and perhaps visitation. To motion and commotion, to desire and longing, I can therefore add invitation and visitation, as a third couple of spirit guises or faces. Not that my spirit is divided in itself but that due to my looking at it directly it is bound to reveal itself to me both face on and in obverse, so to speak. During the course of everyday working and living I would experience these various aspects indiscriminately, and this would then give my work its infinite aspect along with its finite practicality.

*

By way of our distinct imagination we can ensure that our human spirit and nature do not get mixed and muddled up again and again but that their discreteness will be clear to us and their oneness possible and practicable for us. This is easy to say and lends itself readily to the schematic representation which does no one much good. But our attentiveness to our state of mind can do us good. Here clarity is of the essence.

First of all our mind must be clear so that our senses will operate efficiently. What, in any case, is our mind if not the wholeness of our bodily senses?

We might as well review this. We cannot learn anything of our mind in terms of our body, nor can we learn anything of our body in terms of our mind. Both must be referred to our soul, for our soul manifests itself to us as our mind and appeals to us as our body. Our body and our mind are the right and left hand of our <u>soul</u>. It helps to be aware of this when we are once again ready to examine our individual roots and to put roots down more deeply. We are morally obliged to do this at times. My soul at this moment would be offended if I did not make room for it to express itself. It would draw my attention to it in terms of melancholy. In that way I would know that something was up. The useful behaviour for me then would be gladly to suffer this melancholy and perhaps to express my gladness in some way. Usually we are not aware of our soul until it, so to speak, distances itself from us, and then we have a complaint.

310

We have neither head nor taste for business now and may even find a few ailments thrown in so that our suffering might have a focus. At the moment I have a sore tooth and the beginnings of a cold. Also my appetite for food is erratic. Although it is midnight and I feel like dropping into bed, this bit of work will help me get back on track. Neither my mind nor my body is active. Only my soul rests in itself. The evidence it gives of itself is readily picked up by me and noted. Some will say that my mind must be active because I think, or that my body must be active because I write, but I say that my soul does not need to extend itself as body or to express itself as mind. It can do what it does here directly and immediately, through my agency, as I lend myself to its stirrings and above all as I gladly suffer its discomforts and inconveniences. How can I do it gladly? Because I know even now what the outcome will be of my suffering, namely a more profound appreciation of life. For how long should I do this? As long as I wish. I sense no progress, no achievement, nothing. I derive no thought, state no opinion, only jot down what my soul offers. This cannot be too much or too little for me. The measure of it is perfect.

My human nature and my human spirit are united in my soul. They are one in the sense of being reborne (sic). My soul carries them. Just as I am reborn, they are reborne. They exist as they did at the beginning of time, before I confused them. This is a great benefit.

*

While my nature and spirit are one, I am at peace with the world. Being at peace with the world means that I am free to interact with a variety of beings. Why should I bother?

For the sheer <u>pleasure</u> of it. There is such pleasure in this peaceful interaction with beings that no further explanation is needed. Real pleasure is self-explanatory. And one does seem to wish to push through to this pleasure, past all the little pleas-

311

ures of half-heartedness and selfishness which only destroy us and give us no peace.

What we do for the sheer pleasure of it needs no further explanation, no soul-searching, no examination of motives. Our spirit and our nature are one and we are ethically intact. So when you approach me now with some complaint I am perfectly willing to listen and to become a channel for communication for you. Your grief touches me immediately and you will no longer feel alone. I am able to make time for you, to open my heart to you without overwhelming you with answers to questions you have not asked, with solutions to problems you do not really have.

*

What can I do so that my nature and spirit will remain one? That is an important question, because we should not suppose that we are no longer liable to death.

So we must give pleasure to others. And it is a further pleasure to give pleasure to others. We cannot hoard this pleasure, and it does not come apart as particular pleasures. The pleasures of the senses, of the intellect, of the psyche, have nothing to do with it. One almost wishes one had another name for it, but then the other names should really be given to the pleasures, of the psyche, intellect and senses; in other words of the soul, mind or body, when these make separate efforts, as they are bound to try while we ourselves make no progress towards a oneness of our spirit and nature.

So how do we give pleasure to others? Certainly not by trying to give them what they say they want or think they want or feel they want. For here we have again the problem of the disjointed individual, who is not in the possession of his soul, so that neither his body nor his mind, as a consequence, are really and truly his, but he is mental, psychic or sensual, each in turn.

So I may come to you in frustration and talk about my hatred of a person whom I would like to see harmed or I have lost my faith in god and made money my priority and then the worst thing you could do for me is give me money or harm that person because it would only harden me in my misgivings and in my mistrust. What should we call it, when we give someone what they suppose they want when in fact they want what would harm them? We pander to them. Technically we do not even please them. It should mean much more, when we please someone, much more than momentarily satisfying their ego or obliterating their frustration.

When we pander to someone's 'baser passions or instincts', as it used to be said, we make it more difficult for them to become whole persons, and we do the same for ourselves. When we do evil we become evil, though when we do good we do not become good. This is reassuring. It is an arrangement that safeguards our humanity. Humanity, not goodness, is the priority. It is my humanity you should consider, and then you take care of your own too.

So to what extent do we need to judge if we are truly to please one another and give one another pleasure? Before I give you pleasure, do I need to judge your state of being so as not to end up pandering to our fractured self? Not at all. Before you share your pleasure with me, do you need to consider if I am worthy of it? Not so. The pleasure you give me and extend towards me is free. It is not graded by you in accordance with my demand for it and you do not wait to share it with me until I ask for it. Neither can I, in my confused assessment of what would do me good, influence the way you please me. In fact you may please me and I am not pleased at all. After all, our pleasure arises from your oneness of nature and spirit and from your consequent certainty as to who you are and what you amount to, not from any state of being or stated becoming of mine. It is quite true that my weeping, depending on its nature or spirit, may tend to make you weep or laugh or move you to callous indifference, but you may all the same wish to please me – let's use the expression in that new way – in which case you principally bring to bear your wholesomeness of personality on me, which is bound to do me good, whether it momentarily makes me feel good or not.

We notice here the great extent to which pleasure is like love. When you love me you do not ask whether I return that love. Neither do you ask whether I am worthy of your love. In fact if you experience me as your enemy you will know the wisdom of making a special effort to love me, especially for your own sake, though equally for mine.

Certainly we are always able to love one another, because this ability does not depend on our spirit and nature being one. We can be spiritually in a mess and naturally at fault and love someone, intentionally, all the same. This is demonstrated by the fact that we may fall in love, naturally, whereupon we may intentionally love the one we fell in love with and all the magic and egotism disappear while the relationship gains foundation, and similarly we may 'fall out' with someone into a state of animosity, whereupon our intentional love of that person causes the prejudice and criticism to stop and the relationship may begin or resume.

*

Sexual pleasure is in a category of its own. A monogamous relationship of a man and a woman is possible if it is based on love and understanding. Fidelity is of the essence. Erotic pleasure is not excluded but not all are capable of it, and there is no reason why they should be. Erotic pleasure and sexual pleasure are not the same. Fidelity, love and understanding make the difference. It all depends on whether or not someone wants to live and not die. The emphasis on sexuality and sexual pleasure is understandable inasmuch as we all want to be comforted, and well may we ask what causes our discomfort in the first place. The only assumption that makes rational good sense places life at the centre of our being. We want to live. We may not know what life is or what it amounts to but we want to live all the same. We may be totally mistaken about life when we think about it and search for it, when we wait for it or try to grasp it, but within us a hunger and a thirst for life is as real as can be. The hunger and thirst are true and real, we can take that for granted, but our attempts to satisfy them may be misguided. We seek pleasure but we have not yet learned to love. We confuse love with a feeling. We suppose that pleasure might be a thing in itself, available eternally. We mistake sex for gender. We mate as though we had nothing within us except an ignorant craving. As soon as we notice ourselves slipping into dereliction we cobble together a few prejudices and swear by them. Our religions rarely bring us closer to god because after all is said and done we want to feel good, be superior and survive. We want to be happy, as is only natural. But 'only natural' means not spiritual. Then we react and rebel and become 'altogether spiritual'. The struggle begins anew, on a new false basis. We energize our theology until nothing is left of the merciful god for us to perceive, so that finally the systems we build to save us bury us. Then we reflect on what might have been and speak of ideals, irretrievable, imperfectible.

The hunger and thirst for <u>life</u>, with that we have to begin, whether we sense it rationally or not. Before we can even begin to realize an ethical approach to the world and to other beings, we must assume both that the hunger for life exists in us and that it is real. Even our definition of reality may be tied up with that.

In any case, we need a sound centre within ourselves against which we may measure our states of being and our progress towards desirable ends. Our moods overwhelm us if we cannot refer them to a standard of being, so we must have that single standard or fall by the wayside. Not what we make but what is must concern us, especially at the start, when it occurs to us that human life might be meaningful and significant and that it matters whether we behave accordingly or not.

So look around you. You feel miserable and nothing out there interests you. You have only your work. Nothing else stands between you and suicide. And yet how is this 'your' work? Do you want to survive? For what? Do you wish to please others? They are better off without you. Down tools and call it a day.

Suddenly the slightest touch of a breeze brushes your cheek. There is a lightness of heart. The air you breathe seems fresh, the sunshine invigorating. Sparrows chirp, workmen next door scrape a ladder against the guttering. You notice rose bushes, the gleam on metal roofs, washing on the line – as if for the first time. What a pleasure it is to drink this in and to give yourself over to it. Above all there is light, glorious light, the unsurpassable light of day.!

What has happened to your misery, to the vacuum around you? What have you done?

You have believed that death is a transition and that misery is a mercy. You have not misled yourself and others by complaining but you have testified to your knowledge of reality and to your belief in the spirit that sustains it.

So the life for which we hunger and thirst seems to end but in reality it continues, dipping at times beneath the surface of our sensation like a stream underground only to spring up again when we have attested somehow to the fact that this is so, to the truth that a merciful god exists within us as the life for which we hunger and thirst whether we know it or not.

*

So it seems that right at the beginning of that decision to commit suicide (or not) we come across the belief that death is a transition. Tied to it of course is the assumption that not only will we get through but we will be better off afterwards. We suffer our misery, not only to return to a previous ease, but to pass into a new state of fortune. Suffering is tied in our mind to progress. Pain only registers for us the opportunity for suffering. And as we play our mind over this thoughtful topography, we wonder if perhaps we are not much better served, when it comes to that initial discovery of the real life, by what we choose to undergo than by what we decide to make and do. Very likely it comes out to the same and what matters is that, doing or undergoing, we keep a sharp weather eye out for the genuine and authentic element hidden in that longing for life, that desire to really live – whatever that means to us at the time. The truth of the matter surely is that we make a variety of efforts and fail, whereupon we are left with disappointment, frustration, stress and strain, fatigue and tiredness, plus a variety of aggressions and resentments because we blame our failures on others and on circumstances. It appears that perhaps after all our initial doing is invariably uninformed by ethical considerations. But what about our initial non-doing? Is that any better? The alternative to busy activity and ambitious effort seems to be laziness, slovenliness, sensual or psychic indulgence, in other words a slide down the slippery slope of dereliction to destruction. So non-doing, or idleness, whether painful or pleasurable, is no guarantee against failure. We can fail in our being as readily as in our doing.

The rational ethic allows us to apply ourselves as readily to our doing as to our being because nature and spirit are one. At the beginning this ethic helps us come to the realization that yes, spirit and nature are one. Then it allows us to approach this one reality as readily from the side of nature as from the side of the sprit. There is a way for us to do and a way for us to undergo, and they are both the same way. They are the way to the life that embraces death and uses it as transitions.

If we care enough to examine this longing within us that manifests itself to us in so many ways, as a longing for food and drink, for reputation, for sexual gratification, for money and a good mood, then we will discover both life and rational ethics. We will not be disappointed, because any disappointment will immediately be taken up by us on sufferance, just as we will not idle in a vacuum of existentialism but we will take this grand néant as our signal for an act of human-natural faith.

Beings are essential, things are not. Things are not even endurable, not to mention their uselessness. The broad road to destruction, to every calamity imaginable, is paved with things. Our minds, our bodies – we ourselves – become things if we do not work out an ethic that is rational, in other words being-centred.

*

It is incumbent upon me therefore, as upon every individual person, to differentiate between reality and actuality. If we take the mess we have made of things and the distorted image we have of the world for reality, we have no one to blame but ourselves.

We hunger and thirst for life, and this is our basic consideration. We do well to identify this twin disposition in ourselves before we go an further and either throw ourselves into some ambitious program of achievement or else allow ourselves to be drawn into vicarious indulgences blindly.

Even though spirit and nature are one, it is possible for us to be driven by spirit alone, by an unnatural spirit, straight into destruction, or to be carried by mere nature, by a perverse nature, decidedly to our detriment. In broad terms, the oneness of nature and spirit notwithstanding, it is quite possible for us to be unnatural or dispirited. As a matter of fact, as we showed earlier, unless we consciously learn to discriminate between our human nature and our human spirit, <u>so that</u> the oneness of the two may become obvious and evident to us, we are bound to have a very hard time indeed, for it is no longer possible to remain in such ignorance with impunity. A sword enters our wrongheaded or our badhearted lives and we experience the agony of destruction. Calamities are visited upon us indiscriminately and in all our actions we meet with failure. As time goes on we become more hardened against good council and our senses are blunted by misfortune. Then no matter how many clever explanations we have for what happens to us, we all the same deem ourselves not well served.

So while it is quite correct that we must learn to discriminate between our spirit and our nature, between our head and our heart for example, we cannot succeed in this unless we are at the same time aware, truly aware, of the oneness of spirit and nature in reality. Call it a mystery if you like, but only your intellect will be mystified while you insist on its isolation. Or your will is frustrated while you try to bend the world to it.

Our awareness of the oneness of spirit and nature however is the awareness of an accomplishment. It is as if we were gratefully aware of the architect's genius and of the engineer's cleverness and of the workmen's diligence as we cross the bridge over the turbulent stream. We may be architects, engineers or workmen in our life but what unites us is this gratitude for the primal accomplishment.

*

The fact of our hunger and thirst for life is most immanently available to us. It impresses itself upon our attention, rises up in us like a passionate flame, becomes a yearning over the years, an ambition for greatness and mastery , a desire for satisfaction, a longing for comfort. At the same time we may have very little notion of that <u>commonwealth of reality</u> to which we may belong and which may take root in us. So as to participate

319

in that order and to have the benefit of its strength and security, we have to make a small effort in a certain direction, behave in one way and not in others. The path to real being is ethical, and it is a path, this is well enough known by some and has been known for some time. But it is a path of individual discovery of that which does in reality exist. Surely it must be encouraging to hear, from those who have found out and to whom it has been revealed, that it is not a case of undertaking the impossible but rather of bringing oneself round to where one can be in a suitable position to benefit. There was a time when those who knew best on earth realized that notwithstanding their very best efforts they could not get past a certain point in human development quite simply because the time was not ripe. They described this unripeness in a variety of ways, and meanwhile they coped as best they could. The supermarket was closed and although one felt sure that eventually it must open, no one could say when. We should really try to imagine more vividly perhaps how different, crucially different, those times were from ours today. People nowadays refuse to believe that the supermarket is open. This refusal places them in a predicament. In a sense they wait for the saviour who has been and gone and done his job. They look behind every hedge for the supernatural hero, who has not come yet, and so they are blessed with the Napoleons and Hitlers they bring down on themselves.

The supermarket metaphor only tells half the story, of course, because just as the commonwealth of reality becomes more and more the domestic way of life and the home for those who prepare for it and reach out for it, so it becomes an alien force, a hindrance and a snare for those who remain unprepared and do not reach out for it.

Take for example your ability to think. You do not need thoughts in order to be able to think. Nor do you need pictures. You can raise your right arm if you wish and if you are not crippled. Also you can think if you wish. You need nothing to think about. Why should you bother? Because concrete thinking alleviates your adjustment to reality. Concrete thinking is not about anything but if anything comes up, it lovingly incorporates it. It does not manipulate mental pictures or dream images, but if any arise it includes them, overcomes them, even rejects them if necessary.

The same goes for the feeling you can do. In itself it need have nothing to do with feelings, but in the presence of feelings it continues all the same, or rather you may continue to feel, concretely, and then those feelings sort themselves out, into those that support you, those that linger for a while and those that pass away.

Again, what matters here is that we do not mistake a mere act of will for anything useful or substantial. Concrete feeling and concrete thinking are not possible except while we know of the commonwealth of reality, because only then can such thinking and feeling work for us as enrolment in, and engagement with, that reality. While we know of this reality, we are aware that it influences us however we are and whatever we do, and as we think and feel concretely we harvest the true benefit of that influence. We harvest it equally for ourselves and others.

Concrete thinking and feeling after a time is bound to become creative doing.

*

To have in the forefront of our mind the commonwealth of reality – not to ask: Where is it? or : How can I be in it or part of it? – this is more than half the battle, as we work out our individual security and apply to our communal references. Of course we are often attached to appearances, to thoughts and feelings and to psychic phenomena; we may have fabricated a world for ourselves out of these. We may have gone so far as to

321

mistake dying for life. So how can everyone speak to us of this commonwealth of reality and expect a hearing? Clearly it must be the man's bearing and the weight of his words that interest us and arouses our interest in what he means. But the commonwealth of reality breaks into pieces and is yet whole. It performs wonders in secret and surprises us with the clarity of a conviction. It is at once the basis of our conduct and the aim of our performance. We enter this commonwealth as novices in the art of life and never as experts or as professional personalities. The mystery we accept towards clarity takes us there and the facts we state truthfully prevent us from falling out.

The wealth is common to all who gain and treasure it. Of course we may simply ask, inwardly, now that we have a notion of what consists with ethical being and doing. We may ask for happiness, for example, but then we must consider that certain adjustment may be necessary before we can be accommodated. The trials we meet on the road to happiness make sense to us then. Eventually we learn too that happiness is not an end in itself but a commodity to be invested in the communal interest. In a sense we must reach past happiness if we are to 'be happiness'. Then sadness can become the sign of a working relationship for us, not an intimation of guilt because we have erected happiness as an icon.

*

The greatest hurdle and hindrance to ethical advance will always be the misconception of the good as a thing. The good, or god, has an inward root, individually inward or communally inward, and from this root alone can outward goodness grow. At the same time we are influenced by the world and by all beings, and here it makes all the difference whether we reach out and cooperate or remain ignorant. Nothing is more fascinating to people in their ignorance than evil. One wonders why the good does not exercise an equal fascination. Once we have begun to initiate good being in the throes of hypocrisy, evil exerts an influence only so that we may contradict and counteract it. We cannot be good but we can do good, and from the misunderstanding that we can be good arises the challenge of evil. We try to be good and short-circuit our growth towards human strength.

This human strength has really never been properly countenanced. We are all too familiar with demonic strength to be capable of recognizing human strength. It becomes available where our human nature and spirit have been made one by us.

Moral strength explicitly allows us to come out of our individuality so as to enter communality. This is not what we mean by human strength. Demonic strength allows us to triumph over others and to reap a short-lived public reputation. Those who would be good often grovel at the feet of those who have managed to become demonically strong. This is not what we mean by human strength either. We need moral strength to pass from morality to ethics proper, but demonic strength is something we are better off without. Charisma is a popular decoration of demonic strength.

*

The thing about demonic strength is that it impresses, whereas human strength implies and enfolds. We will be able to make better sense of this if we learn about it from the point of view of mortal weakness.

We are mortally weak in the sense that our flesh is not under our control. Neither spiritually nor naturally can we make ourselves carnally superior. Our carnal survival is not in our hands. Often enough however we pretend that it is, because we would like it to be, whenever we refuse to submit to the law of human natural spirit which dictates that first our nature and our spirit must be one, namely that nature and spirit must become one in us. So we pretend that we have what it takes to rise above this merciful law – and so our troubles begin, even though we suppose they have finally ended.

We do not really become sensible to this weakness until we have a go at overriding the merciful law above mentioned. We try to solve a problem by spirit alone, perhaps after some moral success, and suddenly impotence, a feeling or sensation of powerlessness, is upon us. Or we merely address our nature and end by feeling worthless. The impotence and the worthlessness are the two sides of the weakness which we do well to indentify as soon as possible. We are mortally weak then in the sense that we are being reminded forcibly of our liability to dying. They are being forced upon us, these feelings and sensations, and these thoughts and sentiments, or at least we experience it that way. Actually the force merely is a reflection of our own lack of mercy. We have tried to gain a superiority and suddenly we are the underdog – precisely because we tried that. Lucky for us. The longer we are left under the delusion that either sheer willpower or pure self-indulgence can carry the day for us, the worse we will be off in the end when the delusion evaporates or disintegrates. So really if we were smart we would welcome that moral weakness, that sense of impotence and worthlessness, because it signals an opportunity for us, an opportunity for <u>human strength</u> – which bears immortality and eternal life.

Feelings of powerlessness, in the face of events; thoughts of worthlessness, in the presence of beings; moods of frustration and defeat, when our plans misfire and our ambitions run cold: these are the symptoms of body, mind and soul that essentially inform us – not so much of the fact that we have become spiritually or naturally unbalanced, though that is a part of it, as witness our anger, our rage and our accompanying shame or guilt, but of an opportunity for human strength.

If we go wrong now, misreading these signs, we do so by overindulging or by coercing. We either react forcibly to force or we give in to temptation.

*

So here once again it matters that we give the correct ethical significance to the apparent misfortune that besets us. Usually circumstances match our states of being. We are downcast because someone broke into our house or stole our car. We feel defeated because we cannot achieve some goal we have set ourselves. Now if we could see the circumstance and our state of being as separate, or if we could imagine, truly, that the causal relation is really an accidental fabrication, we might stand a chance of knowing and recognizing the <u>weakness</u> we experience in a true light, so that we might patiently bear it on its own grounds and see it through.

In comparison to the relief we experience whenever we demonically force the issue, this patient, knowledgeable bearing of our weakness seems unattractive, for we have no immediate foretaste of anything like victory. We hold out, because we know in our hearts that although we cannot 'sense' it we are making real progress.

I say that we cannot sense it, but we may look for and possess a distinct sense of comfort as we exercise patience in our weakness. This comfort would leave us right away if we strayed into the demonic satisfaction, because then we would 'have our reward'. Human strength is not a reward. It is as essentially our natural and spiritual birthright as the eternal life that accompanies it.

Demonic strength however is 'all the rage'. We pretend nowadays that demons and evils are old-fashioned superstitions but we subscribe to them more fervently than ever. We suppose we have harnessed them and pride ourselves on having mastered them almost completely, and in that way precisely we subscribe to them, because whether we oppose them, tolerate them or profit from them, we still behave in terms of them and with reference to them, hence they define us.

*

And is it fair, or even accurate, to say that the world is demonic, and then to call it this world? A late Christian bias that conquered public and private minds for a time has left the coast clear now for either a perception of the world as created being or a misconception of the world as demonic states. We have decided for the former and are therefore able to discern <u>demonic states</u> as just that and nothing more.

How these demonic states come into existence, this is one particular study, and knowing that might help us avoid – or rather might help us behave in such a way that they are less likely to come into <u>our</u> existence. In other words we might learn how to keep our existence clear, pure and sober, so that it does not become demonic. However it is what we do, not what we refrain from doing, that keeps our existence clear, pure and sober. A clear body, a sober mind and a pure soul are therefore of the essence, and while we exist we are vulnerable.

Make a difference in your understanding between <u>existence and life</u>. To what should we compare the two in order to highlight that difference? Death is the thing. We exist in the face of death: we live notwithstanding death. While we live, demonic states cannot impinge upon us. While our existence is a preparation for life, we are vulnerable to such states, so this is where ethics comes into it, that we might learn to choose the path to life while avoiding the pitfalls of demonic states, and just as important, that we might prepare the conditions for life without leaning on demonic states to help us and without resisting demonic influences as we perceive them.

During and throughout our ethical existence towards life we are bound to encounter demonic states. It will not help us to analyze these states. To bear them, to bear up under them, this is needful.

We make this difference at the moment between existence and life so as to be able to understand better what is meant by human strength. We can lean on this human strength and we can draw on it, but we are bound to fail in this if we do not learn to recognize the demonic states that tend to beset us. And it will always and again be a case of our choosing human strength instead, when confronted or undermined by demonic states or influences. First we recognize these, then, without further ado, we simply go for human strength. That works. Nothing else really works. Once we begin to negotiate with the evil in our presence we are lost, if only for a time. The way back may be arduous.

So the trick is to learn how to lean and draw on human strength. Some will say: Why do we need to wait for demonic states before we can be strong? The answer is, we do not, we must not wait. Our business is to act with strength and in strength. However, demonic states occur; not because we wait for them but suddenly there they are. It is as if our life suddenly came to an end and we are thrown back on bare existence. We cry, in some manner: "Why have I been forsaken?" and the answer always is: "So that you may have more life." But that answer is available on the other side of the suffering we first have to do. This suffering is our portion, and if we refuse to do it we are left with the pain, the worthlessness and the impotence. In short we are left with death, as an end in itself. And this <u>death</u> as an end in itself is <u>the demonic state per se</u>, the utter misconception.

I demonstrate human strength as I write these words. This strength cannot be talked about. It must be exemplified. It is the strength to suffer. It is not popular but the opposite. Never suppose you will be admired for it. It has nothing to do with the popular values or virtues. People do not recognize it. And why should anyone wish to be admired or recognized for it, since it is not an end but the means per se?

Finding ourselves thrown back on our bare existence, as it were forsaken by life, we naturally panic and are spiritually assailed. Demonic states present themselves, as countermeasures, as relief, as delusions. The time has once again come to suffer, but we are much more likely to overcome our reluctance to suffer, and to refrain from behaving in terms of any available demonic states, if we know that we can rely and depend on human strength.

Why call this strength human? Why not simply say: Rely on god?

We mistake god for God. An idol has been created for us and all too often we are all too ready to accept that idol, mostly on account of its magical attractions. The real god has his human attributes, being merciful love, and real human beings share in this divinity. As nature and spirit were made one in reality and as we may make them one for ourselves, <u>divinity and humanity</u> are in truth no longer separate, opposed or divided. We may therefore speak of human strength in comparison to popular strength, where <u>popularity</u> takes no account of humanity and divinity as one but insists on their opposition and separation. Instead of human strength we could also say christian strength, but then the misunderstandings would multiply even more. The difference between Christianity, as a religion, and christianity, as a soul-economical reliance on the work and achievement of Jesus of Nazareth, is not yet worked out.[i]

*

---

[i] See the author's work: '<u>c</u>hristianity, a Personal Exploration (2016)'

Real existence and suffering go hand in hand. When we refuse to suffer, our existence becomes more unfortunate and more painful. Mind you, it is not so much that we refuse to suffer but that it simply does not occur to us to do so. We see no sense in it. We cannot imagine what it means to suffer joyfully and cheerfully. For that we need strength, or at least the promise of it.

When we barely exist we have neither willpower nor desire. It is as well to become familiar with that state. Of course we have the choice of willpower and desire but these would not help us. We need to make a fine distinction here. Bare existence is a fact and the experience is unavoidable. We have to ask ourselves what that fact means to us and how we intend to deal with that experience. In the absence of willpower and desire we are weak. While we barely exist, in other words while we have no life except the past experience and the present hope of it, we are remarkably at the mercy of other beings. Merciful spirit acts upon us through those other beings. We notice this in that we are weak. The myriad ways in which we might be weak all point to this affection of other beings for us. Should we remove ourselves from that affection or resist it? Should we insist on popular strength? Should we be ashamed of that weakness in the face of idealist pretentions?

What do we stand to gain by holding out? First of all we would have to be convinced that it is possible to continue to be weak without being injured or hurt. To the extent of any doubts we have here we will opt for self-defence. Our self in this case is ourselves in doubt and this doubtful state is then what we would be defending. It makes no sense, does it.

We cannot fail to notice, while we are in a weak, existential state, that we are being urged to do something.

We sense this, quite palpably at times. And of course we can see no reason why we should continue in such a state if it makes no sense to do so. The decision to suffer cannot be based on any part or aspect of our weakness-experience. We must know about it. We must have heard. Perhaps we have seen others who have decided to suffer while weak rather than flinging themselves into some demonic pastime or sliding into morbid self-indulgence. It makes a tremendous impression and a lasting one when someone in a state of existential weakness decides to suffer.

*

The one who suffers says yes to the effect other beings have on him during his time of weakness. But he says yes because he knows that he stands to gain from this. He knows that the effect other beings have on him is due to their natural affection, so whatever the effect, such as the type or kind of weakness, the affection is there for him and waiting to be returned.

We have a classic example of suffering during his time of weakness in Jesus of Nazareth, who knew well that he might bring down wrath on the heads of his enemies (rely on popular strength) but he chose to do what would do him good, which was to extend affection, human natural affection, not sentimental affection, to those other beings which were at that time pressing in on him affectively. What or who were those other beings? Primarily the being of god. The human natural affection of god is such that our very soul, or lack of soul, is laid bare, so that we then might respond appropriate with our soul or, in the absence of a soul, perish. What we have heard about this Jesus and what we have learned from his lips allows us today to recognize this moment or time of our extreme weakness as something we can see through and suffer through – because we know that it has been done and therefore that it can be done. To the extent that this person exists in our mind and memory, our suffering becomes easier. It stands to reason that at a time when we are weak and merely in existence, not living though of course not dead either, we should experience with especial intensity that part and aspect of our nature and spirit which is still at loose ends.

*

"Still at loose ends," – so that is the goal? Should we resist our imagination when it constructs a line of progress towards an end? Or should we go along with that and honestly admit that when it comes to the final achievement as such, we either call that life and live it to the full without concern for past, present or future, or else we create a mythic realm into which we eventually blunder with our eyes half closed through cupidity or fatigue?

We have distinguished between imagination proper and a preoccupation with things pictured, which preoccupation is popularly mistaken for imagination. Our notion of progress towards a goal is inherited from a confusion of the two.

<u>Progress means growth</u> and growth is organic. The notion of a stoppage, of an end not in the sense of a goal but of nothing further, is alien to growth but even the idea of a goal, of something achieved, has to be looked at carefully with respect to its applicability to natural and spiritual growth, to human growth as we might call it, because here too we tend to rest on our laurels with every success, every so-called success or victory, until once again we need to ask: What next? Where to next? Still life as such is not ours. Dreams, myths and vicarious falsehoods still cloud our imagination and we seek life as it were outside and beyond ourselves, though very likely we do not recognize this search or acknowledge it as a search for life.

Once purified and disciplined, our imagination limits itself to life-serving functions, so that the question: What is the proper human aspiration into which all our aspirations should flow as tributaries into an endless ocean? eventually no longer exists because we have learned how to live. We may practice various arts to get us back on course if our imagination has become undisciplined and if we have begun to mistake ambitions, successes and victories as ends in themselves. These arts then tend to pose as ends in themselves too, and we forget their life-serving purpose, whereupon an art is required to set these arts back on course.

When we try to imagine, we make very little real progress, mainly because progress itself is imaginary. Life is to be lived and not to be imagined. As soon as we try to imagine it, some image of progress is, so to speak, vouchsafed us. Such images of progress are therefore merciful stand-ins in case we should come to our senses and live again, whereupon a sober critique of those images comes in handy.

Of course we often incline to demand of others: Well then, show us how to live and how to avoid all these tempting dead ends! Those who know how to live must respond to that demand and it happens to be an essential aspect of their living that they do so; that they testify to the life they live. When we live, we do it out in the open where it may be perceived. Part of the definition of living is that it is advertised by the one who lives. Living is exemplary. We set examples and become living examples. The work we do limits our living. It is an alternate life. Whatever we do encroaches somehow on what others have done before us; only if we do it ethically does it amount to an advance. We say that we get ahead. But there is no need to get ahead for a mature human being, once intercourse with others and the world has been established on a sound footing. What happens then is affectionate intercourse and what is done is exemplary ethics.

Once ethics has become exemplary, it is no longer prescriptive nor proscriptive. What are the moral and ethical implications, they ask, of cloning human individuals? What they are asking is: Should it be allowed? and: How must we go about it so as not to infringe against moral standards? In other words: It seems possible to do, now can we get away with it?

Intellectual curiosity has gone off the rails however long before the invention of weapons of mass destruction and cloning. One finds oneself suddenly not only to some extent, but completely and utterly, in the hands of powers which are in themselves amoral and unethical. If there is a problem, it is not so much that something bad is being done which can be proven to be bad but rather that something is being done which is not good, being neither moral for individuals nor ethical for a community, so that, being neither bad nor good, it is neither here nor there – and therefore nonsensical.

How can this happen, we may well ask, that so much nonsense is being perpetrated so that eventually one is faced with amazing tricks and earth-shattering events such as only nature divorced from spirit or spirit separated from nature could come up with?

When we look at the modern understanding as it has developed over the past two-thousand years, we can see that it began, or rather started, from the discovery that nature and spirit are separable, and then every effort is made to exploit each one separately. This understanding culminates in the sciences of the last two centuries. The truly ethical effort, in comparison, is always to make the two one. Right from the start, during modern times, this ethical effort was just as possible as the unethical, but the power was not the same. Where nature or spirit are exploited separately, the power that becomes available excludes humanity and operates to rid the earth of human beings – to rid the earth of beings in favour of the existence of things. Weapons of mass destruction are one predictable outcome, while the cloning of individuals is another. These are only two extreme examples that illustrate the perpetration of the unhuman and the inhuman. Anyone at any moment is at liberty, however, to enter upon the exploration and pursuit of powerful humanity, which will never be popular or fashionable. Human power manifests as secret life and not as sensation or amazement.

So it makes no sense to ask how mere intellectual curiosity comes about in the first place. It is simply a symptom of neglect. If we neglect to mend our roof, the rain comes in. If we neglect ethics, we automatically behave in an inhuman and unhuman fashion. The trouble is, that one tends and inclines to this neglect of one's best interests and then an addictive energy takes over. So with every one-sided advance, the return to human sense becomes more difficult and less likely, while success and victory, if we but knew it, are our worst enemies. Then comes failure and defeat, breakdown and catastrophe, and we have another chance to begin at the proper beginning.

So the question as to whether or not something we do is moral or ethical usually boils down to whether or not it is worth doing. If the only real and honest answer is: because it can be done and it's fun, then we would definitely be wise to pause and take stock. For action to be ethical it must be ethically motivated. Self-defence is not ethical. Ego-centric knowledge is not ethical. This is not to say that a self-defensive case for ego-centric knowledge cannot be made, or that an ego-centric case for self-defence cannot be made. Such cases can be made with great fervour and dedication.

There is a great difference between the evil we find ourselves doing and then we are appalled and repent, and the evil we find ourselves doing and then we justify ourselves and continue in the same vein.

*

Perhaps we should bear with one another when it comes to our undoubted vulnerability to <u>evil</u>. The trick is not to prove evil in one another but to overcome it in ourselves. Even moral outrage is an evil which has to be settled before we can be morally effective. The crimes we perpetrate and the sins we commit all direct us inward. When our soul begins to ache, we either make an effort to rid ourselves of soul, so as to become hardened in sin and crime, or else we must look to this soul-pain for a reversal of our standards. <u>Soul-pain</u> is elusive. We notice it, we look to it and it seems no longer to exist. Cheerfully we disport ourselves – only to be racked again by that same pain. The lesson to be learned here is, that a noticing and a looking are not enough. The pain goes away not because the damage is repaired but so that we can get on undisturbed with the work of repentance. Perhaps we did not know that we had a soul until it began to hurt. Now that it hurts, let us not insist on ignoring it. There are always a few who are willing to do this work and for them I write.

<u>Soul-pain</u> troubles us so that we might gain confidence in our pursuit of <u>soul-gain</u>. Remember that we are finally to come into the possession of our soul, so as to be able to be of use in the world. While we have no soul, we are snares and pitfalls for others. And truly we have no soul, and therefore no life, while we ignore the soul-pain or even repress it or flee from it. We flee from it into the outer reaches of existence, into 'outer space'. We ignore it by existing hectically, in stress and strain, over a period of time. We repress it by blaming circumstances.

Many who have no soul indulge in much speculation about it. This is one way of dissipating soul-pain, the most ignorant way of all. One invents a psyche, in terms of that pain. The shadow cast by the soul is mistaken for the soul, half intentionally because the honest confrontation of our true soul implies coming to terms with ourselves as potentially evil. Our ego fights a running battle to avoid, by hook or by crook, such a confrontation. The psyche is a product or a result of our self-ishness and when we mistake it for our soul we cut ourselves off from life. The more elaborately we construct and decorate our psyche, the more permanently and thoroughly do we become confirmed in our modern half-life, where pain, passion and suffering are not understood and where the life of action is inseparable from evil.

Soul-pain is like a wound that will not heal. From a modern point of view it seems like that. The modern approach to pain is to view it as an unfortunate interruption of happy being or as a punishment for bad doing.

Let us instead view soul-pain as the indicator of an ethical direction. Let us take note of it and look to it, and then, when it goes away, let us persevere in that direction with good will and insight. But something gets in the way. It denies the very notion of a direction, of an inward realm. It tends to change good will into bad will, insight into mere introspection. It would persuade us that nothing can be done, that the well has run dry, that we are up against a wall and no way through.

This in itself is a phenomenon for us to be recognized. We have arrived at the point of no return and unless we despair now, we may have to use violence. If we despair we once again subject ourselves to circumstances. <u>Violence</u> is the only way out. What is meant here by violence? An intense insistence on our spiritual property, that is what is meant. Our entire being is concentrated on a point and we do this in the knowledge of the fact that what is ours since 'prior to the beginning of time', metaphorically speaking, must now, must manifest itself for our use. Of course fatigue will set in and once again at least the temptation of despair. Each time we must insist nevertheless, with all the faculties at our disposal, on our inward being as rationally in tact and perfectly at ease. These words I write now will probably not make much sense to anyone except 'in extremis', but then he will recall and know what to do rather than give in to despair. Nothing is violated. No one is treated violently. This violence is directed entirely inward and our entire being is involved, so this is not a case of one part of ourselves violating another part, such as we imagine perhaps when we speak of 'mind over matter' or of 'willpower and control'. No, cause and effect are one.

*

Despair is the greatest enemy of life and the sooner we know what to make of it the better. It makes some sense to say that ethics itself, and our rational approach to our existence, is rooted in despair. But in order for this to make sense we have to understand despair and not just exist at the mercy of it. We have to know that something beneficial goes on while we experience or feel despair and that while we are in despair, like being in pain, we are not yet suffering and making that benefit our own.

We can distinguish, for a start, between what goes on within ourselves and the despair that draws our attention to it. The despair is a kind of pain and therefore an attribute of death. It lets us know, not so much that something is amiss but rather that something worthwhile is on offer. The difference between these two attitudes is pronounced. In the one case we want to continue to lead a standard existence and every pain is an annoying interruption, a punishment or a morbid exercise. All we want is to get back to the previous painless state so as to be able to get on with our superficial existence. We fear pain as the threat of death and fleeing from it we rush into the arms of death; our superficial existence is after all deadly. It cannot support life, no matter how much we force it and grasp it.

In the other case we see our existence as the preparation and foundation for life, while pain, though we flinch, indicates the next step forward, so that, through suffering, we may arrive at life and at a greater abundance of it. Initially we fear pain, that goes without saying, but then we recognize that fear, and we remember that we are at liberty to suffer if we choose. We can do this for ourselves and then we can do it for others. Once we have learned how to do it for ourselves, we progress to where we do it for others.

The more important consideration therefore is not how we imagine what goes on within ourselves and on our behalf while we experience despair but rather to suffer the despair so as not to end up in despair and so as to make the universal change that affects us suitable individually and appropriate for ourselves. How do we know that we are involved in universal change? The despair indicates as much. How can we appropriate that change? By way of cheerful suffering. Why should it be cheerful? Better ask: How could it not be cheerful? To be affected by universal change – god moving closer to us – merciful spirit acting on our behalf – real life becoming available or more available to us – is that something to regret? Are we to despair because we find ourselves despairing, thus ending individual despair, or are we to rise cheerfully to the occasion?

What does it take, to be able to do the one rather than ending up in the other? How can we really believe that the truth is the truth and behave accordingly?

Little by little, one incident at a time, we make headway. It would do to speak of this as our ongoing conversion. Of course there is a first time for everything. It is possible however to make too much of this first time, because it could just as readily also be the last time if instead of ethically we respond vainly.

* * *

End of Book Two

338

www.ingramcontent.com/pod-product-compliance
Lightning Source LLC
Chambersburg PA
CBHW060447290526
45791CB00001B/14